CONTENTS

Introduction

I wasn't surprised when my first child was a boy. And then my daughter came along, and I was thrilled, albeit a bit shocked, since I'd been certain it was another boy. But I thought about it and decided that mothering girls couldn't be much different than mothering boys. I obviously had a lot to learn.

Three more boys followed Emily, making her my only daughter. I admit to having expectations for our relationship. I thought we would have things in common—things I had enjoyed doing as a child, such as playing with dolls, reading, and tending my plants and pets. These illusions were shattered when I realized she and I were apples and oranges—two completely different people.

And we stayed that way right up until the day she left home in the middle of her senior year. I was heartbroken because she left under less than perfect circumstances, but also because I always dreamed of having a relationship with her just like the one I had enjoyed with my own mother. My mother had been my best friend. And so, I grieved for what I saw as the loss of my daughter and for the best friend I would never have.

It's been just over a year since she left, and we are now closer than we've ever been. We have many things in common, and, yes, I consider her my best friend. What happened? My heavenly Father heard my prayers and orchestrated the entire reunion. I serve an amazing God.

When I began going through the hundreds of devotionals that women were kind enough to share, I made a wonderful discovery. I read countless stories that made me nod and smile in agreement, and I rejoiced in knowing I wasn't alone. So many mothers had shared my experiences and feelings in the complicated business of raising a daughter.

In these devotionals, you will meet mothers, stepmothers, surrogate mothers, mothers-in-law, grandmothers and, even, aunts and family friends who have been called into action as mothers. We hope this book will encourage, inspire, and bless you, and strengthen your fellowship with God. Daily reading will give you the opportunity to travel through the year with a group of remarkable women who have asked God to be an essential partner in mothering their daughters.

So come and spend a few minutes each day with women who have shared your trials, your triumphs and, perhaps, your tragedies. 365 different stories with one overriding theme—we all serve an amazing God.

JANUARY

Desperately Seeking Susan

*You didn't choose me. I chose you. I appointed you to go
and produce lasting fruit, so that the Father will give you
whatever you ask for, using my name.*

This is my command: Love each other.
JOHN 15:16–17

*W*hen my mother died in 1985, I felt like a rudderless ship adrift on the high seas. Though separated by many miles, we remained close, and her passing left a void that threatened to engulf me. I was happily married and had a darling young daughter, but I longed for the understanding and comfort that only a mother can give. I asked God to send someone to fill the aching emptiness in my heart. I was young and immature in my faith and did not understand that the loneliness I experienced was the Lord's way of drawing me closer to Him.

As the months dragged on, I spent more and more time in prayer. I gained solace from reading my Bible, and I found myself growing closer to the Lord. I began to see Him as a friend and confidant. I continued to pray for a mother figure to enter my life, but none materialized.

Months turned into years, and I stopped badgering God. Perhaps He wants me to go it alone, I thought, and I decided I could handle it. I knew the source of my strength. I still missed Mom, but the terrible ache had subsided, and I had found meaning and fulfillment in raising my own family and teaching school.

Finally, the day arrived when my daughter left for college, and I retired from my career. Adrift again, I sought new ways to anchor my life, to fill my days, and to define myself. "I used to be a teacher," I moaned to my friend one day, "but who am I now?"

I joined a sorority and began a Bible study at church. I lunched with friends and took exercise classes. I swam and hiked with my husband. All these things filled my days, but something was missing. I began to express myself through poetry. In school, I had enjoyed my English classes and been told I wrote well, but I always laughed and said, "I can write. I just don't have anything to say!" And then, the Lord began to pour spiritual truths through my pen that surprised even me. The years spent in prayer and study had paid off. I finally had something to say.

I was hesitant to share my poems, so I hid them in a drawer in my office. Then, one day in a Bible study I met an older woman who was destined to change my perspective—and my life. Maxine was warm and kind, and I was drawn to her immediately. We discovered a mutual love of religious literature, and I sensed the Lord's leading when I offered her one of my poems. I was surprised and delighted by her affirmations. "This is really wonderful!" she said with genuine enthusiasm.

Thus began a friendship that has spanned nearly ten years. We have an unusual relationship in that we rarely socialize, but we visit on the phone periodically. Our conversations always transcend the superficial and cut straight to important matters of the heart. "I believe we are soul mates," Maxine said one day. I breathed a silent prayer of thanks for the precious gift God had given me.

A born encourager, Maxine has always searched for ways to affirm others, and she was the perfect person to whom this nervous neophyte could turn for mentoring. Over the years, I have read many of my poems and devo-

3

tionals to her, and her approval has invariably spurred me on to write more. Without her faith in me, I doubt that I would have continued to write or had the courage to submit my work for publication. She instilled within me the confidence to believe that my work has value. When I was invited to read my work publicly at church, Maxine was the first person I contacted for support and prayer. She called after each session and rejoiced in my success.

Although she was unable to continue beyond high school, she educated herself, particularly in the study of the Bible. She has read all the great theologians, and I marvel at the depth of her understanding and wisdom. When I've had a question about God or a situation in the Bible, I turn to Maxine. Whenever I've faced a challenge in my life, she's been there to listen, to console, and to provide advice. Above all, I have always felt loved like a daughter.

Maxine's time and energy are limited now. She will soon be eighty, and the years have taken their toll on her body, but her mind and spirit remain strong. Her days are spent caring for her husband, whose health is failing, and helping with their granddaughter, who is mentally challenged. Her life has not been easy, but I have never heard her complain. She is selfless, completely devoted to God and her family, and unwavering in her faith. Thanks to her, I have learned to accept life as it comes from the loving hand of God. Her "cup runneth over," and its sweetness has spilled into my life.

—Susan Estribou Ramsden

Endurance Test

*We can rejoice, too, when we run into problems and trials,
for we know that they help us develop endurance.*
ROMANS 5:3

I didn't have to wait long for the first test of endurance with my infant daughter. A few weeks after she came home from the hospital, Emily developed a severe case of colic. Every evening, at five o'clock, as if prompted by an internal alarm, she would begin to cry—pathetic whimpers followed by anguished cries and, even, howls of pain.

One evening, my mother came over. Emily's cries filled the room, and tears of frustration and exhaustion trickled down my cheeks. My mother reached down and took the baby into her arms. Miraculously, Emily grew quiet.

"Sometimes," my mother said, "I think God tries to show us that we do have what it takes. You may not think you're doing a very good job, but Emily's colic has proved that you have the love and patience to be a terrific mother." And then, as if in total agreement, Emily gave her grandmother a big smile.

Our trials and tribulations always happen for a reason.

—SBT

More Than We Think Possible

*Now glory to God! By his mighty power at work
within us, he is able to accomplish infinitely more
than we would ever dare to ask or hope.*
EPHESIANS 3:20

Our five-year-old daughter, Ann, sat on the curb looking at the houses in our cul-de-sac. "I wish we still lived in the other house," she said. "At least I had Mike to play with." She was right. There were no children in the new neighborhood, and I longed to find her a friend.

"Ann," I replied, "let's pray for a family to move nearby, one with a child your age." I sat down beside her, and we joined hands and prayed. Afterward, I had my doubts, but as I soon discovered, they were groundless.

A few months later, I saw a moving van driving down our street. I didn't give it much thought until Ann burst through the door, accompanied by two children.

"Look, Mom!" she said. "This is Barbara and Jason. They just moved in, and we can play and walk to school together. Isn't that great?"

I smiled in delighted agreement as I praised God for answering our prayer with not one friend, but two!

God is able to do much more than we think possible.

—JEWELL JOHNSON

Everlasting Joy

A cheerful look brings joy to the heart;
good news makes for good health.
PROVERBS 15:30

"Come on, Mom," pleaded my thirteen-year-old daughter, Teresa. "Why don't you come to church with me? I know you'll love the people. They're so friendly, especially Pam."

"Maybe next week," I replied as she closed the car door. I envied the smile that lit up her face when she joined the circle of laughing girls standing near the church door. I drove away, holding back tears of self-pity. It had been nearly two years since my husband had been transferred to Salem. And we still had no church—and no friends.

For several months, I observed Teresa's joy grow as she shared the happiness she had found with her church family and friends. At her insistence, I finally agreed to visit. Now, almost twenty years later, our family still attends that same church. My husband and I have wonderful memories, many friends, and a terrific son-in-law, who also attended there from childhood.

God can use our children's joy to shower us with blessings.

—CHARLOTTE KARDOKUS

Butterfly Wings

So don't worry about tomorrow, for tomorrow will bring its own worries. Today's trouble is enough for today.
MATTHEW 6:34

My first pregnancy with my son, Gabriel, had passed without incident—the occasional flicker of worry banished quickly by excitement and anticipation. Unfortunately, Gabriel's birth was followed by two miscarriages, and when I discovered I was pregnant once again, I began to worry. The happiness I had felt during my pregnancy with Gabriel was nowhere in sight, having been replaced by a constant state of apprehension. I prayed constantly for the well-being of my unborn child, but even my talks with God were tainted with the anxiety that had taken over my life.

Then, one day, I felt a familiar tickle in my lower abdomen—a sensation I once described to someone as like the brush of a butterfly's wing. Suddenly, I knew God was in control, and He would do what was best for my baby and me. I vowed to take this pregnancy one day at a time, and I sat there for hours, lost in the miracle of feeling my baby move for the first time.

Don't let worry steal your joy.

—SBT

Weathering Storms

Imitate God, therefore, in everything you do,
because you are his dear children.
EPHESIANS 5:1

The loving hands that cradled me as a child are now frail, but they still possess an unmistakable motherly touch. I guided my mother gently toward the door and pulled her jacket snugly around her shoulders and said, "The wind is really blowing cold today, Mom. Let's bundle you up."

She smiled at me as I wound the scarf around her neck and kissed her gently on her cheek. Her eyes spoke to me: "I used to do this for you," they said, "before you could do it for yourself. Now you're taking care of me. I'm sorry it's come to this."

She waited patiently for me as I opened the door. We step outside, arm in arm, to face the world and the storms together, just as we did when I was just a little girl. She was right. She did this and so much more—all for me. More times than I can remember.

Father, help us to remember that we are your dear children,
at every stage of our lives.

—MICHELE STARKEY

Strength for the Hard Times

For I can do everything through Christ,
who gives me strength.
PHILIPPIANS 4:13

Poised before the microphone, my fifth-grade daughter waited to hear the introduction of her accompaniment tape. Abruptly, the audience sucked in a collective gasp as the instrumental music from the tape was swallowed into a defective tape player. I felt completely helpless as I watched Amelia flee behind the curtain.

For weeks, she had prepared for her vocal solo performance, and I wasn't about to let disaster defeat her. Luckily, my husband had put a spare tape in his pocket, so I rushed backstage and found my weeping daughter. "I can't go back out there again, Mom," she sobbed.

"You are strong in the Lord, and I believe in you," I replied. "You can do this!"

Amelia's rendition of *Put a Little Love in Your Heart* was rewarded by a standing ovation, a sense of accomplishment, and a God-given courage.

We can help our daughters tap into their personal strength
and have confidence in a powerful God.

—EVANGELINE BEALS GARDNER

The Beauty of Big Feet

Even when I walk through the darkest valley,
I will not be afraid, for you are close beside me.
Your rod and your staff protect and comfort me.
PSALM 23:4

About two months before my daughter Emily's due date, we had to move. I wasn't thrilled by the prospect of changing doctors so late in my pregnancy, but I liked my new obstetrician right away. Calmed by her personable and caring demeanor, I confessed my fear that my labor would be a repeat of the frightening, painful ordeal I had endured with my son.

She looked down at my feet. "What size of shoe do you wear?"

"Eight and sometimes nine," I replied with some bewilderment.

"I've delivered over a thousand babies," she said with a big smile, "and women with big feet almost invariably have easier labors. With those feet, you should be just fine."

And then I remembered that, although the size of my feet and the skill and comfort of my doctor would serve me well, it would be God who would give me the courage I needed. He would be right there with me.

God will never let you go through anything alone.

—SBT

11

Back on Track

*The Lord helps the fallen and lifts those
bent beneath their loads.*
PSALM 145:14

A week full of challenging circumstances had left me feeling a bit battle weary and bruised. I tried to stay focused on the Lord and remember His promise to be there for me, but I yielded to distraction. Instead of trusting Him to take me through my trials that week, I allowed myself to become worried and disheartened.

When things settled down a bit, I was relieved, but I couldn't help feel as though my faith had been shaken. It was my daughter, Emily, who helped me get back on track. One morning, she told me about a discussion in which several people had challenged her belief in God. As I listened to her describe the manner in which she had defended her faith, I found myself agreeing and contributing my own comments.

When our conversation ended, I felt as though my relationship with God had been restored and strengthened. Although I had turned to prayer and God's word, I had underestimated the power of fellowship with another believer.

When your faith falters, turn to a fellow believer for encouragement.

—SBT

A Determined Daughter

When they were discouraged, I smiled at them.
My look of approval was precious to them.
JOB 29:24

My daughter, Rebecca, worked hard at everything. However, she couldn't catch or kick a ball well and didn't have a good sense of rhythm for dance. Her passionate desire to be an athlete led us to convince the local swim coach to let her join the team at age five. He kept her on because of her exceptional effort.

Her first race was one pool length. We prayed and encouraged her to do her best. The other swimmers had already finished as Rebecca reached the pool's halfway point. She kept stroking and kicking slowly, while I yelled to cheer her on. Soon her teammates started to cheer, and then everyone joined in. She took about five extra minutes to complete the length of the Olympic sized pool. As she climbed out, the entire crowd stood and applauded. Later, she said, "Mom, I heard your voice and kept going."

Rebecca kept swimming for thirteen years, and we cheered her on at almost all her meets. She became a good long-distance swimmer, a lifeguard, and a swim teacher.

A parent's encouragement inspires a child's perseverance.

—KAREN H. WHITING

13

Persistence Pays Off

One day Jesus told his disciples a story to show that they should always pray and never give up.
LUKE 18:1

Sometimes, we adults forget the significance of childhood accomplishments. We don't remember the thrill of tying our shoes for the first time, riding our bicycle or, even, something as simple as whistling. One day, when my daughter Emily was about four, I noticed her watching me whistle. "I want to do that," she said with a familiar determination in her voice.

Her first whistling lesson did not go well. A lot of air passed between those sweet lips, but not much sound emerged. Subsequent lessons proved equally disappointing. I suggested she try praying to God. "He'll help you whistle," I said, "but you have to keep trying. You can't give up."

A few days later, she ran up to me, pursed her lips, and whistled! "He did it," she announced. "I prayed, and I didn't give up, and He helped me."

I gave her a big hug. "Of course He did," I said, and grinned as she raced down the hall, whistling all the way.

God rewards persistence.

—SBT

Giving from the Heart

*She extends a helping hand to the poor
and opens her arms to the needy.*
PROVERBS 31:20

In an effort to teach my eleven-year old daughter, Hannah, the importance of helping others, we volunteered with Habitat for Humanity to build three houses in three days. She worked endlessly without complaint, helping to move dirt, landscaping, and preparing food. I swung a hammer, painted, and installed siding. After twenty-one hours of laboring in ninety-two–degree temperatures, we both came away changed.

"I've learned a lot about doing for others," Hannah said in a confident voice. "It isn't all about me." My heart overflowed with emotions after witnessing the devastating effects of drugs and death on a family. And yet, these same people expressed awe-inspiring gratitude for just a roof over their heads. Those in need hadn't been the only ones blessed by the experience.

I thought about the number of lives we could change if we gave up our time to help others, and I was reminded of the important role we play in teaching our children to have tender hearts for those in need.

A willing heart is all you need to help others.

—KARLA KASSEBAUM

15

Spoiled Rotten

Now let your unfailing love comfort me,
just as you promised me, your servant.
PSALM 119:76

"If loving you means spoiling you, then you're spoiled rotten." My mother said this to me on numerous occasions while I was growing up but, until I had a family of my own, I never fully appreciated what she meant.

For my mother, loving me meant making sure I knew right from wrong and teaching me to take responsibility for my actions. Loving me meant I didn't get everything I asked for, but I always had the things I truly needed. Loving me meant reading to me until I could read on my own, going on fishing and hiking trips, playing board games, volleyball, and softball.

In my mother's eyes, I was spoiled rotten, and when I had my children, I did my best to spoil them rotten, too—according to my mother's guidelines.

Like our heavenly Father, our mothers spoil us with their
unfailing love.

—KAREN McKEE

Faith-Filled Friends

*And let us not neglect our meeting together, as some people
do, but encourage one another, especially now that the day
of his return is drawing near.*
HEBREWS 10:25

Emily was due on New Year's Eve. I harbored secret fantasies of giving birth to the New Year's baby and winning the prizes donated by local merchants in the area. But my baby had other ideas, and I found myself surprised by labor pains just after midnight on December 22.

Recently, her father, brothers, and I went to a surprise party for Emily planned by one of her friends. I was grateful for the opportunity to celebrate the amazing person she has become. The guest list for the party included some of the reasons Emily has grown into such a wonderful and godly woman.

Since middle school, she has surrounded herself with friends who love the Lord as much as she does. She has told me on numerous occasions how much this has helped her walk with God, how being close to like-minded people has given her the strength and courage to avoid some of the pitfalls of growing up.

Spend time with believers and strengthen your faith.

—SBT

17

What Would I Ask For?

*Give me an understanding heart so that I can
govern your people well and know the difference
between right and wrong.*
I KINGS 3:9

In nine years of home schooling my daughter Mary, I learned as much from her as she did from me. One moment that stands out in my memory happened when she was in kindergarten. In our Bible lesson about Solomon, God asked Solomon what he wanted above all else. After I finished my teaching, Mary and I decided to answer the question God had put to Solomon. What would we ask for if we could have anything we wanted?

I thought and thought, trying to come up with something that would impress and instruct my daughter. Finally, I said, "I don't know. What would you ask for?"

Without hesitation, she said, "Nothing. I just want God."

I almost fell off my chair. Then I laughed and hugged her. What a lesson she taught me that day! Indeed, what more could we want?

Our children have much to teach us if we are willing to learn.

—PAM HALTER

Helping Hands

And we will receive from him whatever we ask because we obey him and do the things that please him.
1 JOHN 3:22

One evening, at dinner, it was my daughter's turn to ask the blessing. We held hands and bowed our heads as seven-year-old Bethany thanked God for food and birthdays in her customary way. Before the final amen, however, she tacked on a heartfelt request that brought a smile to my face. "And dear God," she said. "Please help someone get me a drink because I don't have one."

After a quiet chuckle, my husband and I looked at each other and then at the table. Sure enough, everyone had a drink except Bethany. I immediately got up to pour her a cup of milk.

God has promised to give to those who ask. We should be ready to receive, but we must also be ready to act. We never know when he might work through us to answer the prayer of another.

God often works through us to help others.

—KAREN WITEMEYER

Life Alterations

This means that anyone who belongs to Christ has become a
new person. The old life is gone; a new life has begun!
2 CORINTHIANS 5:17

When I was pregnant with Emily, everyone had a piece of advice to offer. "Nothing will ever be the same after the baby comes," people would tell me with knowing smiles. I suspected they must have been exaggerating. Surely, some things would remain unchanged.

As it turned out, they had been telling the truth. My life was altered in every way imaginable, but it brought me a happiness I didn't know existed. Some of the changes I underwent were internal. I viewed the world in an entirely different light. I had a daughter!

However, nothing could have prepared me for the profound experience of dedicating my life to the Lord. Welcoming Emily into the world may have introduced a new lifestyle and a new way of thinking, but when I invited Jesus into my heart, I became a new person. I became a person capable of doing all things with Christ's help, including tackling the tremendous job of being a mother.

You, too, can have a new life with Jesus.

—SBT

Making Plans

We can make our plans, but the Lord determines our steps.
PROVERBS 16:9

My heart raced as I held the letter. This was it—one simple page that would tell my daughter whether or not the Physical Therapy department accepted her as a student. The university admitted only thirty-two of more than five hundred applicants to the program. Now the letter had arrived, but my daughter was in Oklahoma, spending the Christmas break with her sister. Her last words before leaving home were, "Call me the minute the letter comes."

I prayed as I dialed the number. When my daughter answered, I told her the letter was here. "Open it," she said. With shaking hands, I ripped the envelope open and pulled out the folded sheet of paper. How I dreaded reading it and relaying the news over the telephone. Then I looked at the page, and the longed-for word caught my eye. Accepted! We can hear the same words from our Savior when we let Him determine our steps.

Make great plans for your life, but trust in the Lord for an even more wonderful outcome.

—LeAnn Campbell

Difficult to Love

Most important of all, continue to show deep love for each
other, for love makes up for many of our faults.
1 PETER 4:8

At the age of eighty-six, my Mom was difficult to love. Two small strokes had left her with debilitating physical weakness that tragically curtailed her former, feisty lifestyle. Once totally independent, she was now subject to others and bitter for being at the mercy of their schedules.

I was the closest daughter, and her care fell to me. She was often harsh and critical, and I frequently bit my tongue to avoid a confrontation, but my resentment was obvious. Then she suffered a massive stroke. When friends and family gathered at her bedside, I invited each one to take her hand and speak of how she had blessed their lives. Their testimonies of her love and care for them opened my heart, and my mother and I finally made our peace. I wish it had happened sooner but, thankfully, God was faithful to cover my stubbornness with His grace.

We need to express God's love to
even the most difficult people.

—LINDA BLAINE POWELL

The Living Gift

*And may the Lord make your love for one another
and for all people grow and overflow, just as our
love for you overflows.*
1 THESSALONIANS 3:12

My husband, Tom, has developed a very special bond with one of the newest members of our congregation. My friend Hazel and her ten-month-old granddaughter, Ruby, usually sit right behind us, but Ruby often ends up in Tom's arms. This morning, as I watched Ruby sleep, I thought of my own baby girl, now nineteen, and the countless times she rested, safe and loved, in her father's arms.

I recalled how powerful my love felt during those moments and, yet, how much more potent it became as time passed. The more time I spent with my daughter, the more familiar I became with her personality only served to increase the already overwhelming love I had for her. If someone were to ask me to name the most important quality of a good mother, I would answer without hesitation—love.

And so it is with God. The greatest gift I can give the Lord is my love—a love that grows and strengthens when I spend time in prayer and in studying the Bible.

Get to know—and love—the Lord.

—SBT

You're in Good Hands

The eternal God is your refuge,
and his everlasting arms are under you.
Deuteronomy 33:27

At the end of her sophomore year in college, our oldest daughter, Kathy, enlisted in the Air Force. After basic training, she was chosen to be in a Secret Service squad and, for many months, we didn't know her whereabouts.

One day I received a letter in which she told me that she had visited the DMZ on the 38th parallel in Korea. "Mom," she wrote, "just looking across that barbed wire into the eyes of a North Korean soldier sent chills through me." I prayed and worried, and then worried and prayed. One night, while watching the news, a commercial for a well-known insurance company appeared on the screen. It showed two hands holding a car, and the caption read, "You're in good hands with Allstate."

At that moment, God spoke to a worried mother's heart, and I knew Kathy was in good hands with God. I wrote to Kathy immediately and relayed God's message. Years later, she continues to remind me, "Mom, I'm still in good hands."

You can always find security in the hands of God.

—Gwen Rice Clark

I Can See Clearly Now

Now we see things imperfectly as in a cloudy mirror, but then we will see everything with perfect clarity. All that I know now is partial and incomplete, but then I will know everything completely just as God now knows me completely.
1 CORINTHIANS 13:12

I began wearing glasses in the third grade, so it didn't come as a huge surprise when my eight-year-old daughter began complaining she couldn't see well and thought she might need glasses. Dutifully, I called the optometrist and made an appointment. When the day finally came, she treated the situation more as an adventure than a medical necessity. As soon as we were inside the door, she rushed to the display of frames and began modeling pair after pair. By the time I had checked her in to see the doctor, she had accumulated a small mountain of spectacles.

A couple of puffs from the glaucoma machine dramatically altered her upbeat mood. "Can't we just buy the glasses?" she asked. The dilation drops destroyed her deception. "That's enough," she said. "I can see just fine." The doctor and I agreed. Like a child, we often want things without stopping to consider everything involved. I'm so thankful that God knows what we need better than we do—if only we trust Him.

Our Father really does know best.

—VICKI TIEDE

25

Making Amends

If I had not confessed the sin in my heart,
the Lord would not have listened.
PSALM 66:18

In a completely unexpected bid for independence, my daughter Emily left home just after she turned eighteen. Her departure left me in a state of shock, and when angry words passed between us, I was heartbroken. How could she do this to me? For days, I wallowed in self-pity and guilt. Somehow, the whole thing must be my fault, and I concluded that I must be a terrible mother.

I begged God to bring her home. And then, one day, during my morning prayers, I paused for a moment and a crystal clear thought formed in my mind: "It's not about you." It was as if someone had spoken out loud.

It was then I realized why my prayers, although heard by God, had remained unanswered. My pride and obsession with self had damaged my fellowship with God. I immediately confessed my sins and asked for the Lord's forgiveness. It wasn't long before Emily and I were reconciled and rebuilding the loving relationship we once had.

Come to the Lord with a clean heart.

—SBT

A Winning Combination

*The earnest prayer of a righteous person has
great power and produces wonderful results.*
JAMES 5:16

My daughter Alicia's voice trembled as she spoke. "Mom, I've entered the annual Health and Temperance Oratorical Contest."

"Honey, do you think that's a good idea?" I asked. "You're only twelve, and most of the kids who compete are college age. You still have lots of time."

Alicia answered quickly. "You've always said that if we believe and pray, anything is possible. I'm sure if I pray and really work at this, I just might win."

There was no doubt she had the right spirit. Despite my reluctance to admit her readiness for this project, I was pleased that our numerous conversations on the importance of positive thinking, hard work, and ceaseless prayer had found a place in her heart.

On the night of the contest, Alicia became the youngest first place winner to receive the $1,000 dollar prize. Clearly, when our children have big dreams that require significant effort, we can readily support them by encouraging hard work and prayer.

God hears and answers our children's prayers.

—YVONNE CURRY SMALLWOOD

I Can See Clearly Now

*You prepare a feast for me in the presence of my
enemies. You honor me by anointing my head
with oil. My cup overflows with blessings.*
PSALM 23:5

When my then six-year-old Emily's third brother, Connor, was born, she wasn't exactly thrilled. For months, she had talked about how much fun she was going to have with her new sister, and she refused to listen when I tried to explain that the baby might be another boy. Despite my best efforts to encourage an interest in our newest family member, she remained aloof and indifferent toward Connor.

A few weeks later, as I watched Emily's friends arrive for her birthday party, I went into the nursery. I found a group of adoring little girls clustered around Connor's crib, filling the room with their excited, high pitched chatter. "Oh, Emily, he's adorable," one girl said.

"You are so lucky," someone else remarked, and everyone murmured in agreement.

Emily reached down and stroked Connor's hair, and then she turned to me and smiled. "Can we take him into the living room?" she asked.

"Of course," I replied and uttered a silent prayer of thanks to God for helping Emily to see her blessings through the eyes of others.

Ask God to reveal His bountiful blessings.

—SBT

Tomorrow Never Comes

*How do you know what your life will be
like tomorrow? Your life is like the morning
fog—it's here a little while, then it's gone.*
JAMES 4:14

It seemed like a good idea at the time. My daughter Emily wanted to earn some extra money, and I needed someone to clean up the spare room.

Everything went well until I went into the room to see how she was getting along. My heart sank as I surveyed the room. It was obvious to me that she hadn't listened to any of my instructions. Without giving her a chance to explain, I began to reprimand her. A bewildered and hurt expression appeared on her face, but I continued my tirade. "Maybe I should just do it myself," I said.

"Maybe you should," she replied and went upstairs.

I sat down at my desk and stewed in my self-righteous indignation for a few minutes. When I heard Emily ask her father if she could go to the movies with a friend, I suddenly realized I had to set things straight. Only God knew what the future held, and I couldn't let her leave the house until I apologized and told her how much I loved her.

*God doesn't promise us a tomorrow,
so make the most of today.*

—SBT

29

Piggyback Rides

*I will be your God throughout your lifetime—until
your hair is white with age. I made you, and I will
care for you. I will carry you along and save you.*
ISAIAH 46:4

When my daughter started kindergarten, waking up for school proved to be quite a challenge. "Wake up, Sunshine!" I would sing over and over.

She'd ignore me for as long as she could but, then, she would finally open her arms and whisper, "Piggyback ride?" Rather than risk her slipping back to sleep, I'd offer my back. She'd wrap her arms around my neck, and with her draped over me like a warm blanket, I carried her to the breakfast table. It was as if my strength enabled her to get out of bed.

A few years have gone by but, sometimes, I still use a cozy piggyback ride to counteract a sleepy start. Our routine reminds me of one of God's many promises in which He vows to carry us when we are too weary to continue. What a comfort it is to know that when we feel discouraged or tired, we can still reach out to God and ask him to shoulder our burdens.

*In the midst of troubles and trials, we should remember that
God loves to give piggyback rides.*

—LORI Z. SCOTT

A Woman's Touch

See, I have written your name on the palms of my hands.
ISAIAH 49:15

One evening at church, our pastor asked if anyone had special prayer needs. I rose from my pew and made my way slowly to the front. I was a mother with a heavy heart. As the pastor began to pray, I bowed my head and closed my eyes. Suddenly, I felt the presence of someone behind me and I reached up to find a firm, yet gentle, hand on my shoulder.

This was a woman with soft hands. Who could it be? The prayer was not lengthy, but time seemed to stand still as the woman held my hand. Imagine my surprise when I turned around to see the face of my fifteen-year-old daughter, Amy. We embraced and walked back to our seats. Until that moment, I had never thought of my daughter as anything but my child, but the gentle touch of her hand that night transformed her from my little girl into a grown woman.

Embrace the changing roles of your beloved children.

—LaRose Karr

Blessed Sleep

*Then Jesus said, "Come to me, all of you who are weary
and carry heavy burdens, and I will give you rest."*
MATTHEW 11:28

I thought I knew my daughter, but the lie blindsided
me. In honor of her eighteenth birthday, her father and I
had given Emily permission to spend the weekend at her
best friend's house. However, when I phoned her friend's
house Saturday morning, Emily wasn't there. We soon discovered she had spent the weekend with her boyfriend.

Stunned by her deception, I thought of the hundreds
of times I had told her how much I valued honesty. I
remembered explaining that no matter what she did, lying
about it would only make things worse. While the rest of
the house slept that night, I lay awake. Anger and confusion settled in to keep my sorrow company. Had any of my
words over the years found a home in her heart?

I needed to face the situation in the fresh light of
day, but sleep eluded me. Then I thought of the Lord, His
hands outstretched, inviting me to lay down my burden
and rest. Comforted by His presence and His promises, I
finally slept.

No burden is too heavy for God.

—SBT

A Direct Line to God

At that time you won't need to ask me for anything. I tell you the truth, you will ask the Father directly, and he will grant your request because you use my name.
JOHN 16:23

My kids and I were on a flight to New York for a surprise visit to my parents. As the plane took off, and I watched the buildings below get smaller and smaller, a terrible thought occurred to me. Since Mom didn't know we were coming, she wasn't praying for us, as she always did when we traveled. The plane would surely crash!

I knew it wasn't very rational, but I truly felt that my mother had a direct line to heaven because she prayed so often. I was sure she had more influence with God than I did.

The plane landed safely.

When we arrived at my parents' house, I told Mom what had been going through my head when I was in the plane. She laughed. "My prayers aren't worth any more than yours," she said. "You have a direct line to God, too!"

Through our prayers, we all have a direct line to God.

—MARY LAUFER

I See Where You Are

You are the God who sees me.
Have I truly seen the One who sees me?
GENESIS 16:13

Over the years, my daughters have participated in various competitions and programs for church and school, and I've noticed that the first thing they did on stage is to search for my face in the crowd. This was especially true for my youngest girl.

Whether she was alone or in a group, she invariably scanned the audience until she found me. Always a bit nervous, she would relax as soon as our eyes met. She obviously needed to know I was there for her, and that I knew exactly where she was.

Like my daughter, whenever I come up against an intimidating task or trial, I simply need to make contact with my Heavenly Father. I know He is there for me, and I can face anything with His help.

God knows exactly where I am.

—SANDRA MCGARRITY

A Sandwich for Jesus

*Work willingly at whatever you do, as though you were
working for the Lord rather than for people.*
COLOSSIANS 3:23

My daughter Emily watched as I spread the peanut butter across the bread with smooth, precise strokes. A few minutes later, I assembled the sandwich and handed it to her on a plate. "Can you take that to your dad, please?"

"You sure put a lot of work into a peanut butter and jam sandwich," she said with a grin.

I paused for a moment. "I suppose I do, but it's worth it when you're making a sandwich for Jesus."

"I thought you made the sandwich for Dad."

"Oh, I did," I replied, "but if I imagine that I'm cooking dinner for Jesus or washing His clothes, or sweeping His floor, it helps me realize that my work around here is truly important. It inspires me to do the best job I can. Does that make sense?"

"Yeah, it does. All I know is you make great sandwiches," she said and smiled again. "Now, do you think you could make one for me?"

Working for the Lord is truly a labor of love.

—SBT

FEBRUARY

Just Like Me

For everyone has sinned;
we all fall short of God's glorious standard.

Yet God, with undeserved kindness, declares that we are
righteous. He did this through Christ Jesus when he freed us
from the penalty for our sins.
ROMANS 3:23–24

*M*y mother is perfect. I've been hearing about her qualities and virtues all my life. Here is a partial list:

Popular: She has explained to me how she could orchestrate four dates on a single night, using her sorority sisters to keep suitors from running into each other between the afternoon soda, early supper, early movie, and late party commitments.

Brilliant: To save money, she completed her four-year college degree in three years, with a high GPA. She played a mean game of contract bridge and did double-acrostic word puzzles for casual amusement.

Talented: She was a clever seamstress and hand-smocked elaborate scenes—one, I recall, was a complete farm—on the bodice of my dresses. She made coats for me and for herself. She took an upholstery course and recovered our sofa. She took up cake decorating and created a three-tier wedding cake. One year, she made hand-painted, nativity scene cookies for each member of the Girl Scout troop.

Society queen: As the impeccably dressed and perfectly coiffed wife of a prominent St. Louis intellectual properties lawyer, she handled her social obligations with finesse. She kept track of intricate guest lists and retained a record of the menus, her outfits, and when each guest recipro-cated. She also led the women's group at her church.

Leader: She led my Brownie, Girl Scout, and Senior Scout troops. As Skipper of the Mariner Scout Ship Pinafore, she accompanied us to Mystic, Connecticut, for basic seamanship training and organized a week on a chartered schooner in the Bahamas. The girls flocked around her and brought their boyfriends and fiancés for her approval a decade or more later.

As for me, I've never been beautiful or popular. I'm smart, despite my less than perfect grades at school. I play an adequate game of party bridge, choose comfort over style in dress, and limit my cooking to the microwave. I have never met the standard my mother set and decided—early on—not even to make the attempt.

As the decades rolled by, I have achieved some goals of my own. I obtained a master's degree in special educa-tion and taught for a quarter century. I published several devotionals and stories, as well as a travel book. I have assisted with a Bible study, spoken to women's groups, and helped lead a middle-school youth fellowship. Nonethe-less, I've always assumed I would never be in my mother's category of wife, mother, and woman. I came to the con-clusion that none of my accomplishments would ever be good enough—as far as I could see.

Then I made a fascinating discovery. I was going through some family papers and read a series of letters my mother had written to a friend. And that's when I found a paragraph written by mother in 1945, two years before my birth, while my father was still in the Army. It read,

"I never feel that anyone attractive could possibly like me, and I'm afraid of thrusting myself upon them. If I get close to someone, they might find I'm not as terrific as I think I am and, worse yet, *I* might find out I'm not."

Oh, my goodness, I thought. I felt as though she was describing me! I never knew my mother had felt that way. She always cruised along, accomplishing marvelous things, expecting amazing results and, as I once imagined, readily meeting her own high expectations. And I had always seen myself stumbling behind, admiring her from afar. Now I knew differently. She had been unsure of herself, just as I had so often felt. How remarkable!

I felt like the blind man in the Gospel of Mark. Jesus healed him, but he told the Lord that he saw people who looked "like trees walking around." So Jesus touched his eyes again, and then "he saw everything clearly." (Mark 8:24) He had gained more than physical vision; he had acquired empathy, compassion, and perception.

The words my mother had written cleared my vision. She was a person with great talents, but she, too, had doubted herself on occasion. She was admired, yet she craved approval from those around her. She was a leader, but questioned her identity. In other words, she was a person just like me.

I'm grateful for the understanding that led to a better relationship between my mother and me. Now, I can accept my own shortcomings more readily, be willing to face my own doubts, and celebrate my own accomplishments without having to compare them to my mother's so-called perfection. We are two women, making mistakes along the way, but doing our best. I can live with that.

It occurred to me that my discovery gave me a glimpse of what it's like to see people from God's perspective—through His eyes of love and compassion. No need to compare myself with my mother or anyone else. No need for feeling unable to keep up. If my creator is satisfied, then I should be, too.

—ELSI DODGE

My Rock

You are my rock and my fortress.
PSALM 31:3

"Don't worry, Mom. It's an adventure," my daughter Melody said as we drove to a baby shower in west Seattle. When we passed the Space Needle, I knew we were headed the wrong way. I tried a different road.

"If we pass the Space Needle again, we're doomed," I said just as the Space Needle appeared again. After passing the Space Needle two more times, driving the wrong way on a one-way street, and going through the worst part of Seattle, we finally reached the shower. When someone asked us why we were so late, Melody simply said, "We took a wrong turn."

Life is like that. We have a destination in mind, but things get in our way. Sometimes we are stretched to the limit trying to reach our goal, and we lose our sense of direction. The good news is we can turn to the Lord to get back on the right path.

God hasn't promised us a life without problems, but He has promised to be with us every step of the way.

—MIDGE DESART

Anywhere with Jesus

God is my strong fortress, and he makes my way perfect.
2 SAMUEL 22:33

On the morning of August 11, 2006, I woke to the news of a foiled terrorist attack. My eighteen-year-old daughter, Julie, was scheduled to fly that morning to Connecticut to visit a friend. Petrified, I tried to convince her not to go. I called the airline, hoping they had canceled her flight, but the schedule hadn't changed. We watched television and scanned the Internet. "It's up to you, Julie," I finally said. "I'll support whatever you choose to do." Secretly, I prayed for her to remain at home.

She decided to go. We loaded the suitcases in the car and began the long ride to the airport. I clutched the steering wheel and fought back the tears. As we traveled down the road, a song by Amy Grant filled the car. I heard the lyrics, "anywhere with Jesus I can safely go," and I smiled at my daughter. "That's your confirmation right there," I said. "Go with Jesus, and He'll keep you safe."

We can count on God's protection during every journey.

—CONNIE HILTON DUNN

Running for Safety

He will cover you with his feathers. He will shelter you with his wings. His faithful promises are your armor and protection.
PSALM 91:4

The other day when my daughter arrived for a visit, she headed straight for the chicken pens out back. She knew that a clutch of chicks had hatched the night before, and she could hardly wait to see the new babies.

We stood and watched the hen with her brood, marveling at how the slightest noise sent the tiny chicks scurrying for the safety of their mother's wings. When Emily was about three, she wouldn't leave my side. And then, summoning all of her courage, she would venture out the front door, only to hurry back inside a few minutes later to make sure I was still there.

It wouldn't be long before the chicks in front of us would be wandering everywhere, driving their poor mother to distraction. *I know how that feels, too,* I thought with a smile. Even though Emily no longer ran to me for security and safety the way she did as a child, I knew her Heavenly Father was always there to shelter and protect her.

Find real security under the sheltering wings of God.

—SBT

Good Grief!

*When they walk through the valley of Weeping, it
will become a place of refreshing springs, where
pools of blessing collect after the rains!*
PSALM 84:6

The pressure was mounting as I fought for control of
my emotions. My thirteen-year-old daughter, Elizabeth,
had never seen me cry, and I was determined to keep
it that way. She stood before me with her arms crossed,
wearing a typical teenage, eye-rolling, arrogant look on
her face.

"Mom, I need you to call my flute teacher, now. She
has to know if I can play in the special concert coming
up." It was a simple request, but it put me over the edge
where I had been perched precariously after a jam-packed
day of teaching, chauffeuring, and mothering. Tears of
frustration and exhaustion spilled down my face.

A week later, Elizabeth came home from a new job.
She was sobbing, but instead of escaping to her room and
slamming the door as she usually did, she came to me for
comfort and encouragement. Perhaps she found her tears
less mortifying after witnessing mine.

*Our tears provide an opportunity for those we love to
demonstrate their love and compassion.*

—NANCY MITCHELL

45

Spicy Exploration

Love never gives up, never loses faith, is always hopeful, and endures through every circumstance.
1 CORINTHIANS 13:7

I stood in the doorway of what was once my organized and tidy kitchen, surveying the devastation. Behind my teenaged daughter, I saw a collection of pots and pans on the stove and a sink full of dishes. The countertop was littered with the remains of shredded carrots and potato and onion peels. "What are you making tonight, sweetheart?"

"It's an Indian dish!" Kiri's eyes were sparkling. "It's going to be much better than that other thing I tried last night."

"Sounds delicious," I replied, determined to keep my voice upbeat. I left the kitchen, and once out in the hall, I stopped to mutter and shake my head. Last night's tongue-searing meal was still fresh in my memory, but I loved my daughter so much that I'd rather eat ten thousand inedible meals than crush her joyful spirit of experimentation.

Our Heavenly Father feels exactly the same way. He delights to see His children discover and use the gifts He has given them. He wants us to develop our full potential for His honor and glory.

Sometimes love involves a little indigestion.

—DENA N. NETHERTON

Into the Storm

*Immediately after this, Jesus insisted that his disciples get
back into the boat and cross to the other side of the lake,
while he sent the people home.*
MATTHEW 14:22

My daughter Emily left home a few days after she turned
eighteen. She had no definite plans, no resources—only a
fierce determination to be independent. I remembered our
many disagreements over the chores I expected her to do.
She had often complained that all she did was housework.

"Maybe she'll find out that life around here wasn't as
bad as she thought," I told my husband. Tom just hugged
me. I think he knew that behind my angry words was the
wounded heart of a worried mother.

That evening, he said, "Perhaps God wants Emily to
learn a few things—about herself, her faith and, even, her
relationship with us. All we can do is pray for her and be
here if she needs us."

I thought about Jesus sending His disciples into the
storm because there was a lesson He wanted to teach
them. He watched over them that night and made sure
they reached the shore safely. I knew He would do the
same for Emily.

*God may send us into a storm,
but He will help us reach the other side.*

—SBT

47

Baking a Legacy

And you should imitate me, just as I imitate Christ.
1 CORINTHIANS 11:1

Sourdough bread was a staple in our house when my kids were growing up. I always kept the starter in one of its various stages, and we all savored the aroma of fresh bread baking in the oven.

When our 4-H Leader asked for parents to help teach projects, I knew immediately how I could participate and made arrangements for our first bread-baking lesson. My daughter and the other 4-H members stood around the island countertop. As they began working their hands into the floury mixture, I was surprised at how quickly Anna took to kneading the dough.

Then I remembered the many years she had watched me from her favorite perch on the kitchen stool. It was a welcome reminder of the importance of the many jobs I perform as a mother—tasks that might be imitated when I least expect it!

Our children are watching and learning from our example.

—SALLY FERGUSON

Nighttime Visits

She makes sure her dealings are profitable;
her lamp burns late into the night.
PROVERBS 31:18

The house was dark except for a light over the sink and the one coming from under the door to Aunt Sue's bedroom. Just home from a date, I went in to say goodnight and ended up sitting on her bed and telling her where I had gone and what I had done. Since my parents' divorce, our unmarried aunt had lived with our family to help my mother.

Mom worked hard during the day and was usually in bed when my sister and I came home from nighttime school events or dates, but Aunt Sue was always there with her light on, her door open, and an open invitation to stop by and share our lives. She told us what to do and scolded us when we needed it, but it was those nighttime visits I remember most. I now realize that she was truly a gift from God. I hope, somehow, I enriched her life as much as she did mine.

Loving mothers keep the door open and the light on.

—LAURIE A. PERKINS

Never Give Up

So let's not get tired of doing what is good. At just the right time we will reap a harvest of blessing if we don't give up.
GALATIANS 6:9

My daughter was born with a mind of her own. Stubborn and strong-willed, she questioned everything and often made it difficult for me to know what was really in her heart. Discouraged and disheartened, I worried that, somehow, I had let her down, but I never stopped praying that, one day, we would share our love for the Lord in the kind of relationship I had known with my own mother.

Then, a few months after she left home, she called to tell me that one of her friends from high school had decided to become a missionary. "I could really see myself doing something like that," she said.

My amazement grew as she went on to describe the many ways God had been working in her life, and how the things she had learned at church and at home were beginning to make sense. I shared her joy that day, and in the months that followed, we have shared so much more. And when she tells me she has been praying about something, I remind her to never give up.

Don't lose heart—God is listening.

—SBT

Joint Heirs

God decided in advance to adopt us into his own family by bringing us to himself through Jesus Christ. This is what he wanted to do, and it gave him great pleasure.
EPHESIANS 1:5

Although the topic of adoption was rarely discussed when I was a child, I have always been proud to tell others that our beautiful daughter Kimberly was adopted. I am eternally grateful to her young birth mother for having the wisdom and selflessness to realize that she was not in a position to become a parent. Because ours was a closed adoption, we have never met but, someday, in heaven, I will give this courageous woman a huge hug of heartfelt appreciation for her incomparable gift.

As Christians we are all adopted. In the Bible "adoption" is used to describe the process of salvation through Jesus Christ. God is our Father who graciously adopts us into His spiritual family and grants us all the privileges of being His joint heirs with Christ. When I consider what our Father has done for us through His son, my heart swells with love and gratitude, just as it does when I gaze upon our precious adopted daughter.

Our adoption into the family of God is solely the work of God's love and grace.

—SUSAN ESTRIBOU RAMSDEN

Listening with Your Heart

Turn your ear to listen to me; rescue me quickly.
Be my rock of protection, a fortress where I will be safe.
PSALM 31:2

When the phone rang, I picked it up with one hand and continued to stir the chili on the stove. "Mom!" my younger daughter, Emily, said. "You'll never guess what happened today." She proceeded to fill me in on the latest campus crisis while I set the table. I offered a few words of encouragement, but most of the time, I listened. "I feel better now," she said when she had finished talking. "I have to go to class."

My two daughters know they can call whenever they need to. Some calls come at 2:00 A.M., but even in the middle of the night, I try to listen patiently and pray with them. College-age children don't necessarily want advice. They just need a willing ear to help them sort things out so they can make their own decisions.

Your daughter might need a loving listener,
even when she's grown.

—JANET M. BAIR

Perfect Love

Such love has no fear, because perfect love expels all fear.
1 JOHN 4:18

Only hours after my daughter Emily was born, we discovered she needed a transfusion to correct a blood incompatibility disorder. She was taken by ambulance from our local hospital to a larger facility, and after receiving my frantic phone call, my mother hurried to join us at the hospital.

After listening to the pediatric surgeon describe the procedure that would correct Emily's problem, both my husband and mother appeared relaxed and full of confidence. But I remained terrified, my mind reeling with unthinkable possibilities. "What if something happened to her? What if something went wrong?"

My mother took my hand, and I looked into her eyes. Reflected there was the unconditional love I had known my whole life. It reminded me of the even greater, unfathomable love now surrounding my new baby. My fear fled, leaving me with a peace that could only come from God.

Defeat your fears with God's love.

—SBT

Changing Your Mother Tongue

Those who control their tongue will have a long life;
opening your mouth can ruin everything.
PROVERBS 13:3

I walked in the kitchen just in time to hear my daughter reciting a list of complaints. She finished her rampage with a familiar statement, and I felt my cheeks redden with shame when I realized that she was only repeating what she had heard from me. It was then I knew my influence had set a negative tone in our home.

I asked the Lord to change my words. He answered by changing my outlook. He began by showing me all that was *right* in my life. Instead of dreading the endless laundry, He guided me to thank Him for the people to whom the clothes belonged. Rather than allow me to whine about another trip to the store, He helped me thank Him for the resources to buy what we needed.

As my outlook changed, so did my attitude, and then, finally, my speech. Thankfully, many of the words that now flow from my mouth are positive and full of gratitude.

A mother's words and attitudes
can set the tone for the entire family.

—KENDIS CHENOWETH

Secure in Your Arms

How precious is your unfailing love, O God! All humanity
finds shelter in the shadow of your wings.
PSALM 36:7

It's not easy to be adopted at the age of fourteen. Joy had been abandoned multiple times by people who should have loved her. So, she acted out, trying to prove that when things got tough, we would abandon her too. But we didn't. We simply let God love her through us. We disciplined her, but we never let go.

Sometimes she wanted to be a little girl, perhaps to experience the safe childhood she never had. Sometimes she pushed us away. We took our cues from her. If she wanted to hold my hand or cuddle up next to me on the couch, I welcomed her. I never said she was too old for those moments of affection and security because I didn't want her to remember the hurtful comments she had heard so often as a small child.

Now she and her husband are providing the same security and love to foster children. She knows the power of a love that doesn't let go.

A mother's patient love can provide her daughter
with lifelong security.

—CAROL R. COOL

The Unbreakable Connection

No power in the sky above or in the earth below—indeed, nothing in all creation will ever be able to separate us from the love of God that is revealed in Christ Jesus our Lord.
ROMANS 8:39

I may have been a grown woman with a family of my own, but my mother's death left me feeling like an orphaned child. The loss of her physical presence was reason enough to mourn, but my real sense of loss came from the intense feeling of isolation I experienced after she was gone. We had been parted many times over the years, but the connection between us had never been broken or, even, weakened by our separation. When she died, I felt abandoned and so very alone.

As the fog of grief began to lift, I realized that I was not alone. God was with me, as He always had been. His unchanging, unconditional love continued to sustain and encourage me as I made my way in a world without my mother. I am secure now in my belief that not even death can separate me from this miraculous love. And I rejoice in the knowledge that I will see my beloved mother again someday.

Nothing can break your connection to God.

—SBT

Only Skin Deep

Accept Christians who are weak in faith, and don't argue with them about what they think is right or wrong.
ROMANS 14:1

"Mom, I want to get a tattoo on my nineteenth birthday!"

Could I really be hearing my daughter correctly? After taking a moment to pull myself together, I reply, "Oh really?"

"I want a butterfly on the inside of my wrist."

"Oh, that's gonna hurt!" I say this in a lighthearted voice, but my heart sinks. Is this really something a Christian girl should have, I wonder?

German author and philosopher, Johann Wolfgang von Goethe, once wrote, "We can't form our children on our own concepts. We must take them and love them as God gives them to us."

Putting aside my fear of what my daughter may become, I focus on her heart. I see a sweet, young lady who desires to follow Jesus. I remind myself of her good reputation at work and the way children flock to her. God's grace enables me to accept and love my daughter as He does—complete with tattoo.

We have to learn to look beyond the surface.

—CINDY BOOSE

Acceptance Doesn't Mean Approval

Do not seek revenge or bear a grudge.
LEVITICUS 19:18

My older brother Bob was obviously upset. "Mom, I can't believe you let Becky come by to visit," he said. "Have you forgotten how much she hurt my son? She has no business in your house."

My mother's reply was gentle but firm. "Acceptance doesn't mean approval," she said, "and I certainly don't condone what she did. You have every right to be angry, but she used to be part of our family, and I will always welcome her in my home."

My mother's definitive statement had a profound influence on the way I raised my daughters. I didn't always approve of their friends, their choices, or their habits, but I always welcomed my girls with open arms. I held fast to my beliefs and prayed that God would work out His will for their lives as they matured in their Christian walk.

We should practice acceptance and leave approval up to God.

—JEANETTE MACMILLAN

Lighting Up the World

The Word gave life to everything that was created,
and his life brought light to everyone.
JOHN 1:4

After the birth of my first child Gabriel, I suffered two miscarriages. I struggled to remain optimistic, but found myself becoming increasingly depressed as the months went by without another pregnancy. My mother's declining health only served to further dishearten me.

My faith in God and my love for three-year old Gabriel helped me carry on during those dark days when I wondered if the sun would ever shine again. I rejoiced when I discovered I was pregnant again, and when Emily was born nine months later, it was one of the happiest days of my life.

Emily's birth brightened my family's life, but the birth of our Lord brought an eternal light into the darkness of a spiritually desperate world. The arrival of my daughter gave us great happiness, but the coming of the Messiah gave us the opportunity to walk in the light forever.

Ask Jesus to banish the darkness in your life.

—SBT

Lost and Found

*When he arrives, he will call together his friends
and neighbors, saying, "Rejoice with me because
I have found my lost sheep."*
LUKE 15:6

I wasn't sure how long I had been searching for my three-year-old daughter, Tiffany, but the time had seemed unendurable. I searched the house, my frantic voice calling out her name in every room. I was on the verge of phoning the police, but something prompted me to check her bedroom one more time.

Suddenly, I heard a small giggle, and I went limp with relief. Tiffany had crawled inside her beauty salon play set. While we were desperately searching, she had been waiting for us to participate in her game of hide and seek. Any thoughts of disciplining her were banished by the joy I experienced when I realized she was safe.

The Bible tells us that God searches for each one of us like lost sheep and rejoices when we are found and returned to His loving care.

The Lord is our shepherd.

—DEBBIE ZILE

Flawless Communication

Be happy with those who are happy,
and weep with those who weep.
ROMANS 12:15

Angry tears streamed down my face. Stormy thoughts thundered through my mind. Lord, she's had enough disappointments, I thought. Why didn't she make the team? My twelve-year-old daughter sat next to me in tears. Born with a severe communication disorder that impacted all areas of her life, nothing had come easily to Anna. Nothing but soccer.

When Anna told me that her friend Stephanie had received a congratulatory call from the soccer coach, I was furious that Anna had been left out. "It okay, Mom," Anna said. "I happy Steph make it. I just sad."

I felt like a fool. In three imperfect sentences, my daughter had exhibited the qualities I should have demonstrated to her. I realized that soccer wasn't the only thing that came easily to her. She had proven that she could accept her losses, put her friend's happiness before her own, and maintain her honesty in an emotional situation. That day, I discovered I still had a lot to learn about Anna.

Our daughters have so much to teach us.

—CAROLYN BYERS RUCH

61

Wedding Jitters

*Trust in the LORD with all your heart;
do not depend on your own understanding.*
PROVERBS 3:5

When my daughter, Emily, announced that she and her boyfriend, Alan, were getting married, my initial reaction was anxiety and uncertainty. Although Alan was several years older and had a good job, Emily was only eighteen and had just graduated from high school. Emily's father and I discussed the situation with the young couple, but they were adamant. They wanted to live together, but not without the benefit of marriage.

That night I asked God to show Emily the error of her decision. Then I remembered something she had said earlier that afternoon. "We want God to be in our marriage. We want to live by His word." I thought about the difficulties my husband and I had faced until we invited the Lord into our lives.

Ever since Emily's birth, I had trusted God to guide and protect her. I knew He had a plan for Emily's life. Why should I stop trusting Him now?

We may have facts and opinions, but God has a plan.

—SBT

Standing My Ground

So be careful how you live.
Don't live like fools, but like those who are wise.
EPHESIANS 5:15

I had to say "no." The movie in question had been dismissed for perverting the characters and disregarding the purity of the original story. I felt troubled because I didn't want my daughter Stephanie to be embarrassed when she had to tell her friends she couldn't go.

Then she surprised me. In spite of her disappointment, she agreed with my decision. "You were right, Mom," she said. "Everything I've read about the movie says it lacks moral integrity. Can I go to a different movie with another friend?"

My troubling feelings vanished, replaced by happiness and gratitude. I thanked God for giving me the wisdom not to abandon what I knew to be right in order for my daughter to maintain her status with her friends. Once again, parenting had challenged my desire to please my daughter, but God had provided the necessary guidance.

We must seek God's will despite our worldly desires.

—DONNA L. WICHELMAN

Literal Listening

My children listen to me. Listen to your father.
Pay attention and grow wise.
PROVERBS 4:1

My toddler daughter had dark eyes, pinchable cheeks, and ears that listened verbatim. One evening, her usually cute face was twisted into a pout. Dinner had ended, and it was time for ice cream, but she wasn't getting any. Her daddy's instructions had been precise. "You have to empty your plate before you can have your dessert."

In the kitchen, I prepared dessert. When I returned to the dining room, my husband was laughing. Our little girl's plate was empty, but only because she had dumped her food onto another plate.

Maybe she misinterpreted her father's orders, but in her mind, our daughter had done what she was told. Sometimes when my husband or my Heavenly Father speaks to me, I tune out or half listen. Occasionally, that can lead to trouble. Thank goodness, God and my husband forgive and forget. And I always vow that next time I will listen!

It's easier to follow instructions when we really listen.

—CYNTHIA AGRICOLA HINKLE

A Perfect View

The heavens proclaim the glory of God.
The skies display his craftsmanship.
PSALM 19:1

As a young child, I had been told God lived in heaven, but I wondered how He kept his eye on the hundreds of sparrows that lived in our neighborhood if He was way up in the sky somewhere.

Then one rainy day, my mother and I were out for a drive. Suddenly, a giant shaft of sunlight broke through the dark sky. The beam of radiant light in the midst of the dark and ominous clouds was one of the most beautiful things I had ever seen. "Look," I said to my mother. "I think that's where God must be standing right now. He can see perfectly from there."

She may have been tempted to comment or correct me, but she only smiled. I have come to know some of the answers I sought as a child, but every time I see the sun break through the clouds, I still think of God, standing there watching over all His children—and the sparrows.

The beauty of God's creation should be a marvel to us all.

—SBT

Priceless Prayers

Take delight in the Lord,
and he will give you your heart's desires.
PSALM 37:4

It was only a bracelet, but when it was stolen out of my hotel room, I actually cried. I bought it in Italy when I was the age that my daughter is now and had always planned to give it to her someday.

"I'm sorry, Mom," she said, "but I think it's gone for good."

"Well," I replied, feeling a bit foolish, "I told God if He would help bring it back to me, I would really appreciate it." The look on my daughter's face told me she considered my request rather silly, too.

Weeks later, on a whim, I went online to see if I could find something similar. My search led me straight to an auction featuring *my* hand painted, vintage bracelet. There was no doubt it was mine. I won the bid, and when my daughter saw me wearing it again, she couldn't deny it was a minor miracle.

God wants to hear all of our prayers—even the ones we consider trivial or insignificant.

—DEBRA WHITING ALEXANDER

Blossoming Talent

*In His grace, God has given us different gifts
for doing certain things well.*
ROMANS 12:6

My daughter has always loved art. At the age of two, she colored walls and, a year later, when she sculpted the "Wizard of Oz" characters in clay, I displayed the figures to encourage her creativity. As a teen, she painted flowers on cloth for a contest.

Years later, one of my editors called for an original sparrow picture to accompany an article I had written. I couldn't draw and prayed for help. When my daughter heard of my need, she said, "Why didn't you ask me? You know I can draw birds."

"I'm sorry, I didn't think you had the time."

"Did you know there are seventy-five species of sparrows?" she asked. "Which one should I draw?"

"Let's read my article again," I replied.

An hour later, I had my sparrow picture. We copied the picture and submitted it to the editor. As I watched my daughter beam over her first published piece of art, I thanked God for inspiring me to praise her artistic ability from childhood.

It's never too early to encourage your child's gifts.

—IRIS G. DOWLING

A Divine Calling

Study this Book of Instruction continually. Meditate on it day and night so you will be sure to obey everything written in it. Only then will you prosper and succeed in all you do.
JOSHUA 1:8

Even though I accepted the Lord as my personal savior at an early age, my daughter Emily was born during a period of my life when faith had taken second place to my worldly desires. I still prayed for my unborn child's well-being and praised Him when I delivered a strong and healthy baby, but I only had a vague idea of His profound role in my daughter's life—even before her conception.

After I dedicated my life to the Lord and began to spend time in His word, I made some amazing and life changing discoveries. Even before Emily was born, God had a purpose for her. He knew everything about her and, most importantly, He chose me for her mother.

These revelations brought the awareness that being Emily's mother was far more than changing diapers, worrying about a healthy diet, or deciding on the best education. Like everything else in my life, God had elevated motherhood from the ordinary to the divine.

Everything we do is for the glory of God.

—SBT

A Troop of Daughters

Feed the hungry, and help those in trouble. Then your light will shine out from the darkness, and the darkness around you will be as bright as noon.
ISAIAH 58:10

She's ninety-five years young, and we still call her Skipper. Edna Hollis and the Girl Scout troop she led faithfully over fifty years ago still gather every July at her Colorado cabin. Much has changed in five decades, but not Skipper's love for her girls.

I was eight when my dad left, and we moved to Denver. There, we met Skipper. Her daughter became my best friend, and their parsonage became my home away from home. The money needed for me to attend camp always mysteriously showed up. So did food, hugs, laughter, and learning. Skipper saw to it.

When Janice, a sweet young girl, was turned away from other Scout troops, Skipper welcomed her warmly. Today, they live in the same apartment building, where Skipper cares for sixty-five-year-old Janice, now suffering from a debilitating disease.

Skipper has always modeled a spirit of adventure, a quest for excellence, and unconditional love. Her daughters—all fifty-two of them—have been blessed to call her "Mom."

The fatherless, rejected, and needy
all need a mother's special gifts.
—SANDI BANKS

March

Mothering Is Not for Wimps

For God has not given us a spirit of fear and timidity, but of
power, love, and self-discipline.

2 TIMOTHY 1:7

*S*ometimes, I wonder if the word "passionate" was created to describe my mother. She has always responded to most situations with vibrant feeling. She laughs, cries, celebrates, and mourns with every bit of her soul and often adds a touch of drama for good measure. Even though she possesses a vast spectrum of emotions, staying calm has never been her forte.

However, I recall a time when she kept her cool in a way that exceeded my expectations. When I was fifteen, the parents of the children I had been babysitting returned from their evening out. They offered me a ride because it was dark, but I didn't want to return for my bicycle the next day, so I insisted on going home on my own. They let me leave, but they gave me strict orders to walk my bike.

As I set off on foot, the chill of the evening surrounded me, and I decided it was too cold to walk the remaining half-mile. I hadn't rode far when I felt my bike dip into a well known, but forgotten, pothole. I flew over the handlebars and landed on my chin. I immediately knew something was wrong with my jaw, and with about a quarter of a mile left to go, I walked my mangled bike the rest of the way home.

During the long climb up our steep driveway, I remembered that my father was out of town on business. I knew my mother would fuss and cry and, maybe, even wail a little. She came running as soon as she heard me come in. Her face froze in a shocked expression for a moment, and then I observed something totally unfamiliar. Demonstrating an unnerving air of calm, she settled me on the couch and dabbed at my chin with a cold cloth to stop the bleeding. Time crawled by, and finally she spoke. "I think you might need stitches. Let's go to the emergency room."

I was relieved to be on my way to the doctor, but I wasn't sure she should get behind the wheel. Experience told me that tears and hysterics had to be on their way, and I didn't know what we would do if she broke down while she was driving. The woman in the driver's seat looked like my mother, but she was obviously in control of the circumstances. I didn't know what to make of it. There she was, without a tear in sight, expertly maneuvering the car to the emergency room.

After taking X-rays, the doctor explained the procedure to set my broken jaw and wire it shut until I could see a surgeon the next morning. My mother acted as though she heard similar reports from the doctor every day. I'm sure she wished my father was there for moral support, yet she never expressed any anxiety. She handled the entire episode like a seasoned veteran.

Today, as the mother of two girls, I try to emulate the courage my mother demonstrated that night. I recall how comforting it was to have her take control and, now, when trouble strikes, I attempt to do the same. When I had my first child, I had no idea how often I would rely on bravery and pure faith. It takes courage to watch your preschooler cross the monkey bars alone for the first time, or put your precious treasure on the school bus with a smile the day after a school shooting fills the news. Only faith can get you through the first time your teenager takes the car out for the evening. Mothering is not for wimps. I learned that lesson from my mother in the emergency room when I was only fifteen.

God knows exactly what we need, at the moment we need it, and He provides it in abundance. My mother and I needed her strength that night, and God was there to supply it. He sees our struggles and equips us in ways we don't understand. Whether it is courage or compassion, God makes sure the seeds of character planted deep within us bloom when we need them the most.

—Dianne Daniels

Our Children's Children

But the love of the Lord remains forever with those who fear him. His salvation extends to the children's children.
PSALM 103:17

After being reunited with my birth mother as a young adult, I had the opportunity to meet her mother. When I flew to Morgantown, West Virginia, to see Grandma Norma for the first time, I discovered firsthand that my biological grandmother was a mighty woman of faith. Although she had been paralyzed in her thirties as the result of an automobile accident, Grandma Norma was a woman with a deep abiding trust in the Lord.

This was a woman who had assumed we would never meet, but when I was still in the womb, she had prayed for me and entrusted me into the Lord's gracious care. Now, when I read in the Bible that the faithful will be a blessing to their children's children, I can't help but think of Grandma Norma.

We can be a blessing to future generations.

—MARGOT STARBUCK

Making Things Right

*Always be humble and gentle. Be patient
with each other, making allowance for each
other's faults because of your love.*
EPHESIANS 4:2

"You won't believe what happened," my daughter Emily said as she came through the back door.

"Try me," I replied and joined her at the kitchen table.

It turned out she had argued with her best friend on the bus ride home from school, and by the time she finished telling me about it, there were tears in her eyes. "Leah was so wrong," she said. "I'm never going to speak to her again."

I wasn't sure what to say. I knew how she felt, and I thought about all the times I'd been determined to maintain my position of being right—sometimes at a heartbreaking cost. "Being right can be lonely," I finally said. "I guess you have to ask yourself if it's worth losing your best friend."

Later that night, Emily announced that she had talked to Leah. Her smile told me it didn't matter anymore who had been right earlier that day. It also told me how good it felt to find out what was really important.

*Sometimes making things right feels
a lot better than being right.*

—SBT

My Daughter Rocks On

No one is holy like the Lord! There is no one besides you;
there is no Rock like our God.
1 SAMUEL 2:2

I was fifty-four years old when Shiloh and I went to our first Aerosmith rock concert together to celebrate her fifteenth birthday. Not long after she introduced me to rock music, the true Rock introduced Himself to her.

I had first become a mother in my teens, and my last child was born right before I turned forty. In all those years, the music industry had gone through a multitude of changes. I was unfamiliar with what was going on, music-wise, in my youngest daughter, Shiloh's, life. Thank God, she bypassed the wild punk music and decided she was an 1980's fan.

We found common ground by going to that concert together, and as I listened in on her guitar lessons, our relationship grew. Later, I watched Shiloh yield her musical dreams to the Lord, and I thanked God for leading me to encourage her gift of music.

Rescued by the Rock, Shiloh now rocks out for the Lord.

—DONNA COLLINS TINSLEY

Priceless Gifts

Anyone who loves another brother or sister is living in the light and does not cause others to stumble.
1 JOHN 2:10

Woodcrafts and homemade fudge decorated my booth. It was my first craft fair, and when my mother arrived, she investigated my items with the air of an interested customer. "How do you make your mosaics?" she asked.

I laughed. "You know how I do it, Mom. Why don't you look around and have fun?"

"I might be able to attract some people," she replied. "Other shoppers are always intrigued when they see someone else checking things out." The predicted customers never arrived, but my mother did her best to compensate. She purchased approximately one item per hour. "For gifts," she said each time she bought something.

Sales weren't the only thing my mother generated that day. She gave me hope and perseverance. She demonstrated the value of a support system, but her belief in me was, by far, the greatest gift I could have ever received.

Our support and encouragement is a priceless gift.

—L. A. LINDBURG

Being Myself

I am leaving you with a gift—peace of mind and heart.
And the peace I give is a gift the world cannot give.
So don't be troubled or afraid.
JOHN 14:27

Thanks to my mother's flair for color and style, our home always looked like something out of a magazine. Preparing a dinner for twenty people didn't faze her in the least—she loved to entertain. On the other hand, my house looks like tornado central, and my idea of entertaining is to phone my husband and tell him to pick up pizza on the way home from work.

For years, I tried to be like my mother. It was my Aunt Helen who put a stop to my manic self-makeover. "God doesn't want you to be your mother," she said.

"But I feel like such a failure compared to her."

"Just as she might have felt if she had tried to write a book, raise five children, or care for that zoo full of animals you have."

I decided that maybe my mother and I had more in common than I thought. We both followed our dreams and used the gifts God had given us.

Find your gift and use it for God's glory.

—SBT

Instructions from the Mountaintop

You can be sure of this: The Lord set apart the godly for himself. The Lord will answer when I call to him.
PSALM 4:3

Our younger daughter burst in from a youth retreat with good news. "Mom and Dad, I need you to sit down. I know where I am supposed to go to college."

A battle of the wills had been going on for so long that I had totally given the subject over to God. A couple years earlier, our daughter decided to enroll at a reputable college two states away. I did not want my daughter to live fourteen hours away, even though it was a very good college. I grudgingly prayed. "Lord, I don't want her to go so far away, but if it is Your will for her I accept."

While on the youth retreat in the mountains, she felt led by the Lord to attend college closer to home. With the matter fully settled by God, her freshman year was wonderful. She was not homesick, played on a praise team, and made strong Christian friends who prayed with her daily.

When the Lord whispers, we need to be still enough to listen.

—LAROSE KARR

Comfort Food

So whether you eat or drink, or whatever you do,
do it all for the glory of God.
1 CORINTHIANS 10:31

My daughter and I were overweight and miserable. In the past, we had successfully dieted and lost weight by following a Christian weight loss plan complete with assignments that kept us in God's word. However, when the diet was done, we invariably reverted to our old ways and the pounds piled on faster than they had melted away.

"Why do we do this to ourselves?" Heather asked.

"We know why," I replied. "We allow food to control us."

She nodded. "Instead of going to God for comfort when I'm stressed, I go to food. Then I'm more miserable. Staying in God's word helped avoid that trap."

"Sad isn't it?" I said. "Can you imagine if I had something bothering me and all I did was eat a piece of cake instead of talking to you about it? I wonder how God feels when I put so-called comfort food before Him. I say He comes first in my life, but my eating doesn't always show it."

Jesus is the Bread of Life—let Him be your comfort food.

—DONNA SUNDBLAD

Learning to Laugh

For our present troubles are small and won't last very long.
Yet they produce for us a glory that vastly outweighs them
and will last forever!
2 CORINTHIANS 4:17

Sometimes, I still tease my daughter Emily about her misadventures with high school Latin. At the time, it wasn't a laughing matter, but time has helped both of us learn that getting worked up over something can be a big waste of time and energy. And with the right attitude adjustment, we were even able to see some humor in the situation.

I recall the day she came home with a D on her report card, the first time she had received anything lower than a B. At first, I reacted with disappointment, but Emily's distress was infectious. It wasn't long before I was upset, too. And then I remembered something my mother often said: "What's it going to matter fifty years from now?"

I repeated my mother's words to Emily. Both of us stopped, took a deep breath, and stared at each other for a moment. "I know I can bring up that grade," she said.

"I know you can, too," I replied.

God expects us to do our best—even in Latin.

—SBT

A Lesson from Martha

One day Jesus told his disciples a story to show that they should always pray and never give up.
LUKE 18:1

Watching her mother hauled off to jail and being abandoned by her father might have made Martha bitter, but it didn't. At age eleven, after living in four foster homes, she became my daughter.

One day, she asked, "When I marry will they put my picture in papers everywhere?"

I wondered if she might be longing for her birth parents and hoping they would see her photograph, locate her, and take her away to a fairytale life. Later, I realized all she wanted was a "forever" home of her own someday, with lots of children to love.

Her faith, courage, and hope always inspired me. Today, she is a mother of five, and she continues to teach me lessons. "Mom, she hit me," one of the children complains. "I'm sorry," Martha replies. "Let's pray about it together."

"He doesn't like me," another frets and, once again, Martha suggests prayer.

I prayed a lot *for* my children. Martha makes me wish I'd also prayed more *with* them.

Thank God for the lessons our daughters teach us.

—ELAINE YOUNG MCGUIRE

Much More Than Tea

*All the believers devoted themselves to the apostles' teaching,
and to fellowship, and to sharing in meals (including the
Lord's Supper), and to prayer.*
ACTS 2:42

Mom gave me my first tea set at an age when my daughter was still drinking from her sippy-cup. Whether it's high tea at the Silver Plume Antique shop, Christmas tea parties for a dozen or more women and their daughters in my home, or, simply, tea-for-two—teatime is a special event among the women of our family.

Out come the antique teacups, fancy plates, and the requisite sugar cubes. We share stories, sip delicate jasmine tea or robust red herbal tea from Africa, and munch on delicacies that often include cucumber sandwiches. This is tradition and more. The relaxed camaraderie that teas create strengthens the connection with family and friends.

Tea breaks are the milieu for a multitude of joys and concerns, mile markers, ordinary happenings, laughs, and tears. Time to listen and time to care are just two of the gifts of teatime—gifts I am passing down to my daughter and granddaughter.

*Pour a cup of tea and nurture the relationships
that honor the Lord.*

—SHERRON SLAVENS

Altered Expectations

Don't love money; be satisfied with what you have. For God
has said, "I will never fail you. I will never abandon you."
HEBREWS 13:5

Callie expected a thirteenth birthday that would go
down in the annals of history. Too bad our shoestring bud-
get was frayed. I could manage an ice-skating, hot chocolate
celebration with her friends, but even I knew she wanted
something more exciting. Every time she brought the subject up, my stomach twisted into multiple knots. I asked
God to make Callie's birthday memorable but, as the big
day grew closer, trusting Him became increasingly difficult.

And then something happened that no one had
planned: Callie's special day began with an early morning
visit to the doctor and she was sick. We watched videos,
ate soup, and told each other corny knock-knock jokes
all day. I felt terrible about the way things had turned out
until later that night when I tucked her in.

"Mom," she said, "today wasn't what I hoped for, but I
had the best time ever with you. I love you." I don't know
about Callie's thirteenth birthday, but those words definitely made it into my annals of "mom" history.

God is always right on time with what we need—
even if it's not what we expected.

—MICHELLE GRIEP

Lots of Love in Little Things

The man who finds a wife finds a treasure,
and he receives favor from the Lord.
PROVERBS 18:22

When I was growing up, I would often sit and talk to my mother while she did the ironing. I would detect an air of satisfaction in her demeanor as she worked, and her attitude of contentment was particularly noticeable when she ironed my father's clothes. One day, I teased her for ironing my father's white handkerchiefs. "Why do you bother?" I asked. "Who's going to notice if his handkerchiefs are ironed or not?"

She smiled. "Your dad will notice, and that's all that counts. It's like all the little things I do for him. The things that make him feel important, and let him know how much I love him."

I didn't really understand her point until I became a wife and mother. My days are filled with doing little things for the other people in the family, and although there are times when my efforts feel tedious and trivial, it usually gives me a great deal of pleasure to show my husband and children how much they mean to me.

God sees the love in the little things we do for others.

—SBT

The Strength of Prayer

In the past you have encouraged many people;
you have strengthened those who were weak.
JOB 4:3

"I know you pray," Jenn said, as she handed me the note. "So can I give you my list of prayer requests?" I was deeply touched and doubly blessed when I unfolded the small paper. It not only revealed her heart's desires, but also showed the tender working of God in her life.

Jenn and I did not have the best start when she and my son married at nineteen and twenty years old. I allowed my disappointment in their decision and my fear for their future to prevent me from developing a relationship with her. Two years later, God blessed them with my beautiful granddaughter, and I saw Jenn emerge as a loving, caring woman.

My prayers for her increased with love and thankfulness, and as I prayed, our relationship grew. I discovered that God not only answers prayer, He also does a work of grace in the one who prays!

When we pray to strengthen others, we strengthen ourselves.

—MARIBETH SPANGENBERG

Lists and Lessons

But you must remain faithful to the things you have been taught. You know they are true, for you know you can trust those who taught you.
2 Timothy 3:14

I was delighted when my stepdaughter, Kathy, asked me to help her prepare for a large dinner party. Suddenly, she cried out, "I can't find my menu. I'll never remember everything!"

We created a new list. "Forgetting a dish doesn't ruin a party," I said in an effort to calm her. "On my twelfth birthday, long after the cake was served, my mother discovered a huge bowl of apple salad in the refrigerator. The boys happily consumed salad for a second desert!"

Kathy smiled and taped her new list to the refrigerator as I continued. "Mother often used that party to remind me that making lists may anchor my life," I said, "but living by God's word anchors my soul."

Kathy hugged me. "I like having you in my kitchen." That evening, as I watched my lovely daughter graciously serve her Bible study and ministry group friends, I whispered a prayer of gratitude for the lessons my mother had taught me and for all five of my daughters.

Sharing lessons from the past strengthens the bond within families.

—Liz Hoyt Eberle

Precise Planning

For Herod Antipas, Pontius Pilate the governor, the Gentiles, and the people of Israel were all united against Jesus, your holy servant, whom you anointed.

But everything they did was determined beforehand according to your will.
Acts 4:27–28

When Jason, a young man of about seventeen, began attending our church, he didn't seem too interested in learning anything about the Lord. "Why does he come at all?" my daughter, Emily, asked me. "He spends all his time making fun of the pastor or arguing with everyone."

I shrugged. "Maybe he just needs more time." A short time later, Jason brought his friend, Danny. We were all amazed, a few weeks later, when Danny accepted Jesus as his savior and joined our church. No one was more surprised than Emily. "Is it possible that God used Jason to help Danny find the Lord?" she asked.

"God often uses unbelievers to fulfill His will for someone's life," I replied. "He used ungodly people like Pilate and Herod in His plan for our redemption." Emily nodded. "And what about Jason?" I smiled. "I wouldn't be the least bit surprised if God has a plan for Jason's life, too."

Events may appear random, but God is always in control.

—SBT

Let Go and Let God

*Then Jesus said, "Come to me, all of you who are weary
and carry heavy burdens, and I will give you rest."*
MATTHEW 11:28

The determination on my daughter's face told me she wasn't giving in. I gently grabbed her pudgy fist and turned it over. Chocolate candies peeked out from between her fingers.

Savannah had a way of finding chocolate and hiding it for future enjoyment. "Put them in Mommy's hand," I said. As I tried to break her hold on the candies, she began to cry.

"I need them. I want them!" Her tears trickled down her cheeks as I recited all the good reasons she shouldn't have the candy. I knew what was good for her, but that day I doubted my ability to convince her.

Later, I thought about the similarities in our behavior. I remembered all the hurts, habits, and fears I hoarded. I know it would please God if I put those things in His hands, but I kept them for future resentment, doubt, or guilt. No matter how tightly I hung on, God wanted me to let go.

Turn your troubles over to the Lord.

—JAMI KIRKBRIDE

Sweet Surrender

Give as freely as you have received!
MATTHEW 10:8

I had wanted a bentwood rocker for years, but it carried a price tag of $69.99. So, it remained a pipedream, until an anonymous cash gift made the purchase possible. I adored that chair with it high oval back and woven cane seat. Even my lullabies sounded sweeter. On the evenings we held our meetings downstairs, I nursed Kristin early and rocked her to sleep.

One evening a pregnant woman, new to our group, tiptoed upstairs to the nursery with me. She admired my chair and, at that moment, I knew she should have it. I was baffled by my sudden feelings. I had waited so long for my wonderful chair, and it had been mine for such a short time.

My impulsive notion persisted, along with a growing willingness to surrender my treasured possession. That night in the chair's snug embrace one last time, God seemed to whisper, "Share in *her* coming happiness." Then He made the feeling of joy real in my heart.

Everything is a gift from God.

—LAURIE KLEIN

"I'll Pray for You"

Keep on asking, and you will receive what you ask for.
Keep on seeking, and you will find. Keep on knocking,
and the door will be opened to you.
MATTHEW 7:7

My daughter Emily calls at least once a day, and she often asks for my opinion. When her husband was thinking of changing jobs, we discussed it, and I told her I believed the final decision rested with her and Alan. "But I'll definitely pray about it," I said.

A few days later, she told me that Alan had decided to stay in his current position. "He ended up getting a raise," she said in a voice full of excitement. "Your prayers really helped!"

Her comment made me realize that I didn't verbalize my intention to pray as much as I should. Emily knew that she and Alan were always in my prayers, but I needed to say, "I'll pray for you," more often. It always made me feel better when people told me they were praying for me.

The true blessing came the other day when I told Emily about a problem one of her brothers was having. "I'll pray for him," she said. And I know she did.

The words, "I'll pray for you," lets someone
know you really care.

—SBT

And My Pajamas Still Fit!

The more you grow like this, the more productive and useful
you will be in your knowledge of our Lord Jesus Christ.
2 PETER 1:8

It was Bethany's fourth birthday, and I awakened her with a hug. "You are four now!" I said.

"Yes," she replied, "and I still fit into my pajamas!" She ran out to the kitchen, oblivious to her own wisdom. After breakfast, she checked her appearance to see if she looked bigger.

I can identify. Many times, I have marked great milestones in my life, only to look around and realize that my circumstances haven't changed. I am still surrounded by challenges: the bills, the spills, and the same size pajamas. Just like my young daughter, I want to ask, "Dear Lord, am I bigger yet?"

God does not operate on a schedule, and His work in our lives is often done in a quiet and unobtrusive manner. We may feel that our growth is interminably slow or, worse yet, nonexistent, but when we look back, we see that He had been changing us all along.

God is at work to mature us into the
people He wants us to be.

—ANITA LYNN RAMSEY

Worthy of Adoration

Yours, O Lord, is the greatness, the power, the glory, the victory, and the majesty. Everything in the heavens and on earth is yours, O Lord, and this is your kingdom. We adore you as the one who is over all things.

1 CHRONICLES 29:11

My seven-year-old daughter thinks I'm the best thing going. She tells me of her love multiple times a day and is always ready with a hug or a kiss.

Even though I am not worthy of her adoration, I am blessed and humbled by her innocent, heartfelt gifts of love. I cherish the attention, because I know that, as time passes, my little girl will become more independent and, perhaps, rebel against my love for her.

Do we, as Christians, enthusiastically demonstrate affection toward our heavenly Father? Do we tell Him how much we love Him throughout the day, and hang on His every word? God treasures our devotion and, as loving children, we should give honor to the only one truly worthy of our praise and adoration.

Oh, come let us adore Him!

—KELLY W. MIZE

Home Sweet Home

The Lord is like a father to his children, tender and compassionate to those who fear him.
PSALM 103:13

It's a wonderful blessing when my daughter, Emily, and her husband, Alan, come for a visit, and yesterday was no exception. As usual, the time passed all too quickly, and when I caught Alan glancing at the clock, I remembered he had to be at work early the next morning.

I stood up and stretched my legs. "It might be time to call it a night," I said. Emily's smile disappeared, confirming my suspicion that she was in no hurry to leave. I recalled feeling the same way when it was time to go home after spending time with my parents. I felt so safe and special in their company. Sometimes, it was hard to tear myself away and return to the "real" world.

Emily's good spirits returned as we all said goodnight. Perhaps she had remembered that her Heavenly Father would be with her forever, offering His love and sheltering arms—no matter how far she traveled from our door.

Rest and renew yourself in the loving arms of your Heavenly Father.

—SBT

La Mariposa Monarca

God made all sorts of wild animals, livestock, and small animals, each able to produce offspring of the same kind. And God saw that it was good.
GENESIS 1:25

While traveling in Mexico, my daughter Melissa visited a monarch butterfly sanctuary where *la mariposa monarca* migrates each year, as it has for generations. The postcard she sent home exuded excitement. "Dear Mom, I finally went to see the butterflies. I wish you could have come. It was amazing. The trees were all orange! It's a miracle how they migrate all the way from Canada."

Millions of monarchs cluster so heavily that tree branches often break, and when they swarm, the sky turns orange. Incredibly, each butterfly is a first timer—a descendent of monarchs from the year before. How does the new generation know where to go? Once again, I was left in awe of God's creation.

Melissa was certainly blessed by her adventure, as I was when she shared her experiences with me. God's perfect design continues to amaze generation after generation.

Take the time to see the world through your children's eyes.

—KENDA TURNER

First Things First

*All Scripture is inspired by God and is useful to
teach us what is true and to make us realize what
is wrong in our lives. It corrects us when we are
wrong and teaches us to do what is right.*
2 TIMOTHY 3:16

My daughter has always loved to read. By her seventh birthday, she read well enough for me to buy her a chapter-and-verse Bible. She couldn't wait to read it after school. I hadn't instructed her to do this, and I wondered why she started this habit. "You don't *have* to read your Bible as soon as you get home. You can read it any time," I said.

I worried that I had somehow made her think Bible reading was an item on her chore list.

But my little girl was insistent. "I need to read it right away in case God has something important to tell me."

Her comment and perspective sparked an immediate change in me. Now, the first thing I do in the morning—after making coffee—is open my Bible. I certainly don't want to miss anything important God has to say.

God communicates with us through our Bibles.

—RENEE GRAY-WILBURN

God's Goals

Don't act thoughtlessly, but understand
what the Lord wants you to do.
EPHESIANS 5:17

In my senior year at high school, it seemed as though all my classmates knew exactly what they were going to do after graduation. So, I wasn't surprised when my daughter announced that all of her friends had made college and career plans. "I'm the only one who hasn't decided," she said, and I empathized with the desperation in her voice.

Abruptly, I had an idea. "Why don't you make a list?" I said. "I know you've had some ideas about what you'd like to do, but a job is only one part of your life. Make a list of your other goals. Think about your purpose in life."

Emily nodded. "I like that idea."

"Take your list to God in prayer, and ask Him for direction. But don't forget that He's a lot more interested in the kind of person you become than the career you choose."

"Did you ever make a list like that?" she asked.

"No," I replied, "but I don't think it's ever too late. I'm going to make one, too!"

Take time to discover God's plan for your life.

—SBT

Strength in the Rock

The Lord is my rock, my fortress, and my savior; my God is my rock, in whom I find protection. He is my shield, the power that saves me, and my place of safety.
PSALM 18:2

I enjoying creating scrapbooks and have made one for each of my children for their fiftieth birthday. My daughter Karen turned the tables recently by making one for me.

The decades-old family photographs rekindled fond memories, but I was especially touched by the captions she wrote. One read, "Thanks for always walking toward God. We never had to doubt where you would stand." Later, she said, "Mom, you were a solid rock we could depend on."

With God's help, I was able to stand firm in the face of a screaming toddler or a wheedling teenager. His power made it possible for me to establish age-appropriate boundaries and give my children a sense of true security.

When we rely on God's wisdom and strength, we give our children a sense of being safe and loved.

—JOYCE STARR MACIAS

Without Question

He will shield you with his wings.
He will shelter you with his feathers.
His faithful promises are your armor and protection.
PSALM 91:4

I sat on the spring grass in the courtyard of our small apartment complex. Sunshine chased the chill from my arms as my two-year-old daughter rode her tricycle on the sidewalk. Her blond pigtails caught the wind like ribbons of silk. And then something threw my world into a tailspin—a wasp.

"Stop, Heather," I ordered. "Stay still."

I stood and focused on the wasp, now climbing Heather's chest toward her neck and face. Her tiny, innocent eyes stared into mine. She had no idea any threat existed. I thanked God she obeyed me. Her little feet stayed planted, and I inched closer. As I closed in, the wasp flew away and disappeared overhead. Limp with relief, I picked Heather up and hugged her tight.

Just like a devoted mother, God watches over me even when I don't think I need it. Perhaps I need to be more like Heather and obey without question.

God is present in every circumstance,
even when we don't think we need him.

—DONNA SUNDBLAD

Heavenly Hamburgers

If you help the poor, you are lending to the Lord—
and he will repay you!
PROVERBS 19:17

The woman approached me as I brought my shopping cart to a stop beside our car. "I was wondering if you could spare some money so I could get something to eat," she said.

I had just spent all I had on groceries but, then, Emily spoke up. "I have a few dollars," she said and turned to the woman. "I was just going to go back to the store and get myself a hamburger. Would you like to join me?"

The woman gave a quick nod. "I'd like that."

Emily glanced at me as if asking permission. "I think that's a great idea," I said, "but I'm not very hungry, so why don't I put the groceries in the car and wait for you?"

"That was a very nice thing to do," I said on the way home.

"I hope it blessed her life a little," Emily replied. "All I know is that it blessed me a lot!"

"Funny how it works out that way," I said and smiled.

Giving to others is a blessing for everyone involved.

—SBT

Running on Empty

*Your unfailing love, O Lord, is as vast as the heavens; your
faithfulness reaches beyond the clouds.*
PSALM 36:5

My eighty-four-year-old mother definitely has a mind of her own. This was especially apparent on a trip I traveled with her down California's north coast. One morning, we decided to take a sightseeing trip by car.

My mother has always believed that half a tank of gas really means it is almost empty. I've never agreed with her paranoid attitude, but that day I was driving! The winding mountainous road we chose ended up taxing our gas supply—and our sanity. My mother, upset with me because I didn't fill up before we left, became obsessed with the fuel gauge.

When the warning light came on, I thought I had lost the battle. We both prayed. According to our map, we were nearing a town and, suddenly, there it was! We slid to a halt beside a gas pump. Overwhelmed with relief, we turned to each other and laughingly shouted in unison, "I told you so."

*When we are willing, God can transform our differences
into connecting points of joy.*

—KATHRYN WILSON

Me—A Gift to Jesus?

Jesus prayed, "My prayer is not for the world, but for those you have given me, because they belong to you."
JOHN 17:9

I had been a Christian for twenty-five years and a mother for sixteen, when my friend Lynette showed me the verse in John 17 in which Christ thanks God for believers, calling them gifts. I took a deep breath. Me? A gift to Jesus? I had gladly received Christ's gift on the cross, but thinking of myself as a present to Him felt like blasphemy. Earlier that day, as I fussed at my daughters homework and foolishness, I didn't see myself as much of a gift to anyone, much less the Lord.

Lynette smiled. "Do you consider your three daughters to be gifts?"

I was amazed as I realized how the scripture mirrored my experience as a mother. "I sure do!" I replied.

Later, I read the verse and inserted my name in Christ's prayer. It made me feel unique and treasured, and I mentally signed my own gift card—"To Jesus, Love Pam."

You are a gift of love to Jesus from His Father.

—PAMELA DOWD

A Family Affair

Therefore, go and make disciples of all the nations, baptizing them in the name of the Father and the Son and the Holy Spirit.
MATTHEW 28:19

In the past year, my daughter Emily and her brother, Gabriel, have discovered some common interests and begun to spend more time together. A few months ago, she invited him to stay for the weekend at the apartment she shares with her husband, Alan.

I thought it was a terrific idea, and I hoped that Emily might use this opportunity to share her faith with Gabriel. Both Emily and Gabriel have asked Jesus Christ to be their personal savior, but I knew Gabriel needed encouragement. However, I also knew that Emily could be a positive and supportive influence.

When I asked Emily about the weekend, she shared some wonderful news. "We spent a lot of time talking about the Lord," she said. "Gabriel had a lot of questions, so I got my Bible and we looked the answers up together. It was great." My children have given me so much over the years, but the two of them sitting and talking about God may be the most precious gift of all.

Is there someone in your family who has questions about God?

—SBT

Locks of Love

Sell your possessions and give to those in need. This will store up treasure for you in heaven! And the purses of heaven never get old or develop holes. Your treasure will be safe; no thief can steal it and no moth can destroy it.

LUKE 12:33

When my daughter Emily was ten, her hair grew down to the small of her back. She wouldn't allow me to cut it, even through the hot summer. Then, one day, she saw an article in a magazine about an organization that provides hairpieces to children who have lost their hair as a result of a medical condition.

"Can I donate my hair to 'Locks of Love'?" she asked eagerly.

Her willingness to give away such a treasured part of herself in order to help someone else touched me deeply. I snipped off her shiny hair in sections and flattened the waves under books to make it easier to measure. Each section was over a foot long, exceeding the ten-inch minimum donation. We bundled pieces together with rubber bands and sent the ponytail to "Locks of Love." Emily was thrilled to tell everyone her hair would be made into a wig for a child, and I thanked God for helping my daughter to grow spiritually.

Our child's demonstration of selflessness is cause to rejoice.

—MARY LAUFER

APRIL

The Card

Prophecy and speaking in unknown languages and special knowledge will become useless. But love will last forever!
1 CORINTHIANS 13:8

*S*onya handed me a little handmade card. It read, "I really hope you and my dad get together. I think you are just perfect for each other. I hope you are in my life forever and ever!" Brightly colored hearts and flowers formed a frame around words that, frankly, scared me to death! It's one thing to date a man and worry if someone's heart will be broken. It adds a whole new level of seriousness when a nine-year old girl's heart is at stake as well!

I quickly offered up a silent prayer and asked God to protect this little girl who had already endured so much hurt in her short life. I certainly didn't want to be the cause of more heartache for this dark-haired, dark-eyed little beauty. After thanking her for the card and giving her a big hug, I tucked the precious card in my wallet.

Sonya's dad and I had met at church after his divorce. He was raising his children on his own, and I was a widow with two young boys still at home and two who were already out on their own. Our kids were friends at church before we even started dating. I had even taught Sonya and her brother in Sunday school.

It was obvious that Sonya was looking for a stable mother figure in her life. I knew she would be hurt if her dad and I didn't get married. We had two dates a week, one with just the two of us, and one with all our kids. We tried to be very careful because we knew our choices involved our children as well. The kids thought we were too cautious and called a meeting one night to ask us when we were going to get married.

They held a big celebration when we finally announced our wedding. We explained to them that we weren't just marrying each other; we were bringing two families together. Sonya had to have a beautiful new dress for the ceremony. After her dad and I repeated our vows to each other, we recited vows to the children. We wanted to make sure they knew we would always be there for them, no matter what.

When I moved into the house, I began to add a woman's touch. I delighted in watching Sonya's face when she hurried home from school each day to see the changes I had made. When I helped her redecorate her room, she was thrilled. She seemed so happy to have another woman in the house. I could brush her hair without hurting her scalp as her dad sometimes did. I showed her how to bake cookies and cake. Since everyone else in the house was male, she looked forward to our "girl time." She came up with dozens of questions, as though she had been saving them up for years. Our favorite subject was the Lord. She wanted to know all about Him.

And then she became a teenager. She no longer craved my company and spent her time with friends. Our late night talks were replaced with exasperated expressions and curt, crisp answers. I was saddened by the changes, but my older daughter had gone through the same thing, and I prayed it was a temporary stage. In the meantime, I demonstrated my love in any way I could.

After graduation, she moved out and entered a bad relationship. We made no secret of our disapproval, but we stood by her. Then, she was involved in a car accident, and on the way to a doctor appointment, I tried to talk to her. I told her that even though I wasn't her biological mother, I had always put my heart into raising her—just like a real mom. Later, she told her dad to let me know that I was not her mother and never would be.

Her words hurt me deeply, and to protect myself, I separated myself from Sona and her life. As I struggled through the pain, I wondered if she was testing my love. When her father and I married, I had told her I would always be there—when she fell in love, when she graduated, when she got married, and when she had a baby. She believed me when she was younger. Now that her life had grown more complicated, perhaps she doubted my promises. Maybe she found it difficult to believe I loved her as much as my own children and had decided to push me away before I could hurt her. Suddenly, it occurred to me that I had done the same thing. Even though her life had changed in many ways, it was time to make sure she knew I still loved her. I had meant what I said all those years ago—she would always be the daughter of my heart.

—EVA JULIUSON

A Glimpse of Hope

Why am I discouraged? Why so sad?
I will put my hope in God!
PSALM 42:5

"Who is that girl?" a teacher asked as she pointed to a History Fair booth hosted by the sixth grade.

"That's my daughter, Tanya," I said and smiled.

A group of second graders sat on the floor with their hands folded in their laps and their eyes focused on my daughter. They listened attentively as she explained the use of a ricer and a butter churn and then fielded questions.

Tanya had been struggling in school, and after she repeated the fifth grade, I wondered if she would ever make it. However, none of her difficulties were evident in the way she now captured the children's eager attention in her role as a competent teacher. God gave me a glimpse of hope that day, and I knew my daughter would eventually find her way.

God grants us glimpses of hope in dark seasons.

—LYNN LUDWICK

God's Answer

I tell you the truth, you can say to this mountain,
"May you be lifted up and thrown into the sea,"
and it will happen. But you must really believe it
will happen and have no doubt in your heart.
MARK 11:23

When the doctors told me my mother didn't have very long to live, I followed the Apostle Paul's command to "pray without ceasing." I pleaded with God to give me a few more years with her.

However, my mother died, and because I believed God answers all prayers, I came to the conclusion that his answer had been "no." Even as my grief intensified, I knew God had a reason for everything He did. I didn't understand His will, but I accepted it.

Much later, I began to think about the years my mother had spent dealing with chronic asthma and the horrible side effects of the medicine she needed. When I had prayed to keep her here on earth, I had really been praying for myself. I recalled the countless times I had asked God to release my mother from her asthma and the pain she endured. And those were the prayers he chose to answer with a loving and gentle "yes."

Death has no victory for those who trust the Lord.

—SBT

In His Eyes

Long ago, even before he made the world, God loved us and
chose us in Christ to be holy and without fault in his eyes.
EPHESIANS 1:4

Fifth grade had just begun for my daughter. This meant a return to her old nemesis—long division. In fact, her math work in general suffered as she worked her way through the later elementary grades. For a student used to sailing through her studies, it was a source of daily frustration.

One afternoon, bordering on tears, she handed me her latest test, clearly expecting me to lower the boom. How could I? Thirty years from now, neither one of us would remember that math test. Instead, I hope Lauren will always recall that my love for her and my acceptance of her would never be based on her performance.

That's the way God loves us—unconditionally. If we had to earn His love through our achievements, we would all be in trouble. Relying on continued accomplishments to keep His love wouldn't work out very well, either. Thankfully, God loves us without conditions, and through Jesus, He sees us as perfect.

God's miraculous love is unconditional.

—PAULA WISEMAN

A Wounded Family

Praise the Lord; praise God our savior!
For each day he carries us in his arms.
PSALM 68:19

I didn't want to go. Once again, I had set up a time to meet with my mother to address the issues in our past. In light of hurtful scenarios that had come to light in my younger sister's life, our family had become wounded and divided. I had tried to communicate with my mother regarding this situation for several years, but she just couldn't understand my viewpoint. We were at a dead end once more.

As discouragement settled in my heart, the Lord gently reminded me that I don't have to bear these burdens alone. He alone truly understands the conflicts that arise between mothers and daughters. He extended his hands to carry my load, and He will continue to bear it for me as long as I release it into His care.

There is no load too heavy for
your Heavenly Father to carry.

—JAMIE SPEAK WOOTEN

Wanted: A Sister

For since the world began, no ear has heard and no eye has seen a God like you, who works for those who wait for him!
ISAIAH 64:4

Six-year-old Emily already had two brothers by the time I became pregnant with my fourth child, so she was definitely hoping for a sister. When her father came home after the birth of brother number three, she raced to the top of the stairs to hear the announcement. "It's a boy!" her father said, and she burst into tears and fled to her room. One day, I caught her staring at her new brother with a scowl. "What's wrong, sweetheart?" I asked.

"We have too many kids," she replied. "We'll never get to Disneyland at this rate."

"But you've never said that you wanted to go to Disneyland."

She shot me a patronizing look. "Mommy, everyone wants to go to Disneyland."

Four years later, Emily would end up with four brothers. She may have waited in vain for a sister, but God had something even better planned. She and her brother Dylan were destined to become best friends.

God can turn disappointment into a dream come true.

—SBT

115

Sweet Dreams

This is what the Sovereign Lord, the Holy One of Israel,
says: "Only in returning to me and resting in me will you be
saved. In quietness and confidence is your strength."
ISAIAH 30:15

Occasionally, I dream of my daughter back when she was really little. When I wake up, it feels as if God has given me a very special gift—one more minute with my giggly, little, blue eyed blonde. As new parents, we often heard, "Enjoy them now; they grow up so fast." This was usually announced when the bathroom has flooded with water and naked Barbies were scattered across the saturated linoleum.

Back in those days, in a moment of weariness, I actually tapped the hands on the clock forward just a tad, so bedtime would come a little faster. I only did it one or two times—maybe three. I just needed a little extra time to relax and unwind.

When I made the effort to look after myself, I felt rejuvenated—both in body and spirit. Even if it was just a long soak in the tub and, yes, the Barbies were probably still lying there, I believe it helped me to be a better mother to my daughter.

Care for yourself so you can better care for others.

—JENNIE HILLIGUS

Sounds Familiar

Do everything without complaining and arguing.
PHILIPPIANS 2:14

"God," I prayed, "this isn't fair. Why can't I have daughters who don't fight?" My preschool daughters, Erica and Anna, were in the midst of their third fight of the morning. My patience was fading quickly, and it wasn't even lunchtime. I sent them to separate rooms to calm down.

Abruptly, I realized how much I sound like my children when I complain to God.

"It's not fair."

"How come I have to do this and not them?"

"You give me all the hard jobs."

"Why do I have to do this *every* day?"

"Why do I have to do this *again?*"

"It's too hard."

"It's too much."

"I can't"

"I don't want to."

"If only . . ."

No wonder my children whine and complain. They hear the same thing from me on a regular basis. I wonder if God is as tired of my whining and grumbling as I am of my girl's complaints. I need to stop questioning God's will and start singing praises.

Lord help me to listen better, obey more, and complain less.

—ANGIE VIK

Moment of Awakening

I pray that your love will overflow more and more, and that you will keep on growing in knowledge and understanding.
PHILIPPIANS 1:9

Every morning while Emily was in elementary school, she and I would wait for the school bus together. I remember times when I felt distracted inside by thoughts of the work waiting for me and impatient for the bus to arrive.

Then one day in early spring, we were sitting on the steps, watching the chickens scratch around the yard. I happened to glance at the dogwood tree in front of us and noticed the branches, erupting with thousands of tiny, new leaves. I called Emily's attention to the tree, and filled with excitement, she bombarded me with questions until it was time for her to go.

It was a moment of awakening, not only for the tree, but for me as well. I had taken a moment to thank God for helping me see that the time I spent each morning with Emily was a blessing—an opportunity to get to know the precious gift that was my daughter.

Cherish the special times before they become only a memory.

—SBT

Two Moms—Two Friends

Everyone enjoys a fitting reply; it is wonderful to say the right thing at the right time.
PROVERBS 15:23

My daughter was close to tears. "I don't know what to do, Mom. I've done everything the doctor and the book said to do, and nothing is working!" My grandson wasn't sleeping at night, and my daughter's exhausted voice brought back memories of my own babies.

Although she appeared to be looking for advice, I suspected that what she really needed was sleep. As a single mother, she had more on her plate than I ever did, and that only added to her weariness.

Sometimes, I find myself responding to her with motherly advice when she neither needs it nor wants it. As we've wrestled through the changes in her life and our relationship, I've learned that support, encouragement, and a couple hours of sleep while I watch the baby, go a long way. I'm trying to avoid being a parent while she's learning how to be a mother. By working together, we've discovered that we aren't just two moms anymore; we've actually become good friends.

*It takes wisdom to know when to be a mother,
and when to be a friend.*

—MABELLE REAMER

A Season of Suffering

So we have been greatly encouraged in the midst of our troubles and suffering, dear brothers and sisters, because you have remained strong in your faith.

1 Thessalonians 3:7

Amanda let the telephone ring. Caller ID revealed her mother's number, but she didn't want to speak to her or to anyone else. She couldn't bear to hear someone say, "I told you so." Only last week she had defended him to her mother. "You're wrong about him. He loves me. We're going to get married. You'll see." Well, they had both seen him at the movies with another woman, wrapped in a tight embrace.

Amanda left the ringing telephone and walked out to the mailbox. There was one envelope, addressed in her mother's handwriting. She read the note. "My precious Amanda, This hurtful time is for a season, not for a lifetime. Never believe that you are defined by your mistakes, but know that they make you stronger. And remember that I am here for you—your mother who loves you more than you'll ever imagine." Amanda walked back into her apartment and dialed the phone.

A word of encouragement during a failure is worth more than an hour of praise after a success.

—Ava Pennington

He Adores Me

*Then the way you live will always honor and
please the Lord, and your lives will produce every
kind of good fruit. All the while, you will grow as
you learn to know God better and better.*
COLOSSIANS 1:10

There is a collage of photographs hanging in our upstairs hallway, and in one picture, my mother is holding newborn Emily. It is easy to see from my mother's expression that she is completely enamored of her new granddaughter. Sadly, in eight short months, my mother would be gone.

Emily may not have known her grandmother in person, but she became well acquainted with her through the many stories I've told, the albums full of photographs, and the letters her grandmother wrote to me. One day, I noticed Emily pointing out the picture upstairs to her friend. "That's my grandmother. She adored me."

Just as I've provided Emily with the opportunity to know her grandmother, I've done my best to help her know God. I've encouraged her to spend time in God's word, helped her develop a prayer life, and initiated discussions of a spiritual nature. I want my daughter to be able to say, "That's my God. He adores me."

*Give your children ample opportunity to
become acquainted with God.*

—SBT

Compassionate Discipline

All athletes are disciplined in their training. They do it to win
a prize that will fade away, but we do it for an eternal prize.
1 CORINTHIANS 9:25

When my daughter Jolene first expressed an interest in karate, I hesitated. Did I really want my daughter to learn martial arts skills that could cause bodily injury? Once she started, I discovered that karate requires intense discipline of its students.

Jolene had to attend weekly individual and group classes. Her instructors also expected her to practice at home each day. Katas, a sequence of specific moves, taught her to coordinate mind and body as she memorized the choreography. The Christian teachers exemplified a life-style of discipline and compassion.

Jolene persevered through six months of training. She remained excited about what she was learning and developed self-discipline at the same time. As a result, she completed the test for her *chi-chi* or orange belt. The discipline she learned through athletics taught her perseverance in all areas of life.

We can encourage our daughters to learn
self-discipline through sports.

—DARLENE FRANKLIN

Ladies' Night

*One day in your courts is better than
a thousand anywhere else!*
PSALM 84:10

The boys were off to a ball game so it was time for a girl party. We grew excited as we considered the possibilities.

"Let's have tea!"

"How about dress up?"

"Should we do a craft?"

"Paper dolls?"

We planned out our activities and spent the evening together, with all of the talking, giggling, and listening that went with it. I'm with my girls almost constantly, but I felt as if I knew them better after an evening of princesses, dolls, tea, and bubble bath.

God loves us, and He is with us always. Still, it's important to set aside time to immerse ourselves in the things we know are important to Him. When we listen to His heart, we know Him more intimately than before. And if we apply what we learn during our time together, we become a greater reflection of who He is.

Set aside some time for God and get to know Him better.

—ANITA LYNN RAMSEY

The Joy in Simple Things

Be glad; rejoice forever in my creation!
And look! I will create Jerusalem as a place of happiness.
Her people will be a source of joy.
ISAIAH 65:18

I have a flock of ducks, and several of the girls have disappeared recently, so I invited Emily to help me search for them. As we walked through the pony's pasture, I spotted one of my geese sitting by the fence. I had never seen any mating behavior among the geese, so I thought this one might be hurt. We cautiously approached the bird, only to realize that she was sitting on a lovely, little nest constructed of sticks, grass, and feathers. It was an unseasonably warm afternoon, and Emily noticed the bird was panting. "Poor thing," Emily said. "I think she's overheated." We found a fairly large wooden box and put it close enough to the nest to provide some shade. A few minutes later, we headed back to the house. "Wasn't that amazing?" Emily said. "Maybe she'll hatch some of those eggs!" I agreed and thanked God for giving Emily the ability to find joy in simple things.

Discover the complexity of God's creation
in deceptively simple things.

—SBT

Sisterly Love

Instead, be kind to each other, tenderhearted, forgiving one another, just as God through Christ has forgiven you.
Ephesians 4:32

One afternoon, I walked into the living room and found my youngest daughter with alligator tears dripping down her rosy cheeks.

I noticed she was twisting a broken bracelet in her hands. "What do we have here?" I asked as I sat down beside her and reached for some beads spilled across the floor.

She sucked in a deep breath. "I just wanted to try it on, and it broke," she replied in a trembling voice.

"Let's see if we can fix it. Then we'll wrap it up, and you can give it back to your sister as a present. Why don't you ask her to forgive you?"

In less than ten minutes, the bracelet was good as new. A few moments later, I heard her tiny hands knocking on her sister's door. "I'm sorry," she said. "Forgive me, okay?" When I peeked down the hallway, my two girls were hugging, and it was my turn to wipe away a few tears.

We have the ability to forgive one another because we were forgiven.

—Michele Starkey

The Finish Line

*I press on to reach the end of the race and
receive the heavenly prize for which God,
through Christ Jesus, is calling us.*
PHILIPPIANS 3:1

Mother often spoke of the time she won a trip to the National 4-H Club Congress. "It was a fantastic experience," she said. "We were treated like royalty." At the age of ten, I decided that I, too, would attend the Congress. It would be my personal goal to achieve before graduation.

Her talent had been sewing, but I chose cooking as my ticket to the congress. It was hard work, but Mother happily supported my time-consuming and expensive dream. During the time we spent together achieving an earthly goal, she also instilled a heavenly one in my heart.

We traveled all over our state, entering fairs and other competitions where I baked, created visuals, and gave timed demonstrations of preparing menus using dairy products or strawberries.

In my senior year, I achieved my ambition of winning the coveted prize—an all-expense-paid trip to Chicago where I discovered that Mom had been telling the truth. At the National 4-H Congress, I *was* treated like a princess!

*Wise mothers nurture both earthly
and heavenly goals in children's hearts*

—ELAINE YOUNG MCGUIRE

With A Song in Her Heart

Worship the Lord with gladness.
Come before him, singing with joy.
PSALM 100:2

I couldn't have asked for a better role model than my mother. One of the greatest things she taught me was to see the glass half full, to look for the blessing she insisted was hidden in even the darkest moment.

She brought joy into our home in so many ways. She greeted me every morning with a smile, and I saw that same smile each day when I returned from school. There was always time to discuss something of importance to me, and she had a way of making me see things in a new and positive light.

My mother loved to sing hymns, and the kitchen was her stage. I would often pass the kitchen and she'd be scrubbing a pot, singing her heart out. To this day, I can't stand at my sink without hearing her voice. Every once in a while, I sing a song or two, just to let God know how much I appreciate the mother he choose for me.

Show your love for the Lord with a smile and a song.

—SBT

Piercing Pride

Pride leads to conflict. Those who take advice are wise.
PROVERBS 13:10

When Lacey left for college, the emptiness in my heart settled in like a persistent low-grade fever. Full of eager anticipation, I looked forward to her visit during semester break, but the nose-pierced, tattooed blonde who walked through the door bore little resemblance to the girl who had gone off to school.

The happy reunion turned into a what-were-you-thinking argument. I stomped to my room and slammed the door. Embarrassing, that's what it was. There would be raised brows from relatives and wide eyes from friends. I snatched my Bible off the nightstand, but every verse I read referred to pride. Wait a minute, I thought. This was about Lacey, not me. Or was it?

My choice became clear. I could wallow alone in self-important anger, or I could love my daughter with an open mind and heart. No, that reunion didn't turn out as anticipated. It was even better.

Don't allow pride to poison your life.

—MICHELLE GRIEP

An Answer to Every Prayer

*And now I entrust you to God and the message of his grace
that is able to build you up and give you an inheritance with
all those he has set apart for himself.*

ACTS 20:32

Reality hit me. As the oldest of seven, I'd always been the babysitter and mother's helper. Until now, I didn't worry about motherhood other than the pain of delivery. I stared at my newborn daughter's face nestled against my breast. Insecurities and doubts flooded me.

Apprehension clouded my thinking, and feelings of panic began to stir. Was I ready for motherhood? I was going home today. My daughter would be depending on me, and I wasn't ready. I asked God to help me.

A kind-faced man with thinning hair stepped into my room and introduced himself as a pediatrician. In five minutes, he scribbled notes and talked me through basic principles that answered all my questions. His guiding words replaced my anxiety with peace.

Once home, I thought about how God had answered my prayer earlier that day, and I smiled at my own foolishness. Far too often, I struggled with fear when I didn't need to. God was always ready with an answer to every prayer.

God has the power to erase our fear.

—DONNA SUNDBLAD

129

A Loving Leap of Faith

*So be strong and courageous! Do not be afraid and do not
panic before them. For the Lord your God will personally go
ahead of you. He will neither fail you nor abandon you.*
DEUTERONOMY 31:6

After several satisfying years as the principal of an
elementary school, my father decided to return to school
for his graduate degree. I was about to enter kindergarten
and viewed the entire episode as a grand adventure.

Looking back, I realize it was far more than an exciting escapade for my parents, especially my mother. Helping my father to make his dream come true meant leaving
friends and family. It also meant giving up her comfortable,
familiar home for a year and the security of my father's sal-
ary.

I'm sure she worried about the obvious difficulties
involved, but loving my father meant helping him in any
way she could. Going to Berkley was only one of many
times I watched my mother put the needs of her family
ahead of her own. I know now that her leap of faith came
from her belief that God would watch over our little family and provide everything we needed.

God's love makes it possible to take a leap of faith.

—SBT

A Simple Hug

A time to embrace and a time to turn away.
A time to be quiet and a time to speak.
ECCLESIASTES 3:5, 7

One summer my oldest niece wanted to make more money, so she traveled 700 miles from the small town she called home and came to stay with us near Boston where the wages were higher. Using a sheet for a doorway, we turned our living room into a bedroom for her.

We had no children of our own, and we certainly weren't used to having a twenty-year-old around. I was concerned about filling in as a substitute mother if she had problems. I asked God to help me know how to care for her, but I didn't have to worry. As it turned out, she let me know exactly what she needed.

One day, she came home in tears, and I wasn't sure what to do. "I need a hug," she said, and I gathered her into my arms. That day, I learned that sometimes a simple hug works wonders.

A hug is a healing embrace.

—LAURIE A. PERKINS

Help, But Don't Touch

Direct your children onto the right path,
and when they are older, they will not leave it.
PROVERBS 22:6

I heard my young daughter, Lynette, call to me from her bedroom where she was working on an art project. Her voice had an insistent tone when she said, "Come here, I need your help."

Reluctantly, I left my work in the kitchen and went to watch her color, cut, and paste. After a few minutes, I suggested what I thought were a few simple improvements. She didn't appear to be listening, so I reached toward her paper, but she quickly yanked her creation out of reach. She said, "I want you to help, but I don't want you to touch."

This was a new concept for me. That incident helped me understand that my role was to encourage her personal best without imposing my will. As the years passed, I provided love and support, but I tried to leave the necessary changes to God.

An inspiring presence is far more helpful than interference.

—JEANETTE MACMILLAN

Cherish the Moment

Remember that the Lord will give you an inheritance as your reward, and that the Master you are serving is Christ.
COLOSSIANS 3:24

As my mother's asthma worsened, I visited more frequently. When I arrived in the morning, I often found her in a big chair by the fireplace. She always greeted me with a loving smile and an invitation to join her for a cup of tea. After spending some time catching up with our news, I would ask her what she needed done around the house. For many months, she rejected my offer of help. "As soon as I catch my breath," she said, "I'll get up and get busy."

I became more persistent and, eventually, she began to suggest ways in which I could help. I remember folding laundry, cleaning the bathrooms, and bathing the dog, but I don't ever recall hearing my mother grumble about her situation. She was too busy telling me about the birds she had seen at the feeder or a movie she had watched with my father the night before. Thanks to her, I discovered that every moment is precious—too precious to waste with complaints and self-pity.

Counting your blessings is a lot more rewarding than keeping track of your troubles.

—SBT

Following Directions

The Lord leads with unfailing love and faithfulness all who keep his covenant and obey his demands.
PSALM 25:10

"Mom, I think that God is leading me to go back to school," my daughter Lydia said.

I struggled to keep my voice even. "Oh, really?" I replied. It was only two days before school started. All summer, we had planned to home school Lydia for the sixth grade because of the problems she had experienced in the fifth grade. The other girls had delighted in excluding her, punishing her for being a nonconformist and every teacher's favorite.

When I picked her up after the first day of school, she bounced up to the car with a big grin on her face. "Now I know why God wanted me back here!" she said. "There's a new boy, and I know we're going to be great friends." Her sensitivity to God's direction has been rewarded by a strong and long lasting friendship with the fellow student she met that day.

Allow your children to experience the joy
of discovering God's wisdom.

—EVANGELINE BEALS GARDNER

A Man of Prayer

The eyes of the Lord watch over those who do right,
and his ears are open to their prayers.
1 PETER 3:12

The animated phone call from my daughter Laura, who was halfway through her senior year at Texas A&M, stands out as an all-time favorite memory. "Mom, there's this guy named James. We're just friends, but wait until I tell you about him." Her voice bubbled over with excitement as she continued to chatter. "And you'll never guess what, Mom. When we're in our college group at church and it's time to pray, all eyes turn to James!"

Before I knew his last name, his major, or what he looked like, I learned that James was a man of prayer. I felt blessed that my daughter saw this as a significant quality, and that she recognized it would also be important to me.

Today, Laura is the loving wife of this godly man. It's a joy to hold hands around their dinner table with their three precious children. When it's time to pray, all eyes still turn to James—the husband, the daddy, the man of prayer.

Help your children discover the important qualities to look
for in a life partner.

—SANDI BANKS

Difficult Days

It's better to live alone in the corner of an attic than with a quarrelsome wife in a lovely home.

PROVERBS 21:9

Not long ago, I spent a couple of days trying to make everyone around me as miserable as I felt. My poor husband finally concluded that silence was his best defense, and the children actually cleaned up their rooms.

When my spirits finally lifted, a collective sigh of relief could be heard throughout the house. I was so happy to feel like myself again, but I knew I had some apologies to make.

My family responded with love and understanding, reminding me once again how very lucky I was.

Later that evening, it occurred to me that my daughter Emily might have a husband of her own someday, and I was the most significant role model she had for a wife who was devoted to both her husband and the Lord. I knew I would always have my off days, but I decided that next time, I'd try to remember that she was watching and learning how to be a woman.

Model the woman you want your daughter to be.

—SBT

Created and Sustained

You saw me before I was born.
Every day of my life was recorded in your book. Every
moment was laid out before a single day had passed.
PSALM 139:16

I was adopted as an infant, but I was reunited with my birth mother shortly after graduating from college. Not long after our first meeting, I invited her to lunch to get to know her and share the events of my life. Though she put up a brave front, I could tell she harbored very real fears. Perhaps she worried that I loved her less because of the decision she had made when I was born.

No one could have predicted that our meeting would lead me to fully appreciate what both mothers had done for me. One woman had respected the Creator who gave me life by carrying, nourishing, and delivering me. The other woman had honored God every time she diapered me, drove me to basketball practice, and stroked my hair when I was ill. Each of them had blessed me with the devotion of a loving mother.

A mother's love can take many forms.

—MARGOT STARBUCK

Facing the Real World

So we can say with confidence, "The Lord is my helper, so I will have no fear. What can mere people do to me?"
HEBREWS 13:6

After five days at Christian camp, my daughter Kim returned in a joyful mood. She had grown close to God but, then, reality hit. Following an argument with her friend Alice, she retreated to her room with tears dripping down her cheeks. "Everything was fine at youth camp," she said. "Why are things so different at home? I want to feel like I did at camp."

"At camp, you were with Christian kids," I replied, "and everyone was focused on working hard to be a better Christian. In the real world some people are not focused on the Lord."

"What am I supposed to do now?" she asked.

I explained that she could count on God to help her behave like a Christian no matter what she faced. "It doesn't matter what anyone else is doing," I said.

Kim wiped her tears and grabbed two cherry Popsicles. "I think it's time to pay Alice a visit," she said with a smile.

God can inspire us in any circumstances.

—PHYLLIS QUALLS FREEMAN

You're Among Friends

And let us not neglect our meeting together, as some people do, but encourage one another, especially now that the day of his return is drawing near.
HEBREWS 10:25

After she got married, my daughter Emily and her new husband, Alan, moved into an apartment about an hour's drive away from our farm. I urged them to find a new church home as soon as possible, but Alan's job required him to work Sundays.

He tried to change his schedule on several occasions without luck, and as the weeks turned into months, I became concerned. In recent years, I had discovered how much regular church attendance could enrich my relationship with God, and I didn't like the idea of Emily and Alan going it alone. So, I prayed that the Lord would find a way for them to maintain a fellowship with other believers.

When Emily called and told me she was going to a Bible study at a local college with a close friend, I rejoiced. Once again, God had listened to a worried mother's prayer.

God wants His people in church.

—SBT

A Gentle Answer

A gentle answer deflects anger,
but harsh words make tempers flare.
PROVERBS 15:1

Like most teenagers, my daughter has her share of mood swings, and since I've been going through menopause, I'm not always at my best either. On any given day, we're both a little temperamental. This has only exacerbated our communication problems. She tends to interpret my suggestions as criticism, and I perceive her responses as disrespectful.

One night, my husband pointed out that I had a short fuse. "Why do you speak to her that way?" he asked.

"What way?"

"It's your tone of voice," he replied. "You don't use that tone with me."

After a bit of soul-searching, I realized he was right. I would allow the least little thing to set me off and then lash out at my daughter. I began to listen to her more closely, consider her feelings, and think before I spoke. And when I did talk to her, I avoided a hostile tone—no matter what I had to say.

How we say something is just as important as what we say.

—MARY LAUFER

May

The Tools of Comfort

He comforts us in all our troubles so that we can comfort others. When they are troubled, we will be able to give them the same comfort God has given us.

2 Corinthians 1:4

With tears running down my face faster than my feet could carry me, I raced home from the bus stop. I desperately craved the comfort that had eluded me all day at school. "Mom, where are you?" I screamed. "I need you right now!" I pushed the side door of the house open, threw my backpack down, and searched every room. We collided with a hug in the kitchen and, finally, in the safety of her arms, I could cry and escape a day of elementary school taunting. The solace I found in her embrace was the closest thing I knew to heaven. She spoke sweet words of comfort and reminded me of the Lord's promise to help me make it through that horrible day.

A few decades passed, but the kitchen and the women remained the same. Once again, tears streamed down a delicate face, and once more, comfort was needed. This time, it was my mother's tears flowing to the beat of her broken heart. Her husband of over thirty years faced the toughest battle he would ever fight. Knowing that the days we would share with him were short, we consoled each other and braced for this new unexpected season. My brother and I had begun families of our own and had emptied Mom's nest, but in a moment of family crisis we found ourselves back in the kitchen, huddled together for support and comfort. And, in the midst of heartache, we reminded each other that God was faithful. He would bring comfort and peace—no matter what the outcome of the medical treatment.

As the months passed, I became the child who consoled her mother as she grieved the loss of her husband. It was a role I hadn't chosen, but I knew I was well equipped with the tools of comfort she had demonstrated for years: prayer, hugs, love, and compassion. I had no way to fully comprehend her sorrow. The sting of death brought a different experience for the child than for the wife. But I did my best. I hugged, I cried, and I loved. The ache of pain and the sting of grief found temporary relief with the familiarity of a daughter's embrace, but we both knew deep down that only God could truly comfort her.

When I was a child, my mother's nurturing love molded and shaped me into the woman I had become. We loved each other through car accidents, wedding announcements, pregnancies, surgeries, birthdays, and daily life. She provided the support I needed, taught me to honor and comfort others, and guided me to the Lord for peace and joy.

Now, we enjoy daytime Bible study sessions and coffee breaks. We run errands, buy groceries, and share experiences that range from mundane to exciting. Her house is right around the corner, and our lives are knit together in a remarkable way. The secret of our relationship is that every day is full of special gifts. Our daily routine provides us with countless blessings and reminders of how God uses us to encourage each other.

I rejoice in the fact that my son has had the opportunity to share in the love between mother and daughter. However, I wonder if he comprehends the depth of the relationship he has witnessed between two women from two generations. He wasn't there when I ran home that day, and he was too young to fully understand the depth of a new widow's pain; he has seen ample evidence of the Savior who provides comfort, peace, and joy in every situation. And, when he's having a rough day, he knows that his mother's arms are waiting to hug him, too.

—JENNIFER DEVLIN

Family Harmony

Then all of you can join together with one voice, giving
praise and glory to God, the Father of our Lord Jesus Christ.
ROMANS 15:6

Music is a staple in our home, both recorded and live. One evening I picked up my guitar and began to play worship music. Typically, I begin with several easier songs to warm up my voice and fingers. I strummed softly and worked up to a full voice. As I began to sing about God's love, I heard an echo from down the hall. Elie was drawn to the living room, singing her harmony loud and strong. "God's love endures forever. He is worthy to be praised," she sang.

She selected the next song and, soon, my other girls filtered out to join us. Melodies abounded until my sore fingers cried out for mercy. An evening that started with all of us in separate rooms was transformed into family fellowship in which we lifted our spirits and renewed our hearts. What a joy it is to stand with your daughters and sing praises to the Lord!

Fellowship with our family strengthens our faith.

—CASEY PITTS

Advice for the Lovelorn

*Let us think of ways to motivate
one another to acts of love and good works.*
HEBREWS 10:24

As the mother of three teenagers, I'm convinced that matters of the heart require more of my time and energy than any parenting challenge I've encountered previously.

My son Dylan's relationship with his girlfriend, Bobbijo, had been smooth sailing for over a year when, suddenly, they hit a rough patch. For days, Dylan wandered through his days with sad eyes and a perpetual scowl. His father and I tried talking to him, without much success.

Then, one day, I received a call from my daughter Emily. "Why don't you talk to him?" I said. "I suspect Dylan doesn't believe that we ever went through something like this, and if we did, we've forgotten what it felt like."

When Emily called that evening, I heard the music of Dylan's forgotten laughter, and within a few days, he and Bobbijo had returned to calm seas. I never found out what Emily said, but I feel blessed that she loved him enough to reach out to him in his time of need.

*Sympathetic understanding is a
special part of loving someone.*

—SBT

He's Always Watching

The Lord is watching everywhere,
keeping his eye on both the evil and the good.
PROVERBS 15:3

My daughter, Leah, played the flute in the sixth grade band. On the night of the big spring concert, parents lined up across the back of the auditorium with camcorders ready. The band members entered single file to take their appointed place.

With all of the children dressed in white shirts with black slacks, at first I had a difficult time picking Leah out of the crowd. But it only took a moment for this mother's eyes to find her child. Of all the members of the band, only Leah had my undivided attention.

Just as my eyes remain focused on Leah, God's eyes are always focused on His children. Psalm 34:15 says, "The eyes of the Lord are upon the righteous, and his ears are open unto their cry." God watches over the righteous like a devoted mother watches over her child. Isn't it reassuring to know God's eyes are upon us, and His ears are open to our cries?

We always have the attention of our heavenly Father.

—DONNA J. SHEPHERD

Patient Endurance

*Patient endurance is what you need now,
so you will continue to do God's will.
Then you will receive all that he has promised.*
HEBREWS 10:36

Six weeks before our second daughter's wedding, we took the bridesmaids' dresses to show Gisele, her future mother-in-law. Gisele laid the dresses over the back of a chair in her bedroom. "Leave them here until you come for supper tomorrow night," she said. "They'll be all right."

The dresses were not all right. That Saturday night a flood devastated Tulsa. When we returned to Gisele's ruined mobile home, mud dripped off the blue satin dresses—the borrowed blue satin dresses.

Dry cleaners weren't open in the flood-damaged city that Sunday morning. She and I dumped them in the bathtub and turned on the water. All afternoon we took turns leaning over the tub, rinsing and gently scrubbing. On our knees that day, we learned the meaning of patient endurance. But our efforts paid off, and the last traces of mud went down the drain. The dresses were good as new. Jesus does that for us. His blood washes our sins away and makes us clean.

A seemingly hopeless situation may not be hopeless after all.

—LEANN CAMPBELL

Mother's Day

Let your roots grow down into him, and let your lives be built on him. Then your faith will grow strong in the truth you were taught, and you will overflow with thankfulness.
COLOSSIANS 2:7

When I first became a mother, Mother's Day was a special occasion. It gave me a sense of importance, and I loved being recognized with cards and flowers as one of the amazing women known as mothers—the glowing subject of poetry, cards, and endless commercials on television.

I loved the gifts my children diligently created, and the fuss they made over me, but after my mother died, there was always a moment or two of sadness. Whenever I asked her what sort of present she would like, she always said, "I have everything I need and more than I ever dreamed of having."

Today, I remembered that Mother's Day was only four days away. Earlier this week, when my daughter Emily asked me what I wanted, I couldn't think of anything. As I did my chores this evening, I understood exactly what my mother had meant all those years ago. I realized that there was nothing I needed, and I had more blessings than I could count.

Following the Lord has made every day Mother's Day.

—SBT

Deep Dark Secrets

God would surely have known it,
for he knows the secrets of every heart.
PSALM 44:21

My daughter had just finished basketball practice, and as we left the gym, she recapped the entire session. I felt my heart swell. I knew she would love basketball. Her dad and I had suspected fear was the culprit preventing her from playing, so we worked hard to convince her to give it a try. I knew God gifted her in this area.

On the way home, I tried not to gloat. "So, it sounds like you kind of like basketball now," I said.

I glanced in her direction and caught her rolling her eyes. "Why don't you just come out and say it," she said.

"What?"

"Tell me you were right. Tell me how you're the mom who knows everything."

I wanted to defend myself, but I didn't have a leg to stand on. "I don't know everything," I said.

"That's right," she replied. "You don't know my deepest, darkest secret."

I gulped and prepared myself for the worst.

"I can't do a somersault," she said and smiled.

Our deepest, darkest secrets are safe with God.

—VICKI TIEDE

Godly Counsel

Get all the advice and instruction you can,
and be wise the rest of your life.
PROVERBS 19:20

When our son divorced his wife, I worried about the victims of their breakup—four-year-old Britt and two-year-old Brandon. Many times, I unloaded my grandmother worries on my daughter Jen.

She told me repeatedly, "Mom, ask God every day to take care of the children. Then leave them in His hands and try not to worry. He cares for them more than you do."

For years, Jen had listened to my counsel. Now it was time for me to pay heed to hers. I placed the grandchildren's picture in a prominent place in our home, and each day, I gave them to God. Eighteen years later, I can confirm that Jen's advice worked for Britt and Brandon—and for me. The children are well-adjusted Christian young people and I have maintained a calm spirit.

We never go wrong when we heed godly counsel—even
when it's from our own child.

—JEWELL JOHNSON

Put Your Heart into It

If you look for me wholeheartedly, you will find me.
JEREMIAH 29:13

My daughter's first boyfriend was a nice young man she met at church. It didn't take me long to realize she was more taken with the idea of dating than she was with the young man. My maternal instincts told me he may have captured her interest, but he hadn't touched her heart. Consequently, I wasn't the least bit surprised when the relationship lasted only a few short months.

The first boyfriend was followed by Alan—another pleasant young man she met at church. That's where the similarities ended, and I watched as a young girl infatuated with the freedom and fun of dating become a young woman in love. This time, Emily wasn't just following a teenage trend. She was following her heart.

For many years, I attended church, prayed, and read my Bible, but I was only going through the motions. It wasn't until I gave my heart to Jesus that my own conversion from casual observer into committed Christian took place.

Put your heart into your relationship with the Lord.

—SBT

The Wisdom of a Child

Wisdom is of more value than foolishness.
ECCLESIASTES 2:13

I heard my daughter Teresa scream. "Mom, what are you doing?" Somehow, my foot hit the brake. A tire popped as the car spun around. We stopped on the shoulder of the road in a cloud of dust. I had fallen asleep at the wheel.

We were on our way home from a whirlwind trip to Southern California. With my husband unable to come, I was left to drive—at my own insistence. Teresa had asked to drive numerous times, but I had said no, even though she had a driver's permit and lots of experience.

While my son and Teresa's boyfriend changed the tire, I observed the mountainous terrain. Behind us, just to the right, was a steep drop. If the car had gone over, it would have meant death for all of us. As Teresa drove the last two hundred miles home, I silently thanked God for his protection and for my daughter who had watched over me with her youthful wisdom.

God can use the wisdom of our children for our best interests.

—CHARLOTTE KARDOKUS

Healing Walks and Words

God, the Lord, created the heavens and stretched them out.
He created the earth and everything in it. He gives breath to
everyone, life to everyone who walks the earth.
ISAIAH 42:5

When a truck smashed into my daughter's car, it left her with post-traumatic syndrome. For a long time, she had trouble conversing with me. She had difficulty focusing. Her inability to read more than a paragraph at a time became a problem with her history class.

My walking partner had moved away, so I asked Darlene to walk with me in the park behind our home. She relaxed as we strolled among the trees, and I soon discovered that we could talk. If I read her history book and explained it to her as we walked, she could remember the facts. We lengthened our walks and took more of them. Darlene passed her course, and we found a way to chat about any topic and strengthen our relationship.

Now that Darlene is healthy and married, we don't live close by. However, when we visit, we still find our best talks start when we walk.

Take a walk with your daughter and
open your hearts to one another.

—KAREN H. WHITING

Tongue Tied

Now go! I will be with you as you speak,
and I will instruct you in what to say.
EXODUS 4:12

When my daughter Emily left home, I worried that her bid for independence would wreak havoc with her grades at school, but she maintained her place on the honor roll. However, her numerous absences put her at risk of losing credit for the courses she had taken.

She called and told me that she had to meet with a special board to plead her case. "What am I going to say?" she asked, obviously upset.

"You may feel like you're on your own with this," I said, "but God will be with you every step of the way. If you humble yourself and ask Him for help, you'll know what to say."

A few days later, she called to tell me that the board had allowed her credits. "It was amazing," she said. "I prayed and then I knew exactly what to tell the board. I apologized and promised to do my best for the rest of the year."

"I know you will," I said.

"You bet," she replied. "I promised God, too!"

God is ready to give you the words you need.

—SBT

The Face of Grace

Seeing their faith, Jesus said to the man,
"Young man, your sins are forgiven."
LUKE 5:20

It was graduation morning. My high school had selected me to be a junior escort for the seniors accepting diplomas that day, and I was late. I called out a goodbye to my mom and hustled down the stairs. I turned the key and shifted into reverse while the garage door rumbled open. My mind wandered to the upcoming ceremony as I backed down the drive. Something crunched. Angry with my brother for leaving his skateboard out, I grumbled and pulled forward.

When I got out, my eyes widened with horror. I hadn't run over a skateboard. I'd bashed into the side of my mom's car. As I imagined her disappointment and anger, I began to cry and ran into the house where I confessed between sobs.

My mom listened, surprisingly unruffled. "Don't worry about it, honey," she said. "Just go on." Stunned by her calm compassion, I did. Twenty years later, I can't remember a thing about that graduation service, but the memory of my mother's grace remains vivid.

Forgiveness nurtures the soul.

—KAREN WITEMEYER

God's Love in My Daughter's Arms

The Lord will work out his plans for my life   for your
faithful love, O Lord, endures forever.
PSALM 138:8

I met my daughter's eyes and fell in love. I had waited twelve years for this moment—twelve long years of infertility, dashed dreams, and pleading prayers.

I didn't give birth to the little girl with hair as blond as my husband's and a smile that captured everyone's heart. Although I hadn't carried her in my body, she had been born the same week my husband and I had begun adoption classes nine months earlier. And her birth name was Michelle—the very name we chose fourteen years earlier while we were dating.

Years of wondering why God had denied us a family of our own had left me close to losing my faith. And then He blessed our lives with the tiny girl reaching out to us with arms filled with His love. Nearly sixteen years later, I am still reminded that God was listening to our prayers. He was always there.

God has not forgotten you.

—KATHRYN LAY

Blessed Boredom

This is the day the Lord has made.
We will rejoice and be glad in it.
PSALM 118:24

When I was a young girl, and I happened to find myself feeling bored, I kept it to myself—especially if my mother was around. The word "bored" changed my gentle, loving parent into a drill sergeant with a litany of tasks for me to perform.

I now realize that my avoidance of her zero tolerance for boredom led me to discover many of the interests I still enjoy. Most importantly, I realized the beauty of God's creation through the animals and plants I studied.

Today, as the mother of five children, I no longer feel the need to spend every moment engaged in "worthwhile" activities. I actually welcome the prospect of having nothing to do because it means I can take time for the most important thing in my life—my relationship with God. Sometimes I read my Bible or pray, but I also find great fulfillment in finding a quiet place to sit and reflect on the blessing of being given another day to spend with the people I love.

Every day is an irreplaceable gift from God.

—SBT

Discovering a Daughter

A time to cry and a time to laugh.
A time to grieve and a time to dance.
ECCLESIASTES 3:4

"Mom," my son announced, "Holly and I are engaged!"

Stunned, my husband and I could only stare at each other. Even though our son and his new fiancée were still in college, I was thrilled. I had come to think of Holly as the daughter I had never had. In the days that followed, she included me in all the details of the wedding. So this is what it's like to have a daughter, I thought.

When my son called to tell us that the engagement was off, it hurt to know that our "daughter" was no longer a part of our lives, but I forced myself to focus on the positive memories with Holly. She had given me a renewed joy in many activities I had once enjoyed such as gourmet cooking, shopping, gardening—and chocolate! I hadn't lost a daughter. I had gained an appreciation for the things that mothers with daughters take for granted every day.

Thank God for the "daughters" He has brought into your life—even for a short time.

—CONNIE K. POMBO

The Apple of His Eye

The Lord directs the steps of the godly.
He delights in every detail of their lives.
PSALM 37:23

There are days when I find it hard to believe that my Heavenly Father considers me—His daughter—beautiful. All I see when I look in the mirror are the splotches, wrinkles, and smudges that represent my shortcomings, failures, and sins. I bear no resemblance to the godly woman in whom God delights.

But when my daughter enters the room, I can't help but grin as she pivots and proudly models her latest creative hairstyle. The next day, she begs to show me how to juggle plastic Easter eggs, or ushers me to the kitchen to taste her amazing blue cookies. Her hair looks crazy, she usually drops the eggs, and she always leaves a mess when she cooks. Despite all this, I find it impossible not to delight in this amazing, beautiful, and inventive little girl. My smile returns as I remember how much God delights in me.

Disregard the mirror's reflection and remember that God delights in His children.

—MARGOT STARBUCK

Respect Begins at Home

If you honor your father and mother, "things will go well for
you, and you will have a long life on the earth."
EPHESIANS 6:3

My mother often said, "Respect begins at home." When I was young, my awareness didn't come from verbal instruction, as much as it came from watching my parents interact with each other and with the people that visited our home.

I realize, now, that my parents also taught me about respect by honoring me. They spoke to me honestly, in voices filled with love. They cared about my well-being and put my needs ahead of their own.

As a teenager, I had a curfew. One night, I decided I was old enough to decide when it was time to go home. The next day, my mother was obviously upset with me.

"I can hardly wait for the day when I don't have to answer to anyone," I said.

I will never forget my mother's forgiving smile or what she said. "Chances are, you will always have someone in your life who is entitled to your respect. Even if you are all alone, you will still have to answer to God, and He deserves your best."

When we honor our father and mother, we honor God.

—SBT

Learning by Example

He comforts us in all our troubles so that we can comfort others. When they are troubled, we will be able to give them the same comfort God has given us.

2 CORINTHIANS 1:4

It had been a hard week. Balancing work, marriage, and motherhood was getting the best of me. When I saw the dead sparrow, it pushed me over the edge. Before I knew it, I was sitting on the back steps, sobbing.

Abruptly, my daughter Kristal plopped down beside me, and without saying a word, she snuggled in close and began to rub my back. She was consoling me, not because I had instructed her in how to raise someone's spirits and not because she read a book about it. She knew what to do, because she had received comfort. Her gentle caring and sensitivity to my sorrow gave me the strength to face that day and the days that followed.

God's comfort is a gift we need to share with others.

—KAREN SHERRILL

The Book of Love

For the word of God is alive and powerful.
HEBREWS 4:12

My daughter Savannah raced around excitedly as we prepared for our special time. We assembled our Bibles and blankets and then read our devotions. It was an enjoyable routine, but it was also a great way to make my quiet moments more productive. As I nestled into my spot, I noticed the worried look on her face. "Where's my book that tells me how much Jesus loves me?" she asked. A quick search produced her Bible, and we were ready.

It wasn't until later that I realized the real meaning of her simple request. Her words represented enthusiasm for God's word, but they meant so much more. She had recognized the true purpose of the Bible. We often see it as a book filled with instructions, stories, and laws, but its message is really one of God's love for His children. Perhaps if I view my Bible from that perspective, I will find reading it more of a blessing than a task.

The Bible is a complex book with a simple message.

—JAMI KIRKBRIDE

Divine Discipline

No discipline is enjoyable while it is happening—it's painful!
But afterward there will be a peaceful harvest of right living
for those who are trained in this way.
HEBREWS 12:11

We all wanted our son-in-law Alan to slow down. One day during a trip, my husband drew Alan's attention to the speed limit. "I'm going to feel badly when you get a ticket," he said, "but I'm not going to help you pay for it just because you're doing me a favor."

A few weeks later, Emily called. "Alan got a speeding ticket the other day," she said.

"You don't sound very unhappy," I replied.

"Oh, I'm not the least bit upset. In fact, I'm glad."

"Glad?"

"I figure God got tired of Alan not listening to us, and He decided to give Alan His own warning. The ticket is a small price to pay when you think of what could have happened."

"I like your attitude," I said.

Emily laughed. "Well, I like my husband and family to be safe and sound, so I'm happy that God decided to teach Alan a lesson."

Like a loving parent, God sometimes needs to
chastise his children.

—SBT

Keep It Simple

Jesus replied, "You must love the Lord your God with all your heart, all your soul, and all your mind."
MATTHEW 22:37

My friend Karen knew her daughter had spent a busy day attending preschool, playing tea party, and pushing her dolls around in her carriage. So, she wasn't surprised when four-year-old Jenna collapsed on her bed. "Mommy," she said in a sleepy voice. "I want to talk to God, but I don't know what to say."

Karen knelt down next to the bed and tucked the purple comforter under Jenna's chin. "Just tell God how you feel. Talk to Him as if you were talking to me or Daddy."

There was a long silence. Karen suspected Jenna had fallen asleep, so she lightly kissed her cheek and turned to leave. Just before she reached the doorway, she heard her little girl whisper, "I love You, God. Amen." Later that night, it was Karen's turn to collapse into bed. She remembered the giggles that day—the messes, the struggles, and the cuddles—and she took a deep breath. "I love you, God," she said.

Tell God what's in your heart and on your mind.

—LAURIE MODRZEJEWSKI

The Growth Spurt

*Now that I am old and gray, do not abandon me, O God.
Let me proclaim your power to this new generation, your
mighty miracles to all who come after me.*
PSALM 71:18

Mother often spoke of God's power and told our family about His mighty miracles. Then, in her late seventies, she began to experience dissatisfaction with the church where she had worshiped for twenty years. "I want to keep on growing, learning, and teaching," she said. "I'm just not able to do it there."

My sisters and I were somewhat upset by her announcement, so Mother tried to explain how she felt. "I have wonderful and godly friends in my congregation, but I just don't feel God's spirit moving there."

She sought the Lord's guidance for years before she began attending services in a vibrant spirit-filled congregation much further from her home. She has found happiness and fulfillment speaking to women's groups, completing in-depth Bible studies with young women, and mentoring new friends of all ages. God continues to use her in mighty ways, and although some of her old friends don't quite understand, she has never looked back.

It's a wise mother who teaches her daughter to never stop growing in the Lord.

—ELAINE YOUNG MCGUIRE

Timeless Beauty

You should clothe yourselves instead with the beauty that comes from within, the unfading beauty of a gentle and quiet spirit, which is so precious to God.
1 PETER 3:4

When I was a little girl, I thought my mother was the most beautiful woman in the world. She was tall and slender with thick brown hair and enormous hazel eyes. Her smile lit up the room. When I was a teenager, I would stare at photos of her at the same age and wish I had inherited her striking features and sense of style. If I told her she was pretty, she would smile and say, "Thank you, sweetheart." Somehow, I knew she didn't think of herself as anything but ordinary.

Over the years, my mother's luxurious hair thinned and turned gray, and her stunning eyes were often clouded with pain. Despite this, her smile still made me feel as though the sun had broken through the clouds on a dreary day, and I thought she had never been as beautiful. I had finally come to the realization that I had spent my life seeing her through loving eyes, eyes that looked beyond the surface to an inner beauty, untouched by time.

Inner beauty never fades.

—SBT

He Has My Thighs

But let the godly rejoice. Let them be glad in God's presence.
Let them be filled with joy.
PSALM 68:3

I felt totally amazed and overwhelmed as I stood in the delivery room waiting for the birth of my first grandchild. When my daughter saw the baby, she exclaimed, "He has my thighs." Everyone in the room laughed.

Such times are full of great hope and expectation. It was a blessing to share our happiness with each other and, later, with family and friends. It may have been something that happens every day, but it was a total miracle, nonetheless. A difficult start to the pregnancy made the entire experience even more incredible. As I held a tiny, new life in my arms, I thought about all the joy that lay in store for my daughter.

My daughter and I had progressed from the typical teen-age years of mother-daughter conflict to this great day. When she invited me to be a part of the blessed experience of birth, she allowed me to share in one of God's greatest gifts.

Celebrate the miracle of life.

—SHERRON SLAVENS

The Battle of the Bedroom

And let the peace that comes from Christ rule in your hearts.
For as members of one body you are called to live in peace.
And always be thankful.
COLOSSIANS 3:15

My high school senior's messy bedroom was making me crazy. Katie claimed her clutter was comforting, but I believed she was being stubborn and rebellious. Our struggle finally came to a head when she planted her feet, set her jaw, and declared, "After I go to college, I'll never make a bed or dust a dresser top again!" Eventually, she boxed her possessions and left for school, leaving her room very tidy—and very empty.

Now, when I stand at her door, the stark neatness is far more unappealing than the mess ever was. Sometimes, my memory returns to our conflicts, and I regret that I couldn't understand why Katie wanted control of her personal space during that transitional and unsettling year before college. Now I see that a security blanket can take many forms.

It's amazing how a little time and space between parent and child can change things. These days, I like a room to have that "lived-in" look, and Katie has the tidiest room in her dorm!

Being right isn't always better.

—LINDA CROW

Unique Expressions

For God has not given us a spirit of fear and timidity,
but of power, love, and self-discipline.
2 TIMOTHY 1:7

My four boys have always been very demonstrative with me, but for many years, their sister, Emily, was a different story. She never came to me for physical affection, and if I attempted to hug her, she would stand in a rigid, unresponsive pose. I rarely heard her say, "I love you," and when I did, it was usually because I said it first.

Sometimes, I secretly wondered if Emily loved me. And then, one Sunday, the pastor of our church described how God creates every child as an individual and determines his or her unique characteristics even before birth. Emily was one of a kind, just as her brothers were.

I had to smile at my previous insecurities. Hugs and words of endearment were only two ways to express love, and she had demonstrated her feelings in so many other ways. When she came over for a visit a few days later and handed me a bouquet of daffodils, I decided God might be telling me to forget my foolish worries and trust in His wisdom.

Rejoice in your children's individuality.

—SBT

A Maternal Mentor

You gave me life and showed me your unfailing love.
My life was preserved by your care.
JOB 10:12

I leaned against the bed in a crumpled heap on the floor. My latest parenting challenge had left me feeling defeated and confused. Suddenly the phone rang.

I heard my Aunt Lois' sweet voice. "Hello!" she said. "You were on my mind, so I thought I'd call."

I poured my heart out to her. She listened and quoted to me from scripture. Once again, her timing was perfect, and she knew exactly what to say.

A sense of calm crept over me, and I wiped away my tears. "You're not just my prayer warrior, Aunt Lois," I said. "You're like a mother to me."

I had been so thankful when she took me under her wing after the premature deaths of my mother and mother-in-law. Without her prayers and support, I doubt I could have weathered that difficult storm. She cared enough to fill a huge gap in my life. I wish more women would sense the need to mother. There will always be someone who needs a maternal mentor.

A woman needs maternal love and guidance
long after her mother is gone.

—MARIBETH SPANGENBERG

171

Heavenly Post-it Notes

For God speaks again and again,
though people do not recognize it.
JOB 33:14

While visiting my mother in the days before cell phones, my husband and I spent a day shopping in nearby Nashville. Finally, we stopped at one last bookstore. As I approached the cashier with my pile of books, a Post-it on the front of the cash register caught my eye. It read, "Lanita Boyd—Call your mother."

"Your mom must know you pretty well," the clerk said.

I laughed. "Yes, she does."

In the same way, my heavenly Father posts messages for me to notice. A billboard may bring to mind a friend I need to meet for lunch, a song on the radio may prompt me to write an encouraging note, and a question from my husband may remind me of a shut-in I need to visit. All I need to do is to respond to God's call.

God speaks to us in many different ways.

—LANITA BRADLEY BOYD

A Kindred Spirit

*I tell you the truth, wherever the Good News is
preached throughout the world, this woman's deed
will be remembered and discussed.*
MARK 14:9

After my mother died, I wanted to talk about how I felt. I wanted to tell everyone what a remarkable person my mother had been, and I wanted to recall my wonderful memories. However, the rest of my family preferred to keep their thoughts and emotions private. Since I knew that God understood exactly how I felt, I relied heavily on prayer for comfort.

One day, I asked God to find someone who shared my need to talk about my mother. A few weeks later, my brother happened to mention our Aunt Helen. She was my father's older sister and had always treated me like a daughter. She was delighted to hear from me, and as we talked, the conversation turned to my mother.

For over an hour, we opened our hearts to each other. We laughed, cried, told endless stories, and shared our faith. In the years that followed, I called her regularly, and we always took the time to remember my mother.

*Sharing precious memories can be a great comfort
in times of sorrow.*

—SBT

Bus Stop Blessings

Sing to the Lord; praise his name.
Each day proclaim the good news that he saves.
PSALM 96:2

For several years, I did not own a car, so my daughter Jolene and I traveled everywhere by city bus. During the Christmas season, we went out more than ever. There were presents to buy, meals to plan, and celebrations to attend. Between bad weather and increased traffic, the buses ran at unpredictable times. Consequently, we spent a lot of time waiting at bus stops.

Jolene and I passed the long minutes singing Christmas carols. We'd start with *Silent Night*, continue with *Joy to the World*, and sing a chorus or two of *Oh Come, All Ye Faithful*. We sang with joy and without hesitation, gladly proclaiming the savior whose birth we were celebrating.

Some people stared, some people sang with us, while others smiled. Our impromptu concerts shared Christmas peace and joy as the lowly bus stop became our pulpit for spreading the good news of salvation.

We can celebrate our salvation with our daughters—
wherever we are.

—DARLENE FRANKLIN

Carbon Copy

Imitate me, just as I also imitate Christ.
1 CORINTHIANS 11:1

During a recent worship service at the church where I had grown up, numerous people commented on how much my teenage daughter, Kezia, looks like me. I admit she does bear a strong resemblance to myself at that age. She has brown hair and big eyes, as well as amazing dimples that appear every time she smiles.

Outwardly we may share many physical characteristics, but my greatest desire is for her to resemble Christ in a manner that goes far beyond superficial appearances. As her mother, I set the example of Christ in our home, and she is likely to imitate me in many ways. Knowing this, I am inspired to live a life worthy of imitation.

We might not be able to choose our looks, but we can definitely choose to follow the Lord.

—LORI POPPINGA

JUNE

Legacy of Encouragement

When we get together, I want to encourage you in your faith,
but I also want to be encouraged by yours.

ROMANS 1:12

ven as a small, shy preschooler, I enjoyed visits to Aunt Ede's big green house with the front porch shaded by Virginia creepers. She was not only my mother's best friend; she made me feel about ten feet tall. She always made a point of saying something kind. "Oh, haven't you got the shiniest braids, my dear! And just look at that pretty dress!"

I discovered it wasn't hard to sit still when Mom braided my hair before visiting Aunt Ede, and putting on clean clothes was well worth the extra time. I enjoyed trying to live up to her high opinion of me. Even if I just sat quietly and watched the birds at her feeder while she and Mom visited, Aunt Ede noticed my good behavior. "My, but you are such a quiet little girl. Would you like to look at my big bird book?"

After I started school, I discovered that telling her about my good marks was better than getting a big gold star. "I just knew you could do it!" she would say. She gave me hope that, one day, I might be a confident young woman instead of a timid farm girl.

I couldn't help but reminisce as I prepared to go and visit her. Aunt Ede had recently reached her ninetieth birthday, but I could tell her mind was as bright and lively as ever. She toddled across her kitchen to meet me, her frail, little body bundled in the folds of a fuzzy blue sweater.

"Oh, but don't you look better than ever," she said. "It does my old heart a world of good to see you!"

I was glad I had made the effort to dress up. She wiped away her tears of happiness, and as we visited, I took photos of the birds flocking about her feeder. She still had the bird book I so enjoyed as a child. Her eyes twinkled when she quizzed me about my achievements that, by now, included several books and published articles. "I always knew you could do it," she said. "I just knew."

A few weeks later, Aunt Ede's life began drawing to a close. During her final weeks in hospital, she spoke longingly of being able to watch her many feathered friends as they returned to her bird feeder after the long hard winter. "It would do my old heart good to see that first big black crow of spring flapping overhead." But her dear old heart needed more than the encouraging signs of birds returning from the south, bringing the hopes and promises of another summer.

The minister wove Aunt Ede's love of bird watching into her eulogy. "Not even one sparrow can fall to the ground without God the Father knowing, and she was of infinitely more value than many sparrows." She was my second mother, I thought as I stood in the rural cemetery. The gentle, spring rain mingled with our tears and a returning meadowlark trilled resurrection hope.

Its song reminded me of the many birds Aunt Ede and I had watched when I was young and how, in lieu of a birdfeeder, I had resorted to observing our little flock of chickens on the farm. Aunt Ede had paid attention to me with the reverence of someone listening to a birder who had just caught sight of a rare species. I recall telling her

179

how the baby chicks scurried under their mother's wings when a hawk flew overhead. Safely sheltered there, the chicks found loving reassurance, just like Aunt Ede had given me when I was so young and insecure.

She provided a haven when I wanted to run for shelter from the poverty that hovered over my childhood, or hide from the rude remarks of peer pressure that threatened to swoop down and destroy my teenage years. Not only did I make it through my problems unscathed, I managed to rise above my disadvantages.

In later years, when long standing sibling rivalries threatened our family, I refused to hide under a camouflage of denial. Instead, I appropriated God's grace and genuinely forgave. Aunt Ede would have been pleased. I could almost hear her saying, "I always knew you could do it. I just knew."

And, as I faced the death of my husband, Psalm 91:4, a Bible verse I had always associated with Aunt Ede, came to mind. "He will cover you with his feathers. He will shelter you with his wings." She would have expected me to flee to God for His love and protection, and so that's what I did.

I did my best to pass Aunt Ede's legacy of encouragement on to our own daughter, and I have been blessed to see it thriving in the fourth generation of our family. The other day, our toddler grandson managed to drink his milk without spilling any, and I heard our daughter exclaim, "Good job. I knew you could do it!"

—ALMA BARKMAN

The Sweet and Tender Kiss of a Child

But I lavish unfailing love on a thousand generations for those who love me and obey my commands.
EXODUS 20:6

As I held my toddler close in my lap one afternoon, she tilted her head forward and kissed me lightly on the lips. I've never forgotten that moment. With her innocence fully exposed, my darling child trusted me with her love.

I've often thought about the unique qualities of mothering daughters. We watch our boys climb trees and chase imaginary foes, taking on the world with all their maleness. Our daughters love and care for their stuffed animals and dolls, and as they grow and change, many new people surface for them to love—boyfriends, husbands, children of their own, and of course, the Lord. There is something special with little girls. And there are still times when I long for the arms of a little one and the sweet tender kiss of a child!

May we always remember how fragile our children are and lavish love upon them.

—LaROSE KARR

First Place

*And you must love the Lord your God with all your heart,
all your soul, all your mind, and all your strength.*

MARK 12:30

"I'm sorry I hurt you when I moved out," my daughter Emily said. "I was really selfish, and I hope you can forgive me."

"Oh, sweetheart," I replied, "I forgave you a long time ago."

"You did?"

"Yes, but I can admit now that it didn't happen right away. I was pretty hurt and upset for a couple of weeks."

"What changed your mind?" she asked.

I smiled. "Well, I had the same problem you did. All I could think about was how I felt. I prayed and prayed, but it was always about me. It was only when I decided to put God first that I finally found the comfort and peace of mind I needed so badly."

I could see Emily relax for the first time since she'd arrived earlier for a visit. "So you're not angry with me?"

"You're one of the reasons I always try to put God first in my life. If it weren't for Him, I wouldn't be sitting here with one of the best things that ever happened to me."

The Lord has earned first place in your life.

—SBT

Orchestrating a Miracle

You are worthy, O Lord our God, to receive glory and honor and power. For you created all things, and they exist because you created what you pleased.
REVELATION 4:11

My mother made my birthday so much more than just an excuse to have a party and receive gifts. Years later, I don't remember the parties and the presents all that well, but I do recall how my mother made me feel. Long after the party was over, and the new toys and games had been put away, I was left thinking about how much my mother loved me.

And then, a letter from the "Dear Abby" column of the newspaper turned my birthday into an opportunity for me to thank my mother for everything she had done, including giving birth to me. It made perfect sense to me, especially after giving birth to five children of my own, that my mother was the real star of my birthday.

It also occurred to me that I also should be thanking the creator of all life—the one who orchestrated the miracle that occurs every time a baby is conceived and born.

Remember to thank God—and your mother—
for giving you life.

—SBT

Lost and Found

Trust in the Lord always,
for the Lord God is the eternal Rock.
ISAIAH 26:4

Mom and I went shopping at the mall. When we went into the dressing room, we spotted a piece of paper on the floor. It was a twenty-dollar bill!

Just as I started to get excited over our newfound wealth, Mom said, "Donna, we should report this. Whoever lost it may need it worse than we do." I found that difficult to believe. Mom was a stay-at-home mother with five children. I was the oldest at twelve and mature enough to know we counted every penny. But I didn't argue with her. I also knew she trusted God to meet our needs.

These days Mom is a senior adult with a fixed income. Recently, she lost a fifty-dollar bill. Although she was obviously upset, she said, "I trust that God allowed someone to find it who needed it more than I did." In every circumstance, Mom has always trusted God. That's the kind of person I would like to be!

We may not always understand our circumstances, but
God's plan for us is always for our good.

—DONNA J. SHEPHERD

A Litany of Love

For he loves us with unfailing love;
the Lord's faithfulness endures forever.
PSALM 117:2

I don't think there was anything David enjoyed more than praising the Lord. Reading through the psalms one day, I was struck by the seemingly endless list of reasons he had found to tell God how much he loved Him. But even more significant than David's litany of love was his enthusiastic and unreserved passion.

I ended my Bible reading feeling slightly ashamed. Only the day before, my daughter and I had watched a movie. Long after it was over, we talked about its wonderful qualities and how much we had enjoyed it. I couldn't help but wonder when we had discussed our faith with the same eagerness and excitement. I decided that while I still intended to have lots of conversations with Emily about movies, books, and the other things we both enjoyed, we needed to spend more time talking about God—the real love of our lives.

Stop and think about why you love the Lord.

—SBT

Priceless

Since we are living by the Spirit, let us follow the Spirit's leading in every part of our lives.
GALATIANS 5:25

At the yard sale, I pulled up to the makeshift tent placed near a folding table full of books. The handwritten sign read, "Bag of books for a buck." My young daughter giggled with delight as she quickly began selecting books. "Look," she said, "here's one about a dog." We shopped until the bag was nearly overflowing.

An old woman stepped out of the tent and greeted us. My daughter handed her a dollar, and the woman took it with fingers crippled by arthritis. "Thank you, Missy," she said with a smile.

We headed back to the car with our load of books. Suddenly, my daughter said, "I think we should give her more than a dollar."

Without hesitation, I reached in my purse and pulled out a ten-dollar bill. "You're right, honey," I replied. "We really got a bargain, and we had so much fun. You can't put a price on happiness."

Help us to follow God's lead as He gently nudges us in the right direction.

—MICHELE STARKEY

Unfaltering and Unconditional

Long ago the Lord said to Israel:
"I have loved you, my people, with an everlasting love.
With unfailing love I have drawn you to myself."
JEREMIAH 31:3

I don't think I'm the only woman who found herself completely unprepared for motherhood. I wasn't equipped for the debilitating exhaustion, the frustration, and the feelings of helplessness. I also wasn't ready for the intensity of love that overwhelmed me every time I looked at my new baby.

As the years passed, there were many moments when I didn't particularly like my daughter, Emily, but my love for her never faltered. If anything, it became more firmly entrenched within me—as vital and sustaining as drawing my next breath.

There have been times when I've disappointed, displeased, or offended God, and I wonder how He can continue to love me. At moments like this, I recall the day I told Emily that there was nothing she could do to make me stop loving her. And then I remember that my Heavenly Father feels exactly the same way about me.

Experience the unfaltering and unconditional love
of the Lord.

—SBT

Latin and the Lord

For I can do everything through Christ,
who gives me strength.
PHILIPPIANS 4:13

At the beginning of the tenth grade, my daughter Emily was asked to select a language option. Her older brother suggested Spanish as a useful language to learn, but Emily had her heart set on Latin. "I remember Latin," her father said in a voice that suggested his memories weren't all that pleasant. When Emily gave her father that familiar "What do parents know?" look, I knew she had made up her mind.

Nine weeks later, Emily brought her first report card home—complete with a D in Latin. Tears filled her eyes. "I can't do it," she said. "I never knew it would be so complicated and so hard."

We discussed ways to bring up her grade. "Do you know why I'm so sure you can do this?" I asked. Emily shook her head. "Because I know you love the Lord, and I know He will give you the strength to get through this course. All you have to do is ask."

"I can definitely do that," she said with a smile.

God can help us get through anything.

—SBT

A Hint of Heaven

For everything there is a season,
a time for every activity under heaven.
ECCLESIASTES 3:1

The ceremony had ended. The photographer had whisked the bride and groom off to the garden for pictures. Before joining the reception, I popped into the women's restroom to freshen up my lipstick—and catch my breath. My daughter's wedding day had been filled with a multitude of responsibilities. So many details and decisions! Now, I wanted everyone to have a wonderful time, so I whispered a prayer and headed back to the festivities.

As all eyes turned toward me, I felt a sudden jolt. Faces I loved welcomed me and shared my joy in this holy moment. The presence of God surrounded us, like the warming sun of a winter afternoon. The day captured a wisp of the supernatural. Of all the books I had read about weddings and being a mother of the bride, no one had prepared me for the hints of heaven.

The most satisfying moments in our lives
give glimpses into Eternity.

—SUZANNE WOODS FISHER

Pay Attention

*Teach those who are rich in this world not to be
proud and not to trust in their money, which is
so unreliable. Their trust should be in God, who
richly gives us all we need for our enjoyment.*
1 Timothy 6:17

During a phone call the other day, I asked my daughter if she planned to attend Bible study later in the week. "We only have $10 until payday," she said, "and Alan needs it for gas to get to work."

"I can give you the money," I said. "Do you need anything else? Are you okay for food?"

"We have everything we need," Emily replied. "I'll go to Bible study next week."

"Are you sure?" I asked. "I'd like to help if I can."

"Mom," Emily replied, "do you remember telling me that God would provide for us? Well, we'd like to try and get by with what we have until Alan gets paid."

Humbled, and more than a little embarrassed, I remained silent for a moment. Emily had tried to tell me that God was looking after them, but I hadn't been paying attention. Maybe it was time to start listening—my daughter had a lot to teach me.

*Listen carefully—your child might be
saying something you need to hear.*

—SBT

The Silver Lining

*And we know that God causes everything to work
together for the good of those who love God and
are called according to his purpose for them.*
ROMANS 8:28

My daughter Emily was a typical teenager who avoided chores. I had to remind her to do even minor tasks, such as hang up her coat or bring her dirty dishes to the sink. One afternoon I missed a step and turned my ankle. It turned pink and swollen and hurt so much, I couldn't walk.

While I lay on the couch with my foot up, Emily took over. She made chili for dinner and, afterward, she washed the dishes. She did it cheerfully and efficiently and, best of all, without being asked.

For a few days, I had to crawl up the stairs. My little angel appeared each time, carried my crutches to the top, and handed them to me when I got there. "Thank you!" I said, amazed by the change in her. My injury brought out a wonderful side of my daughter and turned out to be a blessing for both of us.

God can turn trials into triumphs.

—MARY LAUFER

A Loving Farewell

If I could speak all the languages of earth and of
angels, but didn't love others, I would only be a
noisy gong or a clanging cymbal.
1 CORINTHIANS 13:1

When my mother died, I wasn't surprised when my father suggested a small family service. Although I sympathized with his desire to keep his grief private, I couldn't stop thinking about all the people who would want to say good-bye to the extraordinary woman who touched their lives in a multitude of ways.

I went to my father and explained how I felt. He agreed and asked me to place a notice in the newspaper. He also asked me to phone some of my mother's closest friends to invite them personally. Making those calls took the rest of day. I listened to story after story of my mother's generous spirit and loving nature. I heard time and again of how she had reached out in love and friendship.

I finally came to the end of the list, emotionally drained but comforted by the kind words others had shared with me. I knew the church would be filled with people on the day of her funeral, but it would also be overflowing with love.

Loving others can be our greatest legacy.

—SBT

Now I Lay Me Down to Sleep

When I think of all this,
I fall to my knees and pray to the Father,
the Creator of everything in heaven and on earth.
EPHESIANS 3:14–15

I remember vividly the night my mother taught me to say my bedtime prayers. I was only about four, but I felt so grownup and special as I knelt beside my bed and recited, "Now I lay me down to sleep. I pray the Lord my soul to keep. If I should die before I wake, I pray the Lord my soul to take." And then, night after night, my mother waited patiently as I asked God to bless everything and everyone from my goldfish to the man who sold penny candy at the corner store.

A few months later, I underwent a tonsillectomy and had to spend a night in the hospital. The nurse had given me strict instructions to stay in bed. Suddenly, I remembered my prayers and scrambled out of bed to say them. The nurse returned and scolded me for not obeying her instructions. When I explained that I hadn't said my prayers, the angry expression on her face vanished, and then, just like my mother, she waited until I was finished.

Every small prayer pleases the Lord.

—SBT

Nourishment for the Heart

Wise words satisfy like a good meal;
the right words bring satisfaction.
PROVERBS 18:20

When I was growing up, mealtime was an invaluable part of my family life. While my friends ate pop tarts and cereal for breakfast, I had bacon and eggs most mornings of my premarried life.

When I went away to a nearby college, I came home on most weekends. No matter what time of day I arrived, there was something delicious to eat, miraculously kept warm for me. While I ate, I told my parents about my week at school. Those meals not only provided physical nourishment, but also gave me the essential emotional comfort that only my mother and father could give.

I have since learned that my mother doesn't really enjoy cooking. The meals she prepared were a labor of love. Much more important than the food itself, family mealtime gave me a sense of security. It is one of my greatest goals as a mother to give my own children the same feelings of being safe and loved.

Love and encouragement will nourish your children
for the rest of their lives.

—KELLY W. MIZE

A Simple Truth

Then he said, "I tell you the truth, unless you turn from
your sins and become like little children, you will never get
into the Kingdom of Heaven."
MATTHEW 18:33

I think my daughter's first few days of school were harder on me than they were on her. As we waited for the bus on her first day, I tried to cover every possible contingency that might occur on the short ride to her school. Emily listened patiently, nodding and smiling in agreement, but then she reached out and touched my arm. "You know, Mom," she said, "everything is going to be okay. I promise."

I wish I could be so poised, I thought and smiled at my self-confident child. "Of course, everything will be all right," I said. "I'm glad you're not nervous about the bus ride."

"I don't need to be nervous," she replied. "Jesus will be riding the bus, too."

The simple and beautiful truth of her statement silenced me for a few moments. The bus arrived, and I gave her a quick hug. "Have a great day," I said.

"You can stop worrying now," she called out as she hurried to meet the bus.

We need to come to our Lord with the
heart and mind of a child.

—SBT

195

Persistence Pays

I press on to reach the end of the race and
receive the heavenly prize for which God,
through Christ Jesus, is calling us.
PHILIPPIANS 3:14

Recently, I commissioned my artistic daughter to add some color to the bare walls of our spare bedroom. A few days later, I commented on her excellent progress. "Oh, Mom, it's awful! I just can't get it right," she replied, obviously discouraged.

"Keep working," I said in what I hoped was a heartening tone. "You'll get it if you stay with it." Our conversation reminded me of a sermon I once heard about persistence. The pastor's illustration had been from the world of sales. He said 48 percent of salespeople made one phone call and stopped. Only 22 percent made two phone calls, and 15 percent made three calls. The remaining 12 percent phoned again and again. Their efforts resulted in 80 percent of all sales.

We all need to persevere to reach our reward
waiting at the finish line.

—DENA N. NETHERTON

Moving Forward in Faith

Jesus and his disciples left Galilee and went up to the villages near Caesarea Philippi. As they were walking along, he asked them, "Who do people say I am?"
MARK 8:27

All my children love to talk, and my daughter is no exception. I don't think I realized how much she enjoyed talking until she left home. When I answer the phone and hear Emily's voice, I know I might as well get comfortable because she always has a lot to say. And when she comes over, we often get no further than the kitchen table where we often sit and visit for hours.

One of the most inspiring conversations we ever had occurred by chance one day when I told Emily about something God had done for me. Not just the God of the Bible, but the Heavenly Father I had to come to know. I tried to explain who I imagined God to be, how I felt about Him, and how I believed He felt about me. Emily's thoughts on the subject made me realize how much I love getting to know my daughter as she moves forward in her life—and in her faith.

Talk to someone about God.

—SBT

Giving Up the Guilt

My guilt overwhelms me—it is a burden too heavy to bear.
PSALM 38:4

I'm quite certain guilt is a frequent visitor to most mothers' hearts. I've put out the welcome mat for guilt on many occasions during my relationship with my daughter, even though I knew it was a waste of time and would accomplish nothing—except to open the door for other negative, defeatist emotions.

I discovered that being human and very flawed made it difficult to achieve perfection as a mother. Despite my best efforts, sometimes things didn't work out quite the way I'd hoped or planned. That's when I allowed guilt to manipulate me and make me think that somehow I had failed. It damaged my fellowship with God by blinding me to the blessings that surrounded me.

I'm learning to replace guilt with prayer. When I ask God for help, He opens my eyes to the overwhelming joy that being a mother has brought me and reminds me of the countless times that doing my best has been good enough.

Don't let guilt steal your joy.

—SBT

Words to Remember

Everyone enjoys a fitting reply; it is wonderful to say the right thing at the right time!
PROVERBS 15:23

My children peered over my shoulder as I scribbled in my pocket notebook. "What are you writing Mommy?" someone asked.

I had developed the habit of writing down the funny things my children said. I knew if I had to rely on my memory, their delightful versions of the English language would be one day forgotten. Eventually, our convoluted conversations became a family game. We teased each other about twisting our words and came up with new phrases. "Ketchup" became "catchup," the word broccoli was transformed into "trees," and "popcorn" was known as "pop pop." We used the invented names even when we were out in public.

Those sayings offered plenty of comic relief during the turbulent teen years. They provided additional proof that our family has a history—a history in which words are cherished and people are celebrated.

Remembering laughter can brighten a dark day.

—SALLY FERGUSON

The Morning Mope

Listen to my voice in the morning, Lord. Each morning
I bring my requests to you and wait expectantly.
PSALM 5:3

While my daughter Emily was growing up, I grew accustomed to the sight of her thumping down the stairs, wearing an indignant expression, and usually muttering something unintelligible. Sometimes, I grew impatient with her morning mope, but in my more tolerant moments, I tried to explain that getting up with a good attitude might help her whole day run more smoothly.

And then it occurred to me that I didn't always start my day with the best outlook. I often opened my eyes with a groan and my mind already crowded with a list of things I needed to accomplish.

I decided to start my day by saying good-morning to God and thanking Him for keeping my family safe for another night. Not surprisingly, I discovered this was just what I needed to help my day run more smoothly and that included being more patient with my grumpy girl.

Say "Good Morning!" to God and keep Him
in your heart all day.

—SBT

Real Riches

What sorrow awaits you who are rich,
for you have your only happiness now.
LUKE 6:24

My mother grew up during the Great Depression, and I imagined that the years of poverty and insecurity must have deeply affected her. And then, one day, she told me about going to the movies every Saturday afternoon with her sisters. "We really couldn't afford it, but your grandmother knew how special it was for us. She probably did without something so we could go."

"Sounds like fun," I replied.

"It was," she agreed. "Times may have been hard, but God was good to us. Your grandfather found a job nearby, so he didn't have to leave to get work. We always had something to eat, and we had each other."

"But your life is a lot easier now," I said.

My mother smiled. "In some ways. I know it couldn't have been easy taking care of a family during those years, but I always felt loved and safe."

Just like the way you've always made me feel, I thought. It was then I realized my mother had never lacked for anything that really counted.

Real wealth can't be found in a bank account.

—SBT

Humble Hospitality

When God's children are in need, be the one to help them out. And get into the habit of inviting guests home for dinner or, if they need lodging, for the night.
ROMANS 12:13

It's always a blessing to see my daughters extend their hospitality to those in need. One of them may invite a family to lunch after church and another might welcome a group of friends over for an evening of board games.

In 2007, the Midwest had two ice storms that downed power lines and left many people without electricity. During both storms, one of our daughters and her husband opened their home to her husband's nephew and his wife and three children for several days. Our grandsons shared their bedrooms, and some people spread sleeping bags on the floor, but everyone stayed warm.

While the entire town struggled without power, another daughter and her husband went door to door to check on people. My husband and I didn't have heat and stayed with one of our girls. None of these acts of hospitality required elaborate preparations—just caring people reaching out to those who have a need.

Selfless gestures result in blessings for everyone.

—LeAnn Campbell

Having It All

I said to myself, "Come on, let's try pleasure.
Let's look for the 'good things' in life."
But I found that this, too, was meaningless.
ECCLESIASTES 2:1

I don't have much time for regular television, but my children can't seem to resist its lure. However, I do enjoy watching movies with my family, and one day I heard my daughter calling me into the playroom. "Look," she said and pointed to the television, "it's that actor you really like."

I listened in shock as a reporter described the actor's recent suicide attempt. I stared at the photo of a handsome, seemingly happy man who had spent several years starring in one hit movie after another. The phrase "everything to live for" popped into my head and, then, I corrected myself. Only on the surface, I thought.

"I bet everyone figured he had it all," Emily said. "I wish I could tell him that there's always hope."

"I wish you could, too," I replied. "Maybe that's exactly what he needs to hear."

When you love the Lord, there is always hope.

—SBT

Time for Traditions

*Tell your children about it in the years to come
and let your children tell their children. Pass the
story down from generation to generation.*
JOEL 1:3

Like many mothers, I tried to picture the kind of home my daughter Lucille would have once she was grown and on her own. One day, I found my answers, handwritten by Lucille before she got married and left home. At the top of the paper I read, "Things we did that I want to do with my family."

Her list included: family night once a week for fun and games without television, family dinner every night, Sunday dinner together, prayer time every night, singing Christmas carols on Christmas Eve, filling Christmas stockings and opening gifts together one by one, hiding Easter baskets, and having homework and reading time.

There was no mention of expensive vacations, shopping for designer clothes or, even, eating out. There was far more time than money involved and family definitely came first.

*Family times become traditions passed
from generation to generation.*

—JEANETTE MACMILLAN

Focus on Flavor

And now, dear brothers and sisters, one final thing. Fix
your thoughts on what is true, and honorable, and right,
and pure, and lovely, and admirable. Think about things
that are excellent and worthy of praise.
PHILIPPIANS 4:8

I spent two years in high school trying to hide a mouth full of braces, so when my daughter Emily was blessed with a picture perfect smile, I was thrilled. The blessings continued with each checkup, but when she was eighteen, our dentist decided that her wisdom teeth needed to come out.

Emily was understandably upset and nervous, so I attempted to reassure her. "Do you know what I do when I have to get a cavity filled?" I asked.

"What?"

"I don't think about what's happening. I focus on the good things in my life like you and your brothers or the dogs. Or, I thank God that I can get my teeth fixed and think about how good it will feel when it's all over."

She smiled. "The dentist told me I'd have to eat soft foods for a few days. I could think about the ice cream flavors I want to try." I laughed. "Yes, you can definitely think about that, too."

Ask God to fill your mind with
beautiful and excellent thoughts.

—SBT

Emily's Angel

For he will order his angels to protect you wherever you go.
PSALM 91:11

When my daughter Emily was in kindergarten, we moved from a small farm to a house in town. Both Emily and her older brother Gabriel were thrilled by the prospect of living within walking distance of their friends. On the day we moved in, I made some quick sandwiches and called the children for lunch. Gabriel came running, but Emily had vanished.

After searching our new home from attic to basement, my husband and Gabriel decided to start knocking on doors and searching nearby yards. I remained at home in case Emily returned, and tried to replace the terrifying thoughts swarming into my mind with a constant prayer that she would return, safe and sound.

When Gabriel found her over a block away, playing at the home of a school friend, I went limp with relief. Frightening possibilities vanished as I thanked God for sending the angel who had watched over my little girl and brought her home to me.

God sends His angels to show His love.

—SBT

The Faithful Fish

Your own ears will hear him.
Right behind you a voice will say, "This is the way you
should go," whether to the right or to the left.
ISAIAH 30:21

"Are you enjoying your swim in the sunshine?" I asked and then laughed at myself for conversing with our new fish. After my husband left, my two daughters and I visited the pet store. We already had two cats and a dog, so we decided to buy three beta fish—one for each of us. We decided that Solomon, Moses, and Jonah would help ease our sorrow. A few days later, I bragged to the girls. "Look how they respond to my voice!"

I could tell they weren't very impressed. "You're feeding them, Mom," someone said. "They want food."

"Yeah, but look how they swim in the direction of my voice. Doesn't that remind you of Jesus? He was a fisher of men. Maybe the fish are trying to remind me how important it is to follow His voice."

One of my daughters grinned. "Whatever you say, Mom," she replied, and we all laughed.

God is faithful to feed our spirit when we follow His voice.

—EVANGELINE BEALS GARDNER

Deceptive Desserts

The Lord doesn't see things the way you see them.
People judge by outward appearance,
but the Lord looks at the heart.
1 SAMUEL 16:7

When I was a little girl, the glass cases at the local bakery offered countless temptations, but I was always drawn to something called a Charlotte Rousse. It came in a small cup full of frothy mountains of whipped cream and topped with a tantalizing maraschino cherry. Anything that looked that wonderful just had to be delicious, but whenever I asked for one, my mother would persuade me to pick something else.

One day, she relented and let me try one. I dipped my spoon carefully into the cup, but when I pulled it out, I stared at the contents in disbelief. Beneath the enticing exterior was a tiny piece of plain yellow cake. "That's it?" I said and looked up at my mother.

She smiled. "I figured you might be disappointed. "Some things look great, but there's not much on the inside."

"Well, next time, I'm going to have a jelly doughnut," I replied. "That way, I'll know what I'm getting."

God is not deceived by outward appearances.

—SBT

Back Door Blessings

God blesses those who are poor and realize their need for him, for the Kingdom of Heaven is theirs.
MATTHEW 5:3

As my Aunt Helen and I looked through my grandmother's Bible, I noticed that numerous passages had been underlined, including the verse above. "Your grandmother had a special place in her heart for people who were down on their luck," my aunt explained. "I remember a steady stream of hungry men coming to our back door during the Great Depression. They were in the city looking for work and had heard that your grandmother never turned anyone away."

I pointed to the verse in the Bible. "They might have been poor," I said, "but Grandma knew they were special in God's eyes."

My aunt nodded. "She told me that God was using her to feed His people."

I thought about my grandmother sharing her love for the Lord with her back door visitors. "I bet she fed their spirits as well as their stomachs," I told my aunt and she smiled.

Find a special place in your heart for those in need.

—SBT

A Port in the Storm

So we have not stopped praying for you since we first heard about you. We ask God to give you complete knowledge of his will and to give you spiritual wisdom and understanding.
COLOSSIANS 1:9

The storm on San Carlos Lake in eastern Arizona blew in without warning while my daughter, Julie, and her husband, Mike, were fishing. Huge waves and torrential rain threatened to fill and sink their boat. Thunder roared and lightening cracked the sky. Mike reassured Julie as they prayed and struggled to make it back to the dock. "It's okay," he said repeatedly. "We'll make it."

Drenched and shaken, they landed their boat. When Julie called to tell me what had happened she said, "Mom, I knew you were praying for me." Since she was a little girl, she knew I prayed for her just as her grandmother and great-grandmother had prayed for their daughters. Now Julie carries on her own legacy of prayer in the lives of her three boys.

Our prayers create a refuge in the storms of life.

—BETTY L. ARTHURS

JULY

Getting on with the Game

*The Lord will guide you continually, giving you water when
you are dry and restoring your strength. You will be like a
well-watered garden, like an ever-flowing spring.*
ISAIAH 58:11

*I*t was a hot July afternoon in 1985. Having already experienced the wonder of five precious grandchildren, I was a bit more relaxed as the birth of my youngest daughter's first child drew near. Everything had gone well during her pregnancy, so I waited at home for my son-in-law to phone with the good news. But when his call came, I heard the alarm in his voice. "Can you come right away?" he asked.

"What's wrong?" I asked. Part of me wasn't sure I wanted to hear his answer.

"The doctor isn't sure yet, but I'd like you to be here when they bring Cindy down from the delivery room."

"I'm on my way," I replied.

My mind whirled as I drove the short distance to the hospital. How quickly things can change, I thought. What could be wrong with our new little one? Would it be something too hard for us to handle? I believed in God and had trusted in Him since I was a child, but nothing drastic had ever touched my children. Did I believe that God was in control of this problem, no matter how serious it might be? I chided myself for entertaining the doubts that were blurring my thinking.

Mark was pacing in Cindy's room when I arrived. She was still groggy from the medication she had been given during the caesarean section, but she realized the baby had a problem. Mark guided me back to the corridor. "What's wrong, with the baby?" I asked, but his answer sounded vague.

"They're saying she's too little."

"What does that mean? Cindy only weighed five pounds when she was born, so what's the big deal?"

"But our baby is only fourteen inches long." Mark opened his hands in an estimated measurement. "The doctor is doing some tests. He said she might have dwarfism." As he spoke, I realized my son-in-law was distracted. He knew he had to find a way to tell Cindy of the doctor's suspicions. They had prayed and planned for this child. Everything had been ready until ominous clouds appeared to threaten their happiness.

A few minutes later, I stood beside my daughter's bed. I felt tears roll down my face, but an indescribable peace settled upon my soul. Even as I shared her grief, comforting scriptures came to mind. "Be still and know that I am God" (Psalm 46:10), and "I will not leave you comfortless" (John 14:18). Cindy stirred. I cupped her face and kissed her forehead. "How do you feel, Sugar?"

"Like a freight train hit me," she replied. Then, her hazy gaze fixed on her husband, and she asked the dreaded question. "Mark, is something wrong with our baby?"

"The doctor isn't sure yet. Try not to worry about it now; just rest and get your strength back." But Cindy persisted, so Mark told her everything he knew and held her in his arms while they both wept. It was their private moment of grief, so I slipped into the hall to shed my own tears.

It wasn't long before we discovered that baby Jessica suffered from dwarfism, although the exact type was unknown. Otherwise, she was healthy—just very tiny. Her arms and legs were proportionate to the rest of her body, and the doctor told us that was a good sign. There were still so many unanswered questions.

In the months that followed, I watched Mark and Cindy love and care for their baby. They fussed over her as any new parents might do and treated her no differently than if she had been of normal size. When they needed me to babysit, I doted over every inch of her.

Cindy made few, if any, concessions for her baby. Jessica was allowed to crawl, pull up, and fall down, as all babies must do. Her accomplishments were right on target. Watching her scoot on one knee and take her first steps was a delightful sight. When she learned to walk unassisted, people stopped to watch as if she were a real walking doll.

Many years have passed since that breezy July day filled with so much anxiety and heartache and, through it all, God has stayed in control. In His infinite wisdom, He blessed us with Wonder Woman and Tarzan's Jane all wrapped into one tiny package. Jessica's zest for life and quest for self-sufficiency has never diminished, and her personal motto continues to inspire me. "Don't question the hand you were dealt. Just get on with playing the game."

—IMOGENE JOHNSON

Healing Words

When she speaks, her words are wise, and she gives
instructions with kindness.
PROVERBS 31:26

I was a pudgy kid. My mom and sisters were thin, but I was destined to wage a life-long battle of the bulge. Mom was my encourager. The day another child called me names, she told me I was beautiful. When I had a meltdown at the mirror, she hugged me and insisted I was lovely. The day a teacher's words made me feel ugly, my mom's words made me feel better. And when I walked down the aisle wearing a size-six wedding gown, she said I was gorgeous.

It didn't matter if my weight went up or down. Mom's loving acceptance was never based on how many pounds, pimples, or freckles I sported. I may have appeared to disregard her opinion, but my heart treasured her unwavering belief in me. She has been gone for twenty years, but her unspoken message still speaks volumes.

A mother's words can heal long after they're spoken.

—SANDI BANKS

Video Victory

*But to answer your question, you know the commandments:
"You must not murder. You must not commit adultery. You
must not steal. You must not testify falsely. You must not
cheat anyone. Honor your father and mother."*

MARK 10:19

When my daughter Emily broke the handheld video system she had borrowed from her younger brother Connor, I waited to see what course of action she would take. One morning, she called and told me that she had sold the broken system for $37. "I'm going to give Connor $10," she said.

"How much was Connor's system worth before you broke it?" I asked. "Oh, about $60."

"I see. And you're going to give him $10."

I heard a big sigh, and then there was silence on the other end for a few moments. "I guess I should give him $60, right?" she finally asked.

"It's up to you," I said. "You're an adult now, and I trust you to make good decisions. But Connor's learning how to please God by watching the people he looks up to— people like you."

A few days later, she gave Connor the money. "Thanks for helping me see things from his perspective," she told me.

I smiled. "Thanks for showing him how to do the right thing."

What are people learning about the Lord from you?

—SBT

Caring Conversations

And now, in my old age, don't set me aside.
Don't abandon me when my strength is failing.
PSALM 71:9

My elderly mother lives on the other side of the country, over two thousand miles from me. I get a chance to visit her about once a year. My sister, who lives much closer, checks on Mom daily and makes sure she has everything she needs.

When my sister had to go out of town to attend her son's wedding, Mom was alone for a week. My other siblings looked in on her frequently and brought her meals. What could I do? I usually telephoned Mom weekly. Since my long-distance calls were free, I decided to phone her every day.

At first I didn't know what we would talk about but, soon, we were reminiscing, and an hour would pass quickly. I realized I had never known my mother as a person, only as a mother. And I had wrongly assumed that she didn't need me. When my sister returned, I continued to call Mom often. We both looked forward to our time together.

Mothers and daughters never stop needing each other.

—MARY LAUFER

In His Image

*So God created human beings in his own image. In the image
of God he created them; male and female he created them.*
GENESIS 1:27

I may have been adopted, but I was raised in a home
with parents and a brother who looked a lot like me. We
were all light haired, fair complexioned, tall, and muscu-
lar. Despite this, there was no one who shared my unique
features. Years later, when my own baby was born, my
adoptive mother remarked on her chunky arms and adorable thigh folds. "Just like you when you were a baby," she
said. When my daughter's wispy baby hair finally grew, I
recognized my own thick brown wavy locks.

Although I loved to see myself in my child, I came to
understand that being created in God's image had nothing to do with hair color or shoe size. I had been made to
see, hear, and speak with the Lord's eyes, ears, and lips.
My arms and legs had been formed to serve. And because
I so often fell short, God continued to work in my life,
transforming me into the image of His son.

A true family resemblance is found in the heart.

—MARGOT STARBUCK

Welcome to the Family

You will tell his people how to find salvation through
forgiveness of their sins.
LUKE 1:77

When my daughter Emily moved out, I found myself missing having another woman around. With four boys and a husband, I often felt outnumbered. Then, my son Dylan brought his new girlfriend, Bobbijo, home, and I soon thought of her as an answer to my prayer for female companionship. Bobbijo slipped into our family as if she had lived with us her entire life.

She came over at every opportunity, always wearing her beautiful smile and blessing us all with her kind and generous disposition. She began to call me "Mom," and my heart responded in kind. God had given me another daughter.

Bobbijo had gone to church sporadically throughout her life, but that changed when she entered out lives. One day, several months after she began attending regularly with us, she made a decision to accept Jesus Christ as her personal savior. God brought her into our home to bring us all joy, but He brought her into His family to give her eternal life.

God has given us the power
to make a difference in someone's life.

—SBT

219

Lost and Found

In the same way, there is more joy in heaven over one lost sinner who repents and returns to God than over ninety-nine others who are righteous and haven't strayed away!
LUKE 15:7

My daughter Emily and I were going through a difficult time. After school, she hurried upstairs where she would stay for hours. When I tried to engage her in conversation, she either remained silent or answered me in petulant, impatient monosyllables. I prayed for guidance and tried to remain patient.

Then, one day, I discovered the pony was missing. I called Emily and, within seconds, she was downstairs, putting on her jacket. Visions of the pony on the nearby highway tormented me and a few tears trickled down my cheeks. Suddenly, I felt Emily's arm around my shoulder. "Don't worry, Mom, we'll find her."

As we searched, we had our first real conversation in weeks. By the time we found the wayward pony, Emily had told me what had been bothering her. "And I haven't been praying," she said. "I feel terrible about that and about the way I've been treating you."

"I'm just happy to have my Emily back," I replied. "Now, why don't you go and have a talk with God? He wants His Emily back, too."

God is waiting to say, "Welcome back!"

—SBT

The Princess and the Tree Climber

You made all the intricate parts of my body and knit them together in my mother's womb.

*Thank you for making me so wonderfully complex!
It is amazing to think about. You were there when
I was being formed.*
PSALM 139:13–14

I have two daughters—a Princess and a Tree Climber, and I treasure both of them. The Princess is a blonde, blue-eyed beauty. The Tree Climber is a brunette, brown-eyed cutie. My Princess loves every minute of school, but my Tree Climber considers school an unnecessary inconvenience. My Princess prefers to handles life with caution whereas my Tree Climber runs at life full speed ahead. My Princess is a planner, as opposed to her sister who worries she might miss out on what is coming next. My Princess reads about trees while my Tree Climber is busy climbing the real thing.

My challenge has been to nurture these two totally unique personalities but, early in their lives, I realized that God created each of them with a specific purpose. Now, I pray daily for God to show me specific ways to treasure and encourage their differences.

God molds each of His children with unique qualities to bring glory to His name.

—LINDA BLAINE POWELL

221

The Freedom of Faith

Some people brought to him a paralyzed man on a mat.
Seeing their faith, Jesus said to the paralyzed man,
"Be encouraged, my child! Your sins are forgiven."
MATTHEW 9:2

I love the account of the men who brought their paralyzed friend to Jesus for healing. When they realized the crowd was too large to enter the building in the conventional way, they lowered their friend through a hole in the roof. Impressed by their faith, Jesus told the man to pick up his bed and go home.

I've never been physically paralyzed, but I've been frozen with fear, crippled by uncertainty, and immobilized by anger and resentment. As a child, it was my mother who encouraged me to break free of these debilitating feelings. "You can do it," she would say. "Jesus believes in you, and so do I."

When my mother died, my earthly source of support and encouragement may have come to an end, but my eternal spring of inspiration remained unchanged. Jesus will always be ready and willing to say, "You can do it!" He believes in me—now and forever.

Jesus can release you from your paralysis.

—SBT

Heavenly Sounds

*Praise the Lord! How good to sing praises to our God!
How delightful and how fitting!*
PSALM 147:1

I stood in the foyer of the church and listened to my thirteen-year-old daughter Tiffany sing. I had always loved music and singing, but my children didn't seem drawn to following in my footsteps. And then, Tiffany decided she wanted to be a singer like her mother.

I felt a familiar and comforting sense of divine peace as the notes echoed across the pews. The melody sounded heavenly and her lyrics were full of feeling. My eyes filled with tears as I listened to my child singing praise to our God. My happiness reminded me of how much it pleases God when he hears His children make "a joyful noise unto the Lord." It doesn't matter if we have the voice of an angel or sing completely off key—God is honored by our acknowledgment of His glory.

Experience the joy of singing God's praises.

—DEBBIE ZILE

A Multitude of Miracles

*I want you all to know about the miraculous signs and
wonders the Most High God has performed for me.*
Daniel 4:2

"Miracles happen every day." That's what my mother
used to tell me when I was growing up but, at first, I was
a bit skeptical. My mother had read to me from the Bible,
and I went to Sunday school. I knew miracles were awe-
some, spectacular events such as Moses parting the Red
Sea and Jesus raising Lazarus from the dead. I didn't want
to refute my mother's claim, but I frankly hadn't seen anything resembling a miracle in my neighborhood.

And then, I started to understand what she meant.
She showed me the tiny green shoots poking through the
earth in early spring. I watched a chick struggle out of its
shell. I saw the skies open up and bring a yearlong drought
to an end. I realized that I was surrounded by the miraculous.

Years later, when I became part of a truly amazing
miracle and gave birth to my daughter, I promised I would
make sure she knew that miracles happen everyday.

Become aware of the many miracles in your life.

—SBT

His Greatest Work

*For we are God's masterpiece. He has created
us anew in Christ Jesus, so we can do the good
things he planned for us long ago.*
EPHESIANS 2:10

I think sewing must skip a generation. My mother was a talented seamstress and made all my clothes as I was growing up. I expressed no interest in learning to sew—I was too busy riding my horse—but my daughter Emily asked for a sewing kit when she just a little girl. A kind neighbor provided sewing lessons, and Emily quickly proved she had inherited her grandmother's skill.

One day, I watched her at work on a new dress. With methodical precision, she placed the pattern on the cloth she had laid out. Showing no hesitation, she cut into the cloth, and her satisfied smile told me she knew exactly what the dress was going to look like. It was wonderful to think that she could imagine and create something beautiful from pieces of paper and a pile of fabric.

I couldn't help but reflect on the meticulous care God uses to transform the sinner who chooses to follow Christ into one of His children. We are His *magnum opus*, envisioned with joy and created with love.

Have you become a new person in Christ?

—SBT

A Glimpse of the Nest

*Teach me to do your will, for you are my God. May your
gracious Spirit lead me forward on a firm footing.*
PSALM 143:10

My teenage daughter spent six weeks on staff at a Christian camp, three hours away from home. It was the longest period of time she had been away and, for the first time, I received a glimpse of the empty-nest syndrome headed my way. She had been at camp for three weeks when we visited her for a day. The morning after we arrived, I woke her just as I had always done since the day she started school.

Abruptly, I began to cry. I realized how much I had missed her since she left for camp and how much I would miss her when the day came for her to leave home permanently. At that moment, I knew that it was right and good for her to grow up and become the person God intended. A silent prayer stirred in my chest, and I asked God to bless my daughter's life according to His will and lead her according to His ways.

*When the time comes, we must let go and
trust God to direct our children's paths.*

—DONNA L. WICHELMAN

Craving Conversation?

Don't worry about anything; instead, pray about everything.
Tell God what you need, and thank him for all he has done.
PHILIPPIANS 4:6

One of the most significant things I discovered in my walk with the Lord was the importance of prayer. I craved the intimacy I knew would come from frequent and heartfelt contact with God. But first, I had to learn how to pray. Initially, I prayed twice a day in a rather stiff and formal way. And then, I read how the Apostle Paul had commanded his followers to pray without ceasing. It occurred to me that while it was vital to have a special time and place to pray, what God really wanted was ongoing communication. He wanted a conversation.

One morning, my daughter Emily called, and as we talked, I shared my thoughts about prayer. "I've decided I'm going to spend more time talking to God," I said. "About everything."

"I talk to God all the time," she replied.

"You do?"

She laughed. "You know how much I love to talk. Besides, God's always there and He's a great listener."

When was the last time you had a conversation with God?

—SBT

Give It to God

*No, dear brothers and sisters, I have not achieved it, but
I focus on this one thing: Forgetting the past and looking
forward to what lies ahead.*

PHILIPPIANS 3:13

Sometimes, I find myself trapped in the past, reliving old hurts and regrets with such clarity, as if I had a DVD playing in my mind. Years after my mother died, I continued to torment myself with memories of an argument we once had. It was my mother who finally came to me after three days and made amends. I responded in kind, and we eagerly forgave each other. I knew God had forgiven me the moment I asked, and yet, I couldn't seem to let go of what had happened.

We were talking about forgiveness at Sunday school and I told my story. A close friend spoke up. "You have to accept God's forgiveness before you can lay that burden down. I suspect you are reluctant to give it up because you haven't forgiven yourself."

She was right. My guilt and shame had never allowed me to release the stranglehold of the past. "God's ready and waiting to carry your load," she said. "It's time to set yourself free."

*Relinquish your burdens to God
and move forward in freedom.*

—SBT

Substitute Mom

We love each other because he loved us first.
1 JOHN 4:19

When I first saw Alicia sitting in the back of my church, the Lord prompted me to greet her, but the sour expression on her face made me feel like running the other away. Yet, by reaching out, I broke down her wall. She told me she was far from home, studying pre-law at our local university.

My visits with Alicia soon became a rewarding part of my week, especially after she joined the ladies' Bible study. With a little encouragement, she became the one who reached out to others. All she had needed was a substitute mom to help her face four lonely years.

Now Alicia is about to take the bar exam and realize her dream of becoming an attorney. Even if she was my own child, I couldn't imagine being any more pleased with her accomplishment. By following God's will and loving Alicia, I've been blessed with the daughter I never expected.

Follow the Lord's promptings and discover His blessings.

—LAURA L. BRADFORD

The Pleasure of Her Company

*If I decided to forget my complaints,
to put away my sad face and be cheerful.*

*I would still dread all the pain,
for I know you will not find me innocent, O God.*
JOB 9:27–28

When my daughter Emily lived at home, we argued frequently about her role in helping around the house. I grew weary of her grim expression, her monosyllabic responses, and her half-hearted efforts. She complained to anyone who would listen that she didn't have time for anything besides the endless chores I assigned her.

Emily had always attended church with the family, but when she got married and moved out, she and her husband rededicated their lives to the Lord. In the weeks that followed, I began to notice changes in her.

One evening, she and her husband came for supper. "Can I give you a hand with anything?" she asked as they came through the door. Not only did she help me prepare the food, but she also insisted on cleaning up after the meal. "I wish I could come over and help you more often," she said.

"I wish you could, too. It's a pleasure to have you here," I said, and I meant every word.

Complaining enhances nothing but a bad attitude.

—SBT

The Borrowed Daughter

Seek the Kingdom of God above all else, and live righteously,
and he will give you everything you need.
MARK 6:33

The annual mother and daughter banquet was coming, and I wasn't going to be able to attend. God had blessed me with two precious boys, but I couldn't talk either of my sons into going as my daughter. My friend had three daughters and offered to "loan" me one, so I invited the youngest girl, Mary. I had prayed with her to receive Christ, and she was my "daughter in the faith." The banquet became the first of many dates for Mary and me.

She grew up to become a beautiful young woman inside and out, but my husband and I moved and lost track of her. One day my youngest son called to tell me he had run into Mary at a coffee shop. I rejoiced at the opportunity to become reacquainted with my "borrowed daughter." She has since become my daughter-in-law and the mother of three of my grandchildren—no longer borrowed!

God knew I needed a daughter for more
than just a luncheon.

—ALICE M. McGHEE

The Last Word

And "don't sin by letting anger control you." Don't let the
sun go down while you are still angry.
EPHESIANS 4:26

"Don't go to bed angry." I heard the expression long before I discovered its original version in the Bible. I made it part of our family's guidelines, along with the "rule" that no one should leave the house angry.

My resolve to rob anger of its power was severely tested the day I caught my daughter in a lie—one with potentially serious consequences. I was furious. My pride had suffered a blow and, worse yet, Emily had placed herself at risk. I didn't trust myself to speak, so I banished her to her room. She could stay there for a few weeks, I thought. One of her brothers could deliver her meals.

I tried to work, but I couldn't stop thinking about the countless times Emily had made me happy and proud. The room grew dark around me. It would be bedtime soon, so I stood up and headed for the stairs. I wasn't angry anymore, but there were explanations and apologies to make—on both sides.

Don't allow anger to have the last word.

—SBT

A Chorus of Caution

And since we know he hears us when we make our requests,
we also know that he will give us what we ask for.
1 JOHN 5:15

"Watch out for the deer and cows! Be careful of the beet trucks and children crossing the street!" Mom was narrating her usual caution-filled lecture as my sister and I left for school. She rarely missed the opportunity to send us out the door with hugs, kisses, and plenty of reminders. We grew so accustomed to the routine; we would all join in to complete her sentence. Many years later, we would still repeat her litany of warnings when we left her house.

When I imagine my own daughter driving, I understand the anxiety my mother must have felt. It's easy to get caught up in fear, but most mothers will agree that the worry began the day we gave birth. No amount of caution or care will guarantee our children's safety. All we can do is surround them in prayer. We can spend each day trapped by worry or enjoy each moment we share to the fullest.

Prayer is a powerful way to protect our daughters.

—JAMI KIRKBRIDE

My Constant Companion

I can never escape from your Spirit!
I can never get away from your presence!
PSALM 139:7

The other day, I came across one of my mother's hand-written recipes. She's been gone for almost nineteen years, but seeing her distinctive penmanship released a flood of bittersweet memories. I am no longer blessed with her physical presence, but she is still very much with me.

I recall her kind and selfless nature when I hear of someone in need. I think of her faith when I remember the courage and strength with which she faced her illness. And when I find myself laughing for no particular reason, I am reminded of her ability to find joy in the smallest thing.

In the same way, I think of God as I go through my day. He's in the technicolor sunrise that lights up the sky and in the smiles of my children as they arrive home safely one more time. He's in the food I prepare and the heat that warms my home. Even the priceless memories of my mother come from His concern for my every need. He is my constant companion.

You are surrounded by evidence of God's goodness.

—SBT

The Hard Way

Each of you must show great respect for your mother and father, and you must always observe my Sabbath days of rest. I am the Lord your God.
LEVITICUS 19:3

When Emily was in the sixth grade, she collected Pokemon cards. She kept them in a special binder filled with special plastic pages to protect her prized collection. One day, she asked if she could take her binder to school. A friend had promised to bring his cards, and they planned to do some trading.

I told her that I didn't think it was a very wise idea and explained that something could easily happen to the cards. She promised not to let them out of her sight and adamantly refused to accept that she might be taking a risk. So, I relented, and Emily left for school with the precious binder tucked into her book bag.

She returned that afternoon in tears. The binder had disappeared from her book bag during recess. "I should have paid attention to what you told me," she said and wiped your eyes.

"That's okay, sweetheart," I replied. "Thanks for helping me remember how important it is to be a good listener."

When we listen to God we can avoid learning things the hard way.

—SBT

235

Priceless Gifts

*If you are really eager to give, it isn't important
how much you are able to give. God wants you to
give what you have, not what you don't have.*
2 CORINTHIANS 8:12

This past Christmas, I looked around the house for just the right gift for each member of our family. For our oldest daughter, I found my mother's Bible storybook. It was falling apart, but the inscription on the front page stated that it had been a gift to my mother from her mother and sister more than eighty years ago.

I chose my mother-in-law's Bible for one of my daughters. Her sister received two platters that had belonged to her grandmothers. Another daughter's gift was my mother's thimble and the small scissors that my mother-in-law carried in her purse during the years she worked in a shoe factory. In an effort to make the gifts even more exceptional, I wrote family stories to accompany each item.

These gifts have little monetary value, but they have a special place in our family history. God doesn't expect expensive gifts, either. He is far more interested in gifts that come from the heart.

Give the irreplaceable gift of memories.

—LEANN CAMPBELL

A Matter of Perspective

But thank God! He gives us victory over sin and death
through our Lord Jesus Christ.
1 CORINTHIANS 15:57

When I answered the phone at 6:20 this morning, I heard my daughter's frantic voice. "Alan's been hurt at work." She explained that he had cut his leg on a piece of equipment and was on his way to the emergency room at the hospital. "He said it's not too bad, but it's going to need a few stitches."

"I'm sure he'll be just fine," I replied.

"It's not just the accident," she continued. "This may sound awful—like I don't care about him getting hurt—but I'm really worried about the medical bill."

"Try looking at this in a different way," I said. "Try thanking God for providing medical care. Think about the possible problems if there hadn't been a place to take him for the right kind of care. The bills will always be there, but you've only got one Alan."

There was silence for a few moments, and then I heard a soft whisper. "Thank you, Lord."

Exchange your worries for worship.

—SBT

The Survey

O Lord, you have examined my heart
and know everything about me.
PSALM 139:1

Recently, my preteen daughter presented me with a fill-in-the-blank survey. I answered thirty questions about everything from her preferred color, pop singer, and TV show, to her favorite Bible verse and biggest pet peeve. It was a perspiration-inducing experience. I assumed that my ability to complete the survey correctly would reassure my daughter that I had taken the time and energy required to know everything about her.

After finishing my assignment, I read my answers out loud. I did well—except for the last question. "You missed something," she said. "Who is my idol?" she asked.

"Miley Cyrus," I answered in a confident voice.

"Wrong!" she replied and imitated the sound of a very loud losing buzzer.

"Who is it, then?" I said.

"It's you, Mom! You're my idol," she replied and gave me a hug. "Only Jesus knows me better than you do."

Take delight in discovering your daughter.

—VICKI TIEDE

Taught by the Best

*Then Jesus called for the children and said to the disciples,
"Let the children come to me. Don't stop them! For the
Kingdom of God belongs to those who are like these children."*
LUKE 18:16

When Emily was a little girl, she could read me like a book. If I was having a bad day, I didn't need to say a word. Somehow, she would know and ambush me for her own brand of laughter therapy. If I were feeling less than glamorous, she would invariably announce that I was the most beautiful mother in the whole world.

She said what was in her heart and on her mind without fear of embarrassment or reprisal. And if I took the time to watch and listen, I caught glimpses of the beautiful, miraculous world she inhabited.

No wonder Jesus had a special place in his heart for children with their transparent hearts and their eager trust. The Lord admired these qualities so much that He insisted we all become like children to enter the kingdom of God. Perhaps it's time to recognize the remarkable spiritual qualities of children.

Jesus recognized children as great teachers.

—SBT

239

The Sleepover

Don't just pretend to love others. Really love them.
Hate what is wrong. Hold tightly to what is good.
ROMANS 12:9

One of my first friends was Mrs. Hargreaves, the elderly woman next door. When I got old enough to venture out on my own, I was allowed to visit her. She always made me feel very welcome and extremely special, perhaps because she missed her own granddaughters, living so many miles away.

One night, I announced to my parents that I was going to spend the night with Mrs. Hargreaves. As I recall, they had their doubts, but we packed up my little overnight bag, and off I went on my exciting adventure.

However, as the sun went down, the glittering excitement of spending the night away from home began to pale rapidly. By the time the stars had come out, I was more than ready for a trip back across the grass to my own safe bed.

I couldn't help but feel like a bit of a failure, but Mrs. Hargreaves hugged me and said, "I had so much fun. We'll have to do this again, soon."

Defeated no longer, I nodded and stepped into the welcoming arms of my family.

You haven't failed until you quit trying.

—SBT

Safe from Harm

God is our refuge and strength,
always ready to help in times of trouble.
PSALM 46:1

During the summers I stayed with my Aunt Charlotte and Uncle Jack on their farm, I became their little girl. They were childless, but no parents could have been more loving and devoted than they were.

My days were filled with endless enjoyment but the nights were a different matter. Night in the country was a thick, dark velvet curtain, illuminated by only the moon and stars. And during frequent power outages, the whole world suddenly became very quiet and very black.

On those nights, I would pay a visit to my aunt and uncle's room. My aunt rarely said a word as she picked up her pillow and returned to my bed with me. Snuggled up against her broad back, I felt completely safe, convinced that her presence would keep me from harm.

My aunt is gone now, but if a night turns fearful and uncertain, I have God's everlasting arms to make me feel safe. And I have His promise that He will protect me.

God is our safe haven both day and night.

—SBT

Working for the Lord

And whatever you do or say, do it as a representative of the Lord Jesus, giving thanks through him to God the Father.
COLOSSIANS 3:17

Transporting rocks and dirt across the backyard on a warm fall afternoon didn't enthuse me in the same way it did my mother, Cindy. "Mom, can't this wait?" I asked.

My mother straightened up and placed one hand on her lower back. "No, it can't wait. I want to help your father."

My grandfather always said, "If you want something done, call Cindy." Whenever my father, my siblings, or anyone else called upon my mother for help, she didn't hesitate. It didn't matter if she was needed as a part-time construction worker, babysitter, or a meals-on-wheels driver—she viewed service to others as a blessing and not a burden.

Sometimes, we forgot to acknowledge her selfless acts, but she didn't seem to mind. I realize, now, that her fulfillment came from knowing she was working for the Lord.

Even the most menial task is important
when we dedicate it to God.

—L. A. LINDBURG

Grandmother in Training

These older women must train the younger women to love
their husbands and their children.
TITUS 2:4

I think my mother suffered a small identity crisis when I announced my first pregnancy, but it didn't take her long to get caught up in the excitement. While I was growing up, she had sometimes irritated me with her unsolicited advice, so I wasn't sure what to expect from her as a grandmother. As it turned out, the arrival of my baby helped me recognize what a truly remarkable woman my mother was.

She was always right there, ready and willing to help, but she had the insight to know that I also needed to find my own way—to develop my own style of parenting. Her frequent and heartfelt praise inspired my confidence, and her respect for my new role gave me the courage to be myself.

Although she probably didn't realize it at the time, she was preparing me for the day I have grandchildren of my own. I don't plan to entertain any sort of identity crisis because I know exactly what kind of grandmother I want to be.

Sometimes the best teaching is done in watchful silence.

—SBT

Free Will Haircut

But the wisdom from above is first of all pure. It is also peace loving, gentle at all times, and willing to yield to others. It is full of mercy and good deeds. It shows no favoritism and is always sincere.
JAMES 3:17

My daughter's blonde hair flowed to her waist. I had as much fun styling it as she did wearing it. In second grade, she played Goldilocks in a school play, but in fifth grade, she dropped the bomb. "I want to cut my hair."

Stunned, I tried to clarify that she meant trim—not cut.

"No, I want it about this short." Her fingertips brushed her jaw.

My heart sank. "It will take a long time to grow back," I said and then, I asked myself what would be accomplished if I refused. Who knew? Perhaps she wouldn't regret it. I asked God for wisdom.

We cut her hair and it looked cute, but it didn't take long for her to regret the decision. It gave us many opportunities to talk about living with the results of our decisions. In His wisdom God helped me to allow Heather to exercise free will and to learn from the consequences.

*God often uses worldly incidents
to teach us heavenly lessons.*

—DONNA SUNDBLAD

Taking Action

> *What good is it, dear brothers and sisters, if you*
> *say you have faith but don't show it by your*
> *actions? Can that kind of faith save anyone?*
> JAMES 2:14

My years of being a mother have taught me that my best efforts don't necessarily guarantee the desired results. However, in recent months, I've been blessed to watch my daughter's faith blossom. I've seen my efforts to instill a love of God in Emily's heart reflected in her words and attitude, but I knew this was only the beginning. For her faith to really take root and thrive, she needed to demonstrate it in her actions.

A few weeks ago, a member of our church suffered a back injury. Not only was Lisa unable to work, she also found it increasingly difficult to care for her three young children. When I told Emily about Lisa's dilemma, Emily immediately offered to go and stay with the family for a week.

I reminded her that she had made plans of her own, but she shrugged and shook her head. "I can always make more plans," she said. "Lisa needs me now." It was then I knew that Emily's faith was firmly planted and flourishing.

Reveal your faith today in action.

—SBT

AUGUST

Leaving It in the Lord's Hands

The Lord says, "I will guide you along the best pathway for
your life. I will advise you and watch over you."
PSALM 32:8

hen my daughter Chelsea was only a preteen, she came to an important decision. "Mom," she said, "you need to accept the fact that I will probably live on the coast someday." At the time, I dismissed it as a childhood dream, much like the many ambitions I had entertained while growing up. But ever since she saw the movie *Free Willy* in the fourth grade, Chelsea had been obsessed with whales and dolphins. Her room gradually turned into an underworld habitat as marine life posters, fish tanks, sea-life curtains and bedding and, even, hermit crabs invaded and overtook the pink, feminine decor.

As the years passed, her love for animals grew. She added a hamster, a cat, and a cute little beagle to her zoo. I hoped she might pursue a career as a veterinarian, in part, because I longed to keep her closer to home. But recently, at the age of twenty-two, she confirmed her desire to live on the coast. "I haven't changed my mind, Mom," she said. "I still want to live by the ocean." And then I heard the words I had been expecting for years but wasn't sure I wanted to hear. "Mom, at the marine biology conference I attended last fall, I was offered a paying internship."

Surprisingly, I was happy for her, especially when it came to the "paying" part. We had just finished putting her brother through five years of college. In addition to Chelsea's three years of college, we had already funded an internship for her so she could obtain hands-on experience with dolphins. Then, I realized she hadn't told me where she would be going for this internship. "It's in southern Florida," she said, as if reading my mind. "And if I like it, and they offer me a job, I might just stay there and finish my degree."

We lived in the Midwest, and Chelsea had been staying a few hours from home as she worked toward her goal of a degree in Animal Psychology. She had been employed at numerous animal-related jobs on the side and was currently volunteering at two local zoos working with otters and manatees.

I was still trying to absorb what she had just told me, when I suddenly recalled another recent discussion about the prospect of marriage and children. Chelsea had been seeing her boyfriend for three years, and I had asked her if they were they planning on getting married in the near future. She told me that she wasn't ready to get married, and then she dropped the bomb. "I don't think I ever want to have kids."

At Chelsea's age, I had been a military wife, forced to live states away from my own mother. I remember the day my husband and I moved to Minot, North Dakota, for a two-year tour of duty. My mother cried the day I left, but she blamed her tears on a cold, and I believed her at the time. Now I understood how she felt. She worried that something major would happen to me, and she wouldn't be able to reach me quickly enough.

My mother and I were just starting to get close after surviving the normal rocky teenage years that most mothers and daughters experience. Then, right after we moved to North Dakota, I learned I suffered from an infertility disease. I had wanted to be a mother ever since I was a little girl, and the news devastated me but, thankfully, not for long. Within a few years we had a son, followed by our daughter.

I always imagined Chelsea would turn out like me. She would love cooking, clipping coupons, and being a mom. I assumed she would want to be a wife and mother. I nurtured visions of the two of us having an adult relationship similar to the one my mother and I enjoyed. As I thought of Chelsea as an unmarried, childless career woman, a lump began to form in my throat.

Looking back, I should have expected this. In the eighteen years my husband and I had spent raising Chelsea, we encouraged her to follow her dreams. She never really played with baby dolls or showed much interest in cooking, but as a young girl, she could tell you the difference between a dorsal fin and pectoral fin. Even the word "sea" was in her name. Chelsea had always followed her dream. The only difficulty was that her dream bore little resemblance to the one I had envisioned for her.

I am not disappointed in the woman my daughter has become; she has many strengths I admire. God has always had His own unique plan for her life. My job for the years she lived under my roof was to "train her in the way she should go" (Proverbs 22:6). Not the way I wanted her to go. Our role as parents was to help her discover her gifts and talents, and direct her to the Lord for the wisdom and encouragement to pursue them.

Moving far from home will be a time of spiritual maturation for Chelsea—and for me. Both of us will need to grow closer to the Lord. Chelsea will find herself turning to the Lord for guidance, and I will be spending a lot of time in prayer. I must learn to leave it all in the Father's hands, and that isn't a bad place to leave anything—especially our little girl.

—CONNIE STURM CAMERON

The Comfort of a Friend

Inside the Tent of Meeting, the Lord would speak to Moses face to face, as one speaks to a friend.
EXODUS 33:13

My daughter Terry was ten when we uprooted her from her neighborhood and school. Then one summer day, she came home with a stray dog and a new friend, named Rita, and begged me to accept them both. Well, the puppy was so cute I couldn't help taking her in, but another ten-year-old? It soon became obvious there would always be room for Rita in our house, our car, and especially our church—a completely new experience for her. As a result, Rita gave her heart to Christ.

Rita and Terry's friendship has lasted through weddings, long distance moves, teenage misery, military service, and divorce. God sanctions loving friendships because they fulfill His promise of eternal comfort. Everyone needs a special companion. God wants to be that kind of friend to you today.

A real friend can be closer than a sister.

—IMOGENE JOHNSON

It's All Part of the Plan

*"For I know the plans I have for you," says the Lord.
"They are plans for good and not for disaster,
to give you a future and a hope."*
JEREMIAH 29:11

My mother was only sixty-three when she died, and I admit there were times when I felt cheated. Times when I questioned God's plan and, yes, times when I felt bitter and resentful. I was a young mother who still needed her mother, and I wanted my children to know their grandmother.

It was my Aunt Helen who roused me from my stupor of sorrow and self-pity. "You know," she said, "God doesn't do things to hurt you. He had a plan for your mother, and He has a plan for you, too. And His plans are full of blessings and hope, not pain and desperation."

Her words reminded me so much of something my mother might have said. In the years that followed, Aunt Helen and I developed a close and loving relationship. Of course, she couldn't replace my mother, but she was there for me to share my joys and sorrows, and to remind me on occasion that it was all part of God's plan.

God has your best interests at heart.

—SBT

A Change of Plans

He will not let you stumble;
the one who watches over you will not slumber.
PSALM 121:3

She had taken college prep courses and received excellent grades. Her chosen college had accepted her, and the registration fee had been paid. Our oldest daughter was headed for college, and I was excited. I had loved every minute of my college experience and only wanted the best for her. But two weeks before she left, Lynette came in from work and said, "Mom, I don't want to go."

"What do you mean?" I asked. She explained how going to college had never been her dream and admitted she was only going to please me. "I don't think it's right for me," she said. "I want to stay home and work."

God knew the plans He had for her. After a successful career in an insurance office, Lynette was blessed with the opportunity to use her creativity, and she organized her own video art business. Later, she was hired as an assistant to the church communications director. Obviously, my daughter had found her place in the world by following God's will and not her mother's dreams.

Fulfillment comes from following your heart.

—JEANETTE MACMILLAN

A Journey from Sorrow to Joy

Those who plant in tears will harvest with shouts of joy.
PSALM 126:5

When I became pregnant about eighteen months after my first child, a son, was born, I was thrilled. I suffered a miscarriage but remained determined to try again. I greeted my third pregnancy with a little apprehension and a lot of enthusiasm. My doctor ordered an ultrasound to alleviate my anxiety. Little did I know the simple procedure would precipitate an emotional crisis, the likes of which I had never experienced.

The scan revealed a birth defect incompatible with life, and my baby died. When I discovered it might happen again, I decided to abandon my dream of having more children. The fear was too great. My faith wavered as I wondered why God would deny my greatest wish.

Despite my intention to limit my family, I became pregnant again and gave birth to my amazing daughter, Emily. Perhaps God knew we needed each other. Looking back, I can see how He took me by the hand after one of my greatest sorrows and led me to one of my greatest joys.

Only God can change unfathomable sorrow
into unbelievable joy.

—SBT

Pearls of Wisdom

Never let kindness leave you! Write them down within your heart. Then you will find favor with God and with people.
PROVERBS 3:3

My granddaughter was having a difficult time dealing with a classmate who was making recess unbearable. Every morning, she dreaded going to school and entering the cafeteria and playground. Few mothers have been spared the pain of watching their children suffer insult and rejection. It is a poignant reminder of how much our Heavenly Father grieves when His children are hurting.

My daughter sat down with her little girl and told her the story of the pearl—the tiny object that becomes beautiful when it is scuffed and polished by the irritants and pumice surrounding it. When we find ourselves forced to endure the "grit," our usual responses are distress and sorrow rather than trusting the process to transform us into jewels.

It was a wonderful lesson for my granddaughter. The spiritual "pearls" we teach our daughters and our granddaughters are precious gifts that create lifelong memories.

Our pearls of wisdom may help heal a broken heart.

—VERNA BOWMAN

The Right Thing to Do

Honor your father and mother, as the Lord your God commanded you. Then you will live a long, full life in the land the Lord your God is giving you.
DEUTERONOMY 5:16

When my mother first asked her parents if she and my father could get married, they gave the young couple their blessing, with one condition. My mother was only nineteen, and they insisted that she finish nursing school before any wedding would be allowed to take place. And so, my parents were married a few months after my mother graduated.

When my mother told me this story, I asked her why she and my father had waited. "If you were in love, why didn't you just get married?"

"We wanted to, but my parents told me I had to finish school."

My look of bewilderment obviously amused my mother because she grinned. "I realize it doesn't sound fair, but I knew they loved me, and I figured they had good reasons for asking me to wait. Besides, God expected me to honor their wishes."

"That must have been hard."

"It was a long wait, but as you know, it was well worth it. And it was the right thing to do."

God created His commandments for our benefit.

—SBT

Anything You Want

He makes the whole body fit together perfectly. As each part does its own special work, it helps the other parts grow, so that the whole body is healthy and growing and full of love.
EPHESIANS 4:16

My daughter is good with children. She babysits an autistic boy next door and shows more patience and compassion with him than some adults do. I start imagining her future as a special education teacher, but then I stop myself. She also has the tenacity to figure out complicated chemistry problems. She actually thinks they're fun!

When I was her age, my father believed teaching was a stable job for a young woman. He couldn't seem to understand that I didn't have the traits necessary to be a competent teacher. To please him, I entered the profession, but I didn't last long.

One night my daughter was trying to decide on her college major. "You can be anything you want to be," I said. "Think about what you're good at and what you truly enjoy. Then share your unique talents with the world."

We should encourage our daughters to develop their God-given talents, and let those gifts determine the path they choose.

—MARY LAUFER

Angel's Change of Heart

Therefore, since God in his mercy has given us this new way,
we never give up.
2 CORINTHIANS 4:1

When we first adopted our pony, Angel, she was quite nervous and standoffish. Because I was her caregiver, she quickly grew used to me, but she viewed other people with suspicion. During every visit, my daughter Emily tried, without success, to befriend the pony.

She decided, finally, that Angel wasn't interested in socializing, but I encouraged her to keep trying. Then, last night, Angel began to follow Emily around and behave affectionately toward her. Emily was thrilled and told everyone back at the house about the pony's change of heart.

Sometimes, I am very tempted to give up—particularly in prayer. I presume to know God's will and conclude that He isn't going to grant my request. I need to remember that God has His own perfect timetable, and my persistence lets Him know how important something is to me. His answer may very well turn out to be "no," but if I give up, I may never find out.

Persist in your prayers. God will answer
them all—in His own time.

—SBT

An Extraordinary Invitation

No one will be able to stand their ground against you as long
as you live. For I will be with you as I was with Moses.
I will not fail you or abandon you.

JOSHUA 1:5

"Hey, Mom, want to come over for coffee?"

I tossed the dishtowel on the counter and grabbed my keys. "You bet!"

My daughter Tanya's invitation might not sound so remarkable, but she had spent much of her life mired in a drug lifestyle, so her request brought me exceptional pleasure. We now live a mile apart—quite a difference from when I didn't know if she was dead or alive.

When I arrived at her apartment, she greeted me with coffee strong enough to energize my entire day, and then served me a waffle buried beneath strawberry whipped topping. As we shared this ordinary moment, I marveled at how God had guided us. He rescued Tanya from the clutches of drug addiction and now helped her forge new paths. And when I had suffered through sleepless nights and cried through endless days, God planted hope in my heart and peace in my mind.

Even as we walk through dark valleys,
God will neither forsake nor abandon us.

—LYNN LUDWICK

An Understanding Heart

Wisdom is enshrined in an understanding heart;
wisdom is not found among fools.
PROVERBS 14:33

When my father remarried, I was pleased—and very relieved. He had become increasingly overwhelmed with grief after my mother's death, and I was worried I might lose him, too. My joy was soon replaced with sadness as he and my stepmother slipped out of my life. I resigned myself to the fact that my father and I were now traveling different paths.

It was only through time spent in prayer and in God's word that I found the first peace I had known for years. I resolved that nothing would ever change the love my father and I shared. Although I still missed him deeply, I was finally able to recognize the blessings in his life.

When he died recently, I prayed for God to give me an understanding heart once more. I no longer saw my stepmother as someone who took my mother's place, but as a woman who had loved my father and was now trying to cope with the devastating loss of her husband.

An understanding heart can help you find peace.

—SBT

Kitchen Conversations

The Lord detests the sacrifice of the wicked,
but he delights in the prayers of the upright.
PROVERBS 15:8

Every once in a while, my firstborn will slip into the kitchen just as I'm starting dinner. "Need some help?" she asks, pulling up a stool. I've learned to recognize that signal. She wants to talk.

Granted, my preteen isn't wrestling with heavy life issues yet. Usually she is looking for some affirmation or some reassurance that she said or did the right thing. Other times, she just wants me to understand her world a little better.

As much as I enjoy those times, how much more does my heavenly Father want to hear from me? In Proverbs 15:8, the "upright" doesn't mean only the super-righteous. It includes all of us who belong to God. He delights in hearing from us. I need to take advantage of the privilege of prayer with the same freedom and confidence my daughter has when she comes to me—and not just at dinnertime.

My Father always has time to talk.

—PAULA WISEMAN

No Questions Asked

*So let us come boldly to the throne of our gracious God.
There we will receive his mercy, and we will find grace to
help us when we need it most.*
HEBREWS 4:16

When my daughter left home in the middle of her senior year, I was hurt and angry. For about a week, I made no effort to contact her, but thankfully, God granted me the insight for which I had prayed. I realized that Emily still needed to know she had a mother who loved her and wanted what was best for her. I began to e-mail her everyday and sent messages through her brother, but at first, she didn't respond.

I used to avoid approaching God when I felt guilty or ashamed. That changed when I finally understood that His love was eternal and unconditional. I wondered if Emily felt some remorse or embarrassment and didn't feel confident approaching me. So, I sent another e-mail in which, among other things, I told her that no matter what happened, she would always be my precious girl. Within days, we were talking on the phone.

*We can approach God with confidence, no matter what
we've done or how we feel.*

—SBT

263

Memories of Grandma

For the sake of my family and friends,
I will say, "May you have peace."
PSALM 122:8

As I stood before family and friends at my grandmother's funeral, I struggled to keep my voice even and clear. "I remember two things about Grandma," I said. "Fried chicken and crossword puzzles. Grandma always let me drop the pieces of chicken in a bag of flour and shake them until they turned white."

I took a deep breath and continued. "Then, I would watch as she made gravy from scratch. Once I ate the whole bowl." Gentle laughter filled the room, and I couldn't help but smile at the remembrance of how uncomfortable I had felt after consuming all that gravy.

"Early the next morning," I said, "Grandma and I would work on the crossword from the newspaper before everyone else woke up. How I looked forward to learning new words. She saved those puzzles for our special time together."

My voice turned insistent as my eulogy drew to a close. "Make sure you set aside time for those you love," I said. "You will build a bond that cannot be broken—or forgotten."

Special moments create memories that last a lifetime.

—CASEY PITTS

A Good Night's Sleep

*Then Peter came to him and asked, "Lord, how often should
I forgive someone who sins against me? Seven times?"*

*"No, not seven times," Jesus replied,
"but seventy times seven!"*
MATTHEW 18:21–22

As the mother of three teenagers, I've discovered that
matters of the young heart have the power to disrupt the
entire household. When my daughter Emily broke up with
Brian, we all felt the earthquake, but it was the aftershocks
that proved to be the greatest challenge.

Emily made the mistake of listening to gossip and react-
ing to comments allegedly made by her ex-boyfriend. The
situation spiraled out of control, and I decided it was time for
a refresher course in forgiveness. "Brian hurt your feelings," I
said, "but now you're hurting yourself by having an unforgiv-
ing heart. And you're damaging your fellowship with God."

"But he was telling my friends things that weren't true."
"Forgiveness won't make what he did right," I replied, "but
it will set you free."

"Okay, I'll give it a try," she said.

"I know you can do it. Oh, just one more thing."

"Yes?" I smiled. "You'll sleep a lot better at night, too."

Forgiveness is the key to the prison of anger and bitterness.

—SBT

Steps of Faith

I know, Lord, that our lives are not our own.
We are not able to plan our own course.
JEREMIAH 10:23

After high school, our daughter Erin went to an Illinois college more than 500 miles from home. She met and married her college sweetheart, Phil, and stayed in Illinois.

Last spring, she called home to tell us they were moving. Erin had landed a teaching position not far from home. My thoughts raced with excitement, but I was stunned when she called a few days later and explained that Phil had been offered a coveted teaching position in Illinois. "What should we do?" she asked.

The most difficult thing I've ever done was to tell them to follow God's will, to pray about it, and allow Him to direct their paths. I hung up and cried out to God like never before. The next morning, I braced myself for the news that they were staying. To my astonishment, that didn't happen.

They made the move, and we've enjoyed them every minute! They are still searching for God's guidance, and though it has been an uncertain journey, I thank God they trusted Him to guide their steps home again.

You can't get lost with God as your guide.

—JENNIE HILLIGUS

A Fresh Start

*I have swept away your sins like a cloud. I have scattered
your offenses like the morning mist. Oh, return to me,
for I have paid the price to set you free.*
ISAIAH 44:22

Like most children, I spent my share of time explaining myself to my mother—the judge and jury of childhood misadventures. My infractions were usually minor, and most of them involved my older brother. However, occasionally my transgressions were more serious. Looking back, I realize that my mother was never harsh or unfair although, at the time, I'm sure I thought otherwise.

I don't recall specific punishment, but I do remember my mother making sure I understood why she was disappointed in my behavior. She was far more interested in discussing the situation than she was in sentencing me to some sort of penalty.

But the most memorable aspect of her discipline was that once I had acknowledged my mistake and expressed remorse, the incident was forgotten. I will always be grateful for her gift of a clean slate.

God is ready to forgive your sins and give you a fresh start.

—SBT

267

Comfort and Consolation

This I declare about the Lord: He alone is my refuge, my place of safety; He is my God, and I trust Him.
PSALM 91:2

I watched anxiously as the nurse checked Amy's vitals. My fifteen-month-old daughter looked so fragile as she labored for breath in her oxygen tent. She had been hospitalized for an RSV infection, and my heart broke to watch her struggle. I wanted to hold her and ease her discomfort, but she needed to be in the tent.

"She's doing better. You can hold her for awhile," the nurse said.

I took the baby out of her tent, wrapped her in a warm blanket, and held her close. I needed this as much as my baby did. Amy, knowing she was safe in her mother's arms, snuggled close and fell into a peaceful, contented sleep.

As I enjoyed the comforting closeness of my precious child, I thought this is how God wants His children to be with Him. Trusting. Peaceful. Content. He wants us to find consolation and concern in His presence. No matter what our situation may be, we can rest safe and secure in our Father's loving arms.

We're never too old to sit on our Heavenly Father's lap.

—ANGIE VIK

Once in a Lifetime

And I am convinced that nothing can ever separate
us from God's love. Neither death nor life, neither
angels nor demons, neither our fears for today nor
our worries about tomorrow—not even the powers of
hell can separate us from God's love.
ROMANS 8:38

On the morning of my parent's thirty-fifth wedding anniversary, my mother and I enjoyed an early cup of tea together. I was still in my twenties, and thirty-five years seemed like a very long time to spend with one person. "How do you stay married for thirty-five years?" I asked.

"That's a rather odd question," my mother said with a chuckle.

I grinned. "I think you know what I'm trying to say."

"Yes, I do, and the truth is, I've never really thought about it. I thank God for bringing your dad into my life, and I wake up each morning grateful for the chance to spend another day with him. I guess that's how you stay married for thirty-five years, although it feels like the time has flown by."

Tears filled my eyes. "You and dad are still in love, aren't you?"

"Absolutely, and we both know there's no guarantee of a tomorrow, so we try to make the most of each day."

Today is a precious, once in a lifetime, gift.

—SBT

Defusing Fear

This is my command—be strong and courageous!
Do not be afraid or discouraged. For the Lord your God is
with you wherever you go.
JOSHUA 1:9

Sonya came to the kitchen with a terrified expression on her face. She had been getting ready for school when friends called to tell her some boys were planning a shooting at her high school. Although I didn't want my daughter to be frightened every time there was a rumor of danger, there had been real school shootings lately. My heart began to race as well.

When I checked with the school, I discovered they had taken steps to handle the threats. That was when Sonya reminded me that we had been reading Joshua in the Bible. We recalled the verse in which we are commanded to be unafraid and to remember that God is with us. So we held hands, asked God for courage, and she went to school. Only a small number of students showed up, but all went well. The next time a fearful situation arises, we will both know to turn to God—our constant companion.

There is no fear more powerful than God's love.

—EVA JULIUSON

Love from the Lighthouse

And He will answer, "I tell you the truth, when you refused to help the least of these my brothers and sisters, you were refusing to help me."
MATTHEW 25:45

As a guest preacher, the evangelist Bill Nickel's powerful messages have been a blessing to our entire congregation. Brother Nickel is the field representative for the Lighthouse Children's Home in Kosciusko, Mississippi, a mission that provides homeless and wayward teenage girls with a loving, Christian home.

Several years ago, our church decided to sponsor a girl from the Lighthouse Home. We wanted the chance to let a troubled girl know that we cared very much and wanted her to succeed in life. And it gave the mothers in our congregation the opportunity to tuck another daughter under their maternal wing.

Through her frequent letters, our "girl" has shared her daily life at the home, as well as her hopes and dreams for the future. On numerous occasions, we've rejoiced over the tremendous progress she's made. It has truly been a rewarding experience filled with blessings, and no matter where life takes her, our "daughter" will always have a place in our hearts.

Even a small gesture of kindness can make a huge difference in someone's life.

—SBT

Our Perfect Provider

And God will generously provide all you need.
Then you will always have everything you need
and plenty left over to share with others.
2 CORINTHIANS 9:8

On hot summer days, Mom used to gather the five of us together and ask, "Who's ready to go to the pool?" I would hurry to my room, put my swimsuit on under my clothes, and climb into the car. That's all it took for me to get ready.

Once at the pool, I raced to jump into the cool water. When I grew tired, I found a fluffy blanket on which to rest with my siblings. Mom slathered lotion on our skin and wrapped fresh, clean towels around our shoulders so we wouldn't burn. When our tummies growled with hunger, she doled out sandwiches, chips, and a refreshing drink.

Of course, I now realize it took Mom much longer to prepare for our outings than it did for me. Without any fanfare, she provided for her children. She knew what we would need before we did. In the same way, God supplies our needs, and often provides before we even utter a prayer. He is our perfect provider.

Let's not take our Heavenly father—
or godly mothers, for granted.

—DONNA J. SHEPHERD

Filling the Void

But everyone who calls on the
name of the LORD will be saved.
ACTS 2:21

When I first met my new mother-in-law, Mildred, I addressed her as Mrs. Townsend, but she quickly corrected me and insisted that I call her "Mom." My own mother had been gone for years, and the idea of using that term of endearment felt a bit foreign and awkward. It was as though I had put the word away when my mother died, never expecting to use it again.

I quickly discovered that Mildred had numerous remarkable qualities, many of which she shared with my mother. She treated me like a precious daughter, and her love helped to fill the void the loss of my mother had created. One day, I realized that Mildred had become my "Mom," and while she would never replace my real mother, God had found a way to ease some of the heartache I had lived with for almost ten years.

A real mother is much more than a title.

—SBT

Blessed Brokenness

Each time He said, "My grace is all you need. My power works best in weakness." So now I am glad to boast about my weaknesses, so that the power of Christ can work through me.
2 CORINTHIANS 12:9

I was dusting the shelves in the living room where I kept some treasured Hummels that I had purchased while living overseas. My youngest stepdaughter opened the front door just as the wind blew a raging path through the room. Without warning, the shelf with the Hummels came crashing down on the floor and the sound of porcelain shattering echoed in my ears. Her tiny feet stepped gingerly through the obstacle course that suddenly stretched between us. She reached out as if embracing the wreckage. "Can we glue them back together?"

I wiped the tears from my eyes and stared down at the shattered pieces before me. "No, sweetheart, we can't glue them back together. Some things are never quite the same once they've been damaged. Broken things lose their value, except in God's eyes. He chooses broken people to do wondrous things for His glory."

Your brokenness is an opportunity for God to work a great miracle.

—MICHELE STARKEY

Respect Can Be Rewarding

*But do this in a gentle and respectful way. Keep your
conscience clear. Then if people speak against you,
they will be ashamed when they see what a good life
you live because you belong to Christ.*

1 PETER 3:16

One day, I came across a sweater my mother bought
for me many years ago. I always enjoyed shopping with
her, especially since she usually took me out for lunch. But
there was a more significant reason she made our trips
pleasant and memorable.

It didn't matter if we went to an expensive shop just
to look around, or to a bargain store searching for good
buys. My mother treated everyone we encountered with
a friendly, respectful attitude, and this distinguished her
from many shoppers. In fact, some of the clerks at stores
we visited regularly knew my mother by name.

When I asked her how she maintained her composure,
she said, "Because that's what God expects of me. Besides,"
she added, "most people work hard at their jobs, and they
deserve my respect." A few years later, I found myself dealing with the public all day, and I was very grateful that
people like my mother existed.

There's no excuse for disrespect.

—SBT

He's Standing By

Hear my prayer, O Lord! Listen to my cries for help!
Don't ignore my tears.

For I am your guest—a traveler passing through,
as my ancestors were before me.
PSALM 39:12

She left home before the end of her senior year of high school. My oldest daughter rebelled and, within a week, I became physically ill. The crisis took its toll on my body and threatened to crush my spirit as well. Later, she would regret her hasty behavior but at the time, she really believed she was acting in her own best interest.

Moments in parenting come when we think we cannot go on. Life moves so fast, we feel like giving up. Trials, problems, and temptations arise, and we find ourselves sinking. Then, just as we are about to lose hope, we cry out to God and He is there. He does not sleep, nor is He slow to act. He is a faithful Father standing by, always listening for the cries of his people.

Are you in the midst of a troubling experience?
Take heart—your God is listening!

—LaROSE KARR

My Mistake

Don't copy the behavior and customs of this world, but let God transform you into a new person by changing the way you think. Then you will learn to know God's will for you, which is good and pleasing and perfect.
ROMANS 12:2

Being a teenager has never been easy, but our society's growing obsession with appearance has made it even more difficult. Young girls are inundated with the message that their value as a person is based on standards of beauty determined by the outside world. In raising my daughter, I've done my best to contradict this pervasive and overwhelming attitude but, sometimes, I feel like I am fighting a losing battle. Then, one day, I realized that I might be contributing to the problem.

It occurred to me that I often described people in terms of the way they look and made comments that supported society's twisted view of self-worth. It didn't make any sense for me to remind Emily that God doesn't care about outward appearances, only to remark five minutes later that a woman on a magazine cover is unattractive.

As a mother, I still have a long way to go, but asking God for the wisdom to learn from my mistakes has made the trip a lot easier.

Acknowledge your mistakes and learn from them.

—SBT

Mommy Number Two

He gives the childless woman a family,
making her a happy mother. Praise the Lord!
PSALM 113:9

I worked with children as a librarian, but my husband and I never had a family of our own. When my younger sister gave birth to two daughters, she often told me to think of her children as my children. We were separated from my sister and her girls by 700 miles, but frequent phone calls helped us keep track of our nieces. We saw them twice a year when we went home for visits.

Each niece came to stay with us when they were old enough. I'd take them to the seashore for a "girls only" overnight adventure. We swam, ate out, wrote poetry, and drew pictures as we sat on a bench and stared out at the Atlantic.

When the girls grew up and had children, I always tried to be available to listen and give advice if asked. Now we take our nieces and their families on special vacations to create even more memories. I praise God everyday for a sister whose heart was big enough to allow me to be "Mommy Number Two."

There is far more to being a mother than giving birth.

—LAURIE A. PERKINS

The More the Merrier

Children are a gift from the Lord;
they are a reward from him.
PSALM 127:3

When someone asked me if I regretted the fact that I only had one daughter, I laughed. How could I possibly feel anything but gratitude and joy for God's blessing of four amazing sons? Once in a long while, I found myself overwhelmed by masculinity, especially after my daughter left home. But as my boys grew up, and girlfriends replaced video games and Ninja battles in the backyard, things began to balance out.

When my son, Dylan, first brought Bobbijo home, I confess it was a bit of an adjustment. I had grown used to a house full of males, but within a very short while, I found myself enjoying having another girl in the house—besides my two dogs, that is. One day, as I watched Bobbijo preparing supper, I realized that I might have four more daughters someday. What a wonderful prospect!

Life is full of delightful possibilities!

—SBT

A Princess in Waiting

And so you were adorned with gold and silver. Your
clothes were made of fine linen and were beautifully
embroidered. You ate the finest foods—choice flour,
honey, and olive oil—and became more beautiful
than ever. You looked like a queen, and so you were!
EZEKIEL 16:13

Night after night, in the halo of her Singer sewing lamp, my mother bent over yards of white linen, making a regal, full-length coat for my prom. I had already confirmed that my friends wouldn't be wearing anything over their dresses, so I ignored the hurt in Mom's tired eyes and hurried off that night without a coat—or a clue. I recall Mom watching from our doorway, cradling the coat.

For twenty years, the princess coat hung in her closet, shrouded in plastic. One day, she asked if I wanted it, and I slipped it out of the bag. It was a gorgeous piece, fully lined and adorned with mother-of-pearl buttons. I couldn't believe I had allowed peer pressure to triumph over such an incredible display of my mother's devotion. "Can you ever forgive me," I asked. The loving smile on her face told me she already had.

It's never too late to say, "I'm sorry."

—LAURIE KLEIN

Love's Sacrifice

We prove ourselves by our purity, our understanding, our patience, our kindness, by the Holy Spirit within us, and by our sincere love.
2 CORINTHIANS 6:6

For as long as I could remember, I had wanted a horse more than anything in the world, but my parents made it abundantly clear that owning a horse was a financial burden they couldn't accommodate. Then, when I was fourteen, we moved, and I started tenth grade in a strange, new school. I tried to make the best of a bad situation, but as I became increasingly unhappy, my grades suffered, and I began to skip school.

One night, I overheard my parents talking about buying me a horse. "Susan needs something to focus on besides school," my mother said. "Maybe she'll make friends with some of the girls who love horses as much as she does."

"But we really can't afford it," my father replied.

"I know, but there's ways I can save money. I think this is important enough to make some sacrifices."

Having a horse of my own changed my life, and I have never forgotten the sacrifice that made it possible.

Even while we were yet sinners,
God loved us enough to sacrifice His son.

—SBT

Stay Rooted

They are like trees planted along the riverbank,
bearing fruit each season. Their leaves never
wither, and they prosper in all they do.
PSALM 1:3

A small group of friends and family gathered in our Midwestern home. My husband had accepted a job in Florida and, for the first time, I would be living away from my mom and dad. We shared good food and good laughs, but an underlying sadness mingled with the excitement of a new call on our lives.

Now, we sat crowded in the living room. One of my sisters started to pray and, in turn, prayers were offered one by one. When it was Mom's turn, my throat tightened. I didn't want to leave her and my dad, but knew I must follow the Lord.

Her voice quivered. "Lord, I thank you for all the years we've had Donna nearby. She's been like a strong oak to this family." Tears leaked and dripped from my lashes. If anyone was strong, I thought, it was Mom. Then, she continued. "Please plant her in the lives of the people she meets in Florida, and let her be their fruitful oak in the Lord's work."

When entering a new season in life,
stay rooted in God's word.

—DONNA SUNDBLAD

September

Honey Mouse

I will be your God throughout your lifetime—until your hair is white with age. I made you, and I will care for you. I will carry you along and save you.

Isaiah 46:4

For the greater part of my life, my mother and I have lived together. At first, this arrangement provoked disparaging comments from my friends and colleagues. "I would rather die than live with my mother!" While I pursued my career, my mother kept house. The day I mentioned that Mom was taking down the Christmas tree, my independence-minded friends tempered their tune. When they found out she did the laundry and made sure dinner was waiting for me every night after work, they began to see the advantages of my situation.

But, as my friends suspected, there were some drawbacks. I was a late bloomer, more likely to curl up with a book than launch out on my own and, for many years, our domestic arrangement did little to change my personality. My mother continued to treat me like a child even as I opened my invitation to join AARP. However, my mother's advancing age and growing physical limitations began to change our relationship. I started taking down the Christmas decorations and took over some of the things she had done for years.

It's rarely smooth when mothers and daughters are forced to switch places. It took some time for both of us to grow comfortable seeing each other—and accepting ourselves—in our new roles. For instance, I didn't mind taking over the cooking, but my mother wasn't keen on leaving the kitchen. She had been the cook her whole adult life, and what did I know about food, except to eat it? Eventually, she resigned herself to my culinary expertise, most notably since I started relying on take-out.

My need to assume a few new responsibilities was revealed one morning when I discovered a mouse in the house. Actually, our cats discovered a mouse in the house. When two cats station themselves on either side of an organ console, it's not because they want to hear a recital. While I watched them and entertained the hope that they simply had a cricket under guard, a small, gray creature dashed from its hiding place into full view. "Pounce!" I yelled to the cats as I leaped back several feet into the next room. Unfortunately, the cats retreated as well. The mouse darted under the recliner, and the cats returned to take up surveillance on either side of it. Clearly, both of them were far more interested in watching the mouse than catching it.

My mother had always handled household catastrophes of this kind. Competent, levelheaded, and practical, she would devise a way to send the mouse packing, but when I thought of her sound asleep upstairs, I realized her mouse exterminating days were over. The cats certainly weren't going to be any help. I sighed as the full weight of responsibility landed squarely on my shoulders. After considering my dilemma, I came up with an idea and searched the basement for an empty coffee can among my painting supplies. Armed with the can and its lid, I joined the cats. I decided I would capture the mouse in the can, slam on the lid, and then release it outside. The only problem with my plan occurred when the mouse appeared. I flinched, and it bypassed the can and scurried under the sofa. The cats followed at a nonchalant pace; apparently, their interest in the mouse was waning.

Perhaps I needed to make the can more inviting. He might have a sweet tooth, I thought and poured some honey into the can. A few minutes later, when he dashed toward me, I screamed, slammed the can on top of him, and scooted across the floor with the can until I got to the door. Can and rodent went over the threshold, and the mouse scurried away with honey dripping down his back. I felt terrible. I had made him vulnerable, not only to his natural predators, but to anything out there longing for dessert.

My friends who once claimed they would rather die than live with their mother are finding out that time, age, and circumstance bring changes to the mother-daughter relationship. Daughters aren't so adamant about proving their independence, and mothers aren't so passionate about speaking their mind anymore. A couple years ago, I opened our home to a second pair of cats—one of them an enthusiastic mouser—and my mother offered only mild reproof. When I set up my sewing machine in the dining room, she voiced little consternation. And when I announced my intention to sell the dining room furniture and replace it with a craft table, she just shook her head.

But I still feel bad about that mouse.

—PATRICIA MITCHELL

A Sense of Importance

"Don't be afraid," he said, "for you are very precious to God. Peace! Be encouraged! Be strong!" As he spoke these words to me, I suddenly felt stronger and said to him, "Please speak to me, my Lord, for you have strengthened me."
DANIEL 10:19

One day, my daughter Emily and I went to Walmart, and as we entered the store, I noticed an elderly man sitting on one of the benches by the door. When he looked up and smiled at me, I greeted him. "Hello," I said. "How are you today?" Encouraged by my interest, he told me about his day. We visited for a few minutes before I excused myself to continue shopping. As Emily and I walked away, she asked, "Do you know that man?"

"No," I replied.

"Then why did you stop and talk to him?"

"Because I wanted him to feel important. I read somewhere that, every day, we should try to make another person feel special. Even if it's just saying hello or sending an encouraging card." Emily smiled.

"I saw the expression on that man's face. I think you really lifted his spirits."

"Well, I'll never know for sure. But I do know that I always feel better when I take the time to think of someone else."

When we encourage others, we inspire ourselves.

—SBT

287

The Beauty Within

Don't be concerned about the outward beauty of fancy
hairstyles, expensive jewelry, or beautiful clothes.
1 PETER 3:3

I was dazzled the first time I saw an old photograph of my mother. "Why didn't you become a movie star?" I asked.

She laughed. "A housewife with eight children is lucky if she has the time to **see** a movie," she replied.

As Mom became older, I thought she reminded me more of Jacqueline Kennedy and less like a starlet. Both Jackie and my mother suffered a death in the family. Jackie lost her husband, of course, while my mother lost her seven-year-old son. Despite their sorrow, they both displayed great strength, but I suspected Jackie must have cried at night, too.

When I left home and became a mother myself, my perspective of Mom changed again. As I raised my children, I began to understand the extent to which she had put her family's needs before her own. She no longer made me think of a movie star or Jackie Kennedy. She had been transformed into a selfless woman—someone who lived her life for others.

We should teach our daughters the meaning of true beauty.

—MARY LAUFER

Privileged Children

I will teach all your children, and they will enjoy great peace.
ISAIAH 54:13

My husband, Tom, grew up with nine brothers and sisters. Although money was tight, there was always food on the table, and his mother, Mildred, dedicated herself to giving her children a loving home and a strong faith in God. Every Sunday, she would undertake the monumental task of getting her large family ready for church. Her husband chose not to accompany his family, a fact that I'm sure distressed Mildred, but made her feat even more remarkable.

Her efforts were not in vain. With few exceptions, her children still attend church faithfully. By teaching her family to love the Lord, Mildred gave them a priceless gift to carry them through the joys and sorrows she knew lay ahead. And when my husband recalls his childhood, I don't hear stories of being deprived or missing out on anything. I hear a son remembering how hard his mother worked to give him what was really important.

Money can't buy the things your children really need.

—SBT

How Much Is Cheese in Africa?

If you need wisdom, if you want to know what God
wants you to do ask him, and he will gladly tell you.
He will not resent your asking.
JAMES 1:5

"How much is cheese in Africa? How many pieces of candy can you actually eat before you throw up?" These are only two of the mind-numbing questions my young daughters have asked over the years. On a recent visit to Disneyland, my five-year-old wanted to know where she could find "Chip and Dip," referring, of course, to Disney's famous pair of chipmunks, Chip and Dale.

With three daughters, each ten years apart in age, the questions have been endless. I can remember talking to my oldest child about dating boys while changing my youngest girl's diaper. I never have to wait long for a new question, and the ancient, well-known rule always applies—the only dumb question is the one that doesn't get asked. So, as I continue to attempt to satisfy their insatiable curiosity, I thank God He is there to take care of mine.

God is always ready to share His wisdom.

—DEBORAH SCHEUFFELE

Birthday Blessings

But now Timothy has just returned, bringing us good
news about your faith and love. He reports that you
always remember our visit with joy and that you want
to see us as much as we want to see you.
1 THESSALONIANS 3:6

My mother always made me feel important on my birthday, and after she died, I missed her special touch. Consequently, it meant a lot to me the first time my mother-in-law, Mildred, acknowledged my birthday. She sent me a card and enclosed a small check with strict instructions to spend it on something for myself.

"How kind of her to think of me," I said to my husband.

He smiled and nodded. "She remembers everyone's birthday and all of the wedding anniversaries, too."

I joked that Mildred had a full time job sending cards to ten children, seven of whom were married, and eighteen grandchildren, but I was touched she had included me. I realized that her card and small gift had contained so much more than a birthday message. It was her way of welcoming me to the family, and although she didn't know it, she had brought some of the magic back to my birthday.

God provides for our needs in
wonderful and unexpected ways.

—SBT

Faithful Provision

*And Mephibosheth, who was crippled in both feet, lived in
Jerusalem and ate regularly at the king's table.*
2 SAMUEL 9:13

My daughter, Anna, has PDD—pervasive developmental disorder—a form of autism. When I found out, I went to God and wept and pleaded for healing, but it didn't happen. There was only continued slow development, atopic dermatitis, a lazy eye, and seizures.

Despite all of this, Anna's smile could light up the room. She loved to pray and listen to praise music. My emotions were constantly pulled in two directions as I begged for healing and rejoiced in little accomplishments.

One day I read the story of Mephibosheth. King David wanted to show kindness to anyone remaining in the house of Saul, but found only the crippled son of Jonathan. David brought Mephibosheth into his house, and he always ate at the king's table. God did not take away Mephibosheth's disability. Instead, He provided for him and his family. When I look back, I see God's faithful provision for Anna, and for me, too.

*The Lord does not always remove our afflictions,
but He will always provide for us.*

—PAM HALTER

My So Called Singing Career

But you are a God of forgiveness, gracious and merciful,
slow to become angry, and rich in unfailing love.
You did not abandon them.
NEHEMIAH 9:17

I was about seven years old and playing outside with my friends when they started talking about the citywide music festival being held the following week. Several of my playmates stated proudly that they were entered in the festival and, not wanting to be left out, I said that I was going to sing.

When I went home for lunch, my mother told me that my father wanted to talk to me in the other room. My appetite disappeared as I recalled my lie from earlier that morning. Within minutes, guilt had tied my stomach into knots, and when I saw my father's stern face, I burst into tears.

As it turned out, my mother had inadvertently discovered my lie when talking to another mother in the neighborhood. I asked my father, between sobs, if he planned to punish me, and his face softened. "I think you've punished yourself enough, sweetheart," he said. Then, he gave me a hug, and I walked out of that room thinking that being forgiven was the best feeling in the world.

Stop punishing yourself and ask God for forgiveness.

—SBT

Staying the Course

I will walk among you; I will be your God,
and you will be my people.
LEVITICUS 26:12

The first stop on my mother-daughter journey was an adoption agency. "Here she is," the director said, smiling and handing me a three-day old baby. Tanya's tiny fingers encircled mine, and I became a mother.

We followed the usual childhood routes: the first day of kindergarten, Girl Scouts, and shopping at the mall. Then, adolescence changed everything. Our new course led to rebellion and courtrooms. I sobbed when my daughter entered juvenile hall in handcuffs.

Several times over the following years, I almost gave up, but God strengthened me and, eventually, granted a sweet reward. On Tanya's wedding day, I led the way down the aisle as her matron of honor. Her dark days were over.

Though it had been a long, agonizing passage, I'm glad I stayed the course. I know God always walked with us, even along the roads neither my daughter nor I had consciously chosen.

God walks with us, no matter where our life's journey leads.

—LYNN LUDWICK

Calling for Courage

You will keep in perfect peace all who trust in you,
all whose thoughts are fixed on you!
ISAIAH 26:3

When I graduated from university with my teaching degree, I had several job offers from which to choose. Some of them were a short distance from my parent's home, but the most appealing invitation came from a school district about 800 miles away. Although I knew it was the best choice for me, I found the prospect of being so far from home unnerving.

Even though I knew my mother hated to see me leave, she gave me the courage to accept the position. She could have sympathized with my reluctance and persuaded me to accept one of the jobs closer to home, but she didn't. Right up to, and including, the moment she said good-bye, she remained optimistic and excited about my new life.

Years later, I asked her how she managed to put on such a brave front. "I asked God for the courage to let you go," she said, "and then I put my trust in Him to keep you safe."

Trust in the Lord and He will supply the courage you need.

—SBT

Olympic Opportunities

May your ways be known throughout the earth,
your saving power among people everywhere.
PSALM 67: 2

Jolene and I stood outside the Olympic Stadium in Salt Lake City. The Olympic torch burned beside the five-ringed flag, flapping in the wind. What an unbelievable experience! I could hardly believe we were actually there.

When I heard about a denominational outreach planned for the XIX Winter Olympics, I didn't hesitate. It was the perfect union of my interest in sports with my passion for missions. It was a complete surprise when my daughter expressed an interest in joining me. So, we both applied and rejoiced when we were invited to join the outreach team.

For seven days, we served snacks and traded pins with Olympic workers. I watched with delight—and gratitude—as Jolene shared her faith with everyone she met. By traveling to a gathering of people from every corner of the earth, we had touched the world together.

We should look for opportunities to involve our daughters in
sharing the good news of Jesus Christ.

—DARLENE FRANKLIN

A Bit of Housework and a Lot of Faith

Many Samaritans from the village believed in Jesus because the woman had said, "He told me everything I ever did!"
JOHN 4:39

When her husband died a few years ago, my mother-in-law, Mildred, found herself with a lot of time on her hands. After raising her younger siblings and ten children of her own, she had become a woman used to staying busy.

So, in her late seventies, she began working for a home care company. "I look after elderly women," she told us in a voice that made it perfectly clear she did not see herself as one of their contemporaries. "I drive them around and do a bit of light housework," she added.

What she didn't mention was how much she cared for these women or how much she enjoyed their company. These things became obvious at Christmas and on her birthday when cards and small gifts arrived from the women whose hearts she had touched. Well acquainted with Mildred's powerful and resilient faith, we weren't the least bit surprised to discover that she had also brought God into their lives.

Let your love for the Lord shine in everything you do.

—SBT

A Sense of Belonging

*After that, Abram traveled south and set up camp in
the hill country, with Bethel to the west and Ai to the
east. There he built another altar and dedicated it to
the Lord, and he worshiped the Lord.*
GENESIS 12:8

I came home and found my daughter in tears. "Mom,"
she said, "I'll never fit in this new school."

Lucille was in sixth grade, the year when she would
finally be one of the "big kids on the block." But all of that
had changed with our recent move. Good friends and a
familiar neighborhood had been left behind. I had tried to
understand, but how could I? As a child I had only gone to
one grade school, one high school, and one church. How
could I possibly know how she felt?

I tried to remember what the Bible said about moving.
What did Abraham do when he moved his family? He
built an altar and set up camp. An altar signified a way
of recognizing God's presence. It meant worship and the
preservation of faith. With God, even a temporary camp
represented more than a dwelling place.

*No matter where we live,
God's presence makes us feel at home.*

—JEANETTE MACMILLAN

Debunking the Allergy Myth

And this same God who takes care of me will
supply all your needs from his glorious riches,
which have been given to us in Christ Jesus.
PHILIPPIANS 4:19

As a child, I loved to visit my aunt and uncle's farm. There always seemed to be an orange tabby kitten with my name on it, and I would plead with my mother to let me take it back to the city with us. Her answer never varied. "I know how much you want a kitten, but we can't have one in the house because of your allergies."

I strongly suspected the allergy excuse was a myth she perpetuated to avoid having more pets but, as it turned out, testing proved I was allergic to cats. I had to admit, once again, that my mother had known what was best for me all along. Although I may have missed out on some things I wanted, I never lacked for anything I needed.

Today, God takes care of all my needs. Once again, I don't necessarily get what I want, but I have no doubt that, just like my mother, the Lord only wants what's best for me.

Like a loving mother, God will meet all your needs.

—SBT

Soul Medicine

A cheerful heart is a good medicine,
but a broken spirit saps a person's strength.
PROVERBS 17:22

June always made me laugh. As a little girl, she would twist her face into such strange positions that I nicknamed her "rubber face." I would burst into laughter while trying to discipline her, leading to bizarre statements such as, "Just because I'm laughing doesn't mean I'm happy with your behavior."

Even as a grown woman with children of her own, she still maintains a cheerful spirit that has served her well in difficult times. Both of her children have inherited their mother's fun-loving personality. It's hard to be gloomy in the midst of such joy.

Laughter is a wonderful gift from God. Even medical science agrees that a cheerful disposition aids in the healing process. And it's always a blessing to share laughter with a friend—guaranteed to lift your spirits!

If our hearts sing, others will be cheered by its music.

—JOYCE STARR MACIAS

Charlotte's Devotion

You were cleansed from your sins when you obeyed the truth, so now you must show sincere love to each other as brothers and sisters. Love each other deeply with all your heart.
1 PETER 1:22

There were five children in my mother's family. The eldest child, Charlotte, was twenty when the youngest, Patricia, was born. My grandmother wasn't well when Patricia arrived, and her health continued to decline in the years that followed. Caring for the new baby fell to Charlotte, and it was Charlotte who also ran the household and looked after her two younger sisters.

While her friends celebrated new jobs, marriage, and babies, Charlotte remained at home to care for her family. Even when my mother became old enough to take over, Charlotte stayed. She wanted my mother to graduate from high school and realize her dream of becoming a nurse. And then, when Charlotte was almost thirty, she married my Uncle Jack and began a life of her own.

Charlotte's dedication resulted in a powerful and resilient bond with her sisters that would last for decades. Long after she was grown and married, with a family of her own, Patricia looked up to Charlotte as her second mother.

Strong families are founded in love and selflessness.

—SBT

God Gets to Decide

*We may throw the dice,
but the Lord determines how they fall.*
PROVERBS 16:33

A sense of purpose is just one of the traits I have tried to instill in my eight-year-old daughter, Kyra. Even at her young age, she has wanted to be an artist for six years. In her imagination, she has already designed her art gallery and determined how her business will be run. She tells everyone she sees, "I am going to be an artist!"

Picture my amazement when she came running up to me one day after gymnastics and yelled, "Momma, Momma, I have changed my mind forever! I'm going to be a gymnast."

I hugged her. "Of course, honey, you can be anything you want."

She gave me a stern look. "No, Momma, God gets to decide. I can be anything He wants me to be."

"You're right, sweetheart," I replied. "He does know best." Even if it does take my little girl to remind me, I thought and smiled.

*We may know what we want,
but God makes the final decision.*

—MELISSA FIELDS

Reminders of a Previous Life

And through him God reconciled everything to himself.
He made peace with everything in heaven and on earth by
means of Christ's blood on the cross.
COLOSSIANS 1:20

Almost a century ago, my maternal grandparents left England for a new life homesteading on the prairies of Alberta, Canada. Their first home was a small hut, constructed from pieces of grassy sod. They had only the bare necessities with one extraordinary exception. My grandmother had brought two ornate vases, inherited from her mother, and they sat in the dim and dreary hut like beautiful flowers blooming in a tangle of weeds.

Did they remind my grandmother of the life she had given up to share her husband's dream? Did they make her think of the life she hoped to have in a new country? They now have a place of honor on my mantle, many years and many miles from their humble origins.

Like the vases, the cross of Jesus Christ reminds me of the life I had before I accepted Him as my savior. And it's a powerful symbol of the eternal life that lies ahead—a life He made possible through His sacrifice.

Jesus made the ultimate sacrifice for you.

—SBT

A Family of Talkers

How much better to get wisdom than gold,
and good judgment than silver!
PROVERBS 16:16

I often tell people how much my children love to talk, but the truth is that they come by it naturally. I can still hear my mother say, "Is it possible for you to be quiet for five minutes?"

I've always talked to my children—about anything and everything. When Emily was in third grade, her class went on a field trip to the beach. Later, the teacher told me that my daughter was a surprising and accurate source of information about the beach environment and the animals that lived there. When the teacher asked her how she knew so much, Emily replied, "My mom told me all about it."

Sometimes, I just let my children talk, and even though I may be tired or distracted, it's still a blessing to have children—including three teenagers—who seek me out to tell me something. Maybe it's because they know I want to hear what they have to say.

Communication is the foundation of any strong relationship,
especially the one we have with God.

—SBT

Two Beautiful Words

I focus on this one thing: Forgetting the past and looking forward to what lies ahead.
PHILIPPIANS 3:13

Joanna turned off the television with a sigh. The sit-com about a dysfunctional family wasn't funny anymore. She thought about the mistakes she'd made as she raised her daughter, Kimberly. Now, Kimberly lived five hundred miles away with a teen-age daughter of her own.

If only I knew then what I know now, Joanna thought. I would have done things differently. Maybe, then, we would have had a closer relationship today. The ringing telephone interrupted her thoughts.

"Mom?" Kimberly said. "I just had the most awful argu-ment with Heather. She broke curfew again last night. I lost my temper and said some terrible things. It made me think of you and me." Joanna's stomach tightened into a knot as she remembered similar arguments with Kimberly years earlier.

"Mom," Kimberly continued, "I never imagined how hard it would be to parent a teenager. You did the best you could, and I want to tell you something I never said before." She took a deep breath. "Thank you."

God is the only perfect parent.

—AVA PENNINGTON

She's Not There

And Christ lives within you, so even though your
body will die because of sin, the Spirit gives you
life because you have been made right with God.
ROMANS 8:10

Ten years after my mother's death, I moved across the country. I had been used to visiting her grave about once a month but, of course, that was no longer possible. Although part of me felt as though I was leaving her behind, my heart knew differently. My treasured memories and the countless things she had taught me would be with me for the rest of my life—no matter where I went.

My daughter Emily had only been eight months old when my mother died. One day, she asked me where her grandmother was buried. "That's so far away," she said when I told her.

"Yes, but your grandmother's not there."

"What do you mean?"

"The very moment she took her last breath here on earth, she entered the presence of the Lord. She's with Jesus, now."

Emily smiled. "I'm glad," she said.

"The best part is I'm going to see her again someday. It doesn't get much better than that."

Put your trust in the Lord and spend an eternity
with the ones you love.

—SBT

A Better Way

Restore to me again the joy of your salvation,
and make me willing to obey you.
PSALM 51:12

Sarah, the youngest of our four children and our only daughter, asked me for permission to rearrange her room. School was out for the summer, and I thought a project would keep her out of trouble, so I agreed as I rushed out the door to work. She decided her bed would look best on the wall covered with pictures, but the bunk bed was too tall and covered the artwork. Rather than move the pictures, she decided to make the bed fit and proceeded to saw it in half.

One of her siblings alerted me to the renovations. I assured Sarah that I knew a better way and, later that evening, we did our best to repair the damage. I wondered how often God watches our efforts to "make things fit" and wants to say, "My child, I have a better way." Too often, we resist His instruction and end up like Sarah's bed—covered with splinters and desperately in need of repair.

Resist the impulse to do things the easier way.

—SANDY MOFFETT

Mom Steps In

*Therefore He is able, once and forever, to save
those who come to God through him. He lives
forever to intercede with God on their behalf.*
HEBREWS 7:25

When my daughter Emily was in first grade, she loved school. And then, one day, everything changed. She came home crying because the boy in the desk behind her had begun calling her names.

At first, I suggested several ways she might deal with the problem, including talking to her teacher, Mr. Murray. "Oh, I can't do that," she said. "I don't want him to think I'm a tattle tale."

The next morning, she left for school full of determination to solve her dilemma but, once again, she arrived home in tears. I had hoped to give her the sense of accomplishment that comes with working out a difficult situation but, that day, I realized I had expected too much of her. It was time for me to intercede.

We went to school and talked to Mr. Murray together. He immediately moved Emily's desk, an act that told her he cared about her problems and that gave her the confidence to approach him in the future.

*Jesus always knows when to intercede,
but mothers have to learn.*

—SBT

For Her Own Good

Their children will be successful everywhere;
an entire generation of godly people will be blessed.
PSALM 112:2

"Mom, let me do this for myself, and *by* myself," my daughter said. "Let me do this alone." I never intended to stand in the way of her growing up, but those words made me realize that I was too involved in her life. I needed to step aside and give her space.

I knew I had done the right thing as I watched her walk confidently into the music room and approach the choir director. Then she auditioned to decide if choir was something in which she wanted to participate.

Sometimes letting go is the right thing to do. A sense of peace settled over me when I allowed my daughter to take control. The choir audition taught me a vital lesson in how to support her growing ability to make independent choices and take responsibility for herself.

Knowing when it's time to let go can foster confidence
in our daughters and help us gain more freedom, too.

—DEBRA WHITING ALEXANDER

The Good Fight

*I have fought the good fight, I have finished the race,
and I have remained faithful.*
2 TIMOTHY 4:7

When I was a young girl, I stayed after school twice a week for piano lessons with Mrs. Sullivan. Eventually, I became skilled enough for her to enter me in competition.

The thought of playing in front of a large crowd filled me with unrelenting anxiety. Even so, I was determined to play well and practiced faithfully. As I sat and waited for my turn, I asked God to make my hands stop sweating. I could play the song in my sleep, but I was afraid my hands were going to slip off the keys.

When I came in second, I smiled and accepted my trophy, but I felt terrible. Later, in the car, my mother asked me why I was so quiet. "I hope you're not disappointed because I didn't win," I said.

"We're too happy to be disappointed," she replied. "You did your best, and that's good enough for your father and me. You'll always be a winner in our books."

*Anyone can be a winner if they put
their trust in God and do their best.*

—SBT

310

Walking into a Deeper Relationship

But when you pray, go away by yourself, shut the door behind you, and pray to your Father in private. Then your father, who sees everything, will reward you.
MATTHEW 6:6

My daughter Natalie was moping and staring at the phone, so I invited her to go for a walk. Halfway down the block, she said, "I don't get Jason. He likes me one minute, and then he acts weird. I didn't even see him today. It's like he's avoiding me. I want to call, but I know I'm not supposed to." She bit her lip. She knew the rules.

"Things like that have happened to me," I replied. "When you don't understand something, give it to the Lord. He'll handle your fears, because He knows exactly what's going on. He already knows your tomorrows, too."

Whether the topic is boy troubles, funny stories, or matters of the heart, conversations deepen while my daughter and I walk. It's nice to be alone together without the usual distractions. Perhaps that's why God invites us to pray to Him in secret.

When we divulge ourselves to Christ, heart connections form and deep roots grow in the sacred soil of trust.

—PAMELA DOWD

Poisonous Pride

Live in harmony with each other.
Don't be too proud to enjoy the company of ordinary people.
And don't think you know it all!
ROMANS 12:16

When Emily was a junior in high school, she received excellent grades. On several occasions, she mentioned that she would, probably, be valedictorian for her senior class. Obviously, her academic successes were gratifying, but part of me found her prideful attitude rather unappealing.

Her senior year proved to be a different story. She began to have difficulty in Latin but, more importantly, she fell in love. Just after Christmas, she left home, and the word "valedictorian" was never mentioned again.

I resigned myself to the fact that she probably wouldn't graduate, but God answered my prayers. Emily finished the year and also managed to earn respectable grades. However, my greatest blessing came from witnessing her humility at the graduation ceremony. The self-satisfied smile she used to wear on report card day had been replaced with a grin that said, "Thank God I made it!"

Pride can poison success and ruin relationships.

—SBT

Cries in the Night

In my distress I cried out to the Lord;
yes, I prayed to my God for help. He heard me from his
sanctuary; my cry to him reached his ears.
PSALM 18:6

As a child, I hated going to bed. I thought all kinds of exciting things went on in my house after bedtime. As I tossed and turned, I would often cry to get out of bed.

After my wailing continued for a while, my mother would appear. What happened next depended on her level of patience that day. Most of the time, she would remind me I had school the next day, and command me to stop my nonsense and go to sleep. But occasionally, I would be allowed to get up for just a few minutes. It was never long before I quietly returned to my room.

Looking back, I think I just wanted to know that my mother heard me. She always came in to check on me. As an adult and a mother myself, I have lain in bed and cried out to my Father. I am certain that even when no one else can hear me, my Father heeds my cries and responds to my needs.

Day and night, God hears and answers our prayers.

—DONNA J. SHEPHERD

The Great Physician

*The Lord nurses them when they are sick
and restores them to health.*

PSALM 41:3

When my entire family fell victim to strep throat, I counted my blessings that I hadn't succumbed, but my relief was short-lived. Not only did I contract strep throat, I came down with the flu as well.

I felt horrible but, unlike the other patients in the house, I didn't rest or take special care of myself. One day, I was on the phone with a friend, and she asked me how I was doing. I burst into tears and said, "I want my mother. She always made me feel better."

"Of course she did, and that's because she told you to go to bed, drink fluids, and all that stuff our mothers used to tell us."

My friend was right, but she forgot one thing. A mother's touch has healing qualities that can't be found in a pill bottle. I no longer had my mother, but I did have the Lord. It was His comforting presence that helped me recover—while I rested in bed and took my medicine.

God can heal a broken bone or a broken spirit.

—SBT

Tender Heart Teen

The Lord is good to everyone.
He showers compassion on all his creation.
PSALM 145:9

A collection of brightly colored teddy bears was popular when our children were young. Each bear had a unique character and a tummy graphic to match its personality. All the children's bears had nicknames, and my younger daughter's teddy was known as "Bear-Bear."

When she became a teen, she was still very much like the teddy bear with the heart on his tummy. On the brink of a new world, she discovered that the actions and words of grownups didn't always match. While her heart still functioned as a young girl, her eyes were opened to the flawed and imperfect world of adults.

I chose my words carefully during this critical time. I wanted to make sure that the wisdom I shared came from my heavenly Father and not from my own earthly perspective.

We need to see others through the eyes of the Lord.

—LaRose Karr

God's Territory

But I lavish unfailing love for a thousand generations on those who love me and obey my commands.
DEUTERONOMY 5:10

One day, my daughter Emily told me about a friend who had just given birth to her first child. "Alan and I aren't ready to have a baby," she said. "And I don't think we'll have more than two."

"God may have other plans," I replied with a smile.

"You're right, but I don't know how you manage everything with five of us." She paused, and her face grew serious. "Can I ask you something?"

"Sure."

"Didn't you ever worry you would have enough love for all of us?"

"Oh, no. In fact, something really wonderful happened. Instead of my love being diminished with the birth of each one of you, I discovered that my capacity for love increased. As if my heart was expandable."

"I guess it's kind of like God," she said.

I nodded. "But on a much smaller, human scale. God has infinite love."

"Sometimes, it seems like you have infinite love," she replied.

I gave her arm a gentle squeeze. "Thanks, sweetheart, but infinity is definitely God's territory."

There is no limit to God's love.

—SBT

OCTOBER

Making the Team

The Sovereign LORD is my strength! He makes me as surefooted as a deer, able to tread upon the heights.
HABAKKUK 3:19

Our twelve-year-old daughter, Ann, burst through the door after school. Her eyes were red, and her face was damp with tears. Without a word, she dashed through the kitchen and, moments later, I heard the bathroom door slam shut. Then I remembered. Today the volleyball coach announced the names of the girls who made the team. Evidently, Ann had not been chosen.

"Ann, please open the door," I said. After a little more encouragement, she finally came out of the bathroom. "Sonja and Angie made the team," she said.

"I'm so sorry you didn't make it," I replied. Spending time with friends had always been important to her. The three girls often stayed overnight at each other's homes and had pizza parties. On Saturdays they went to a local park. For Ann to be separated from them for even one activity hurt her deeply.

I searched for a way to soothe her pain. "There will be other things you can do with your friends," I said. "You can have sleepovers, go shopping, and get together after school." I couldn't help but worry how this crisis would affect my usually confident daughter.

As time passed, the hurt appeared to diminish, and Ann returned to her life as a happy sixth-grader. A few months later, she made an announcement. "Mom, Mrs.

Jamison is holding tryouts for the girls' basketball team. And I'm going to be there." She looked at her older brother. "Marcus, will you help me practice after school? I want to be sure to make the team. All my friends are trying out."

"Sure, I'll help you," he replied, "but don't worry. You'll make the team."

I hope he's right, I thought. Later, as I watched Ann dribble and shoot the ball on our driveway, I questioned her ability to make the team. Still, I said a prayer and cautiously encouraged her, "Just do your best and please don't be too disappointed if you don't make it."

The day when the names of the girls who made the basketball team would be posted on the school bulletin board finally arrived. I spent my time watching the clock, baking cookies, and waiting for Ann to come home. "I didn't make the team," she said and plopped down on a kitchen chair.

"That's too bad, sweetheart," I said. Thankfully, this time there were no tears. I put the cookies on the table and sat down next to her. "Do you remember when you campaigned for student government and were elected president?" I asked. "And don't forget that you play first chair flute in band. Try to see the whole picture. Basketball isn't everything."

"But all my friends made the team. I feel so stupid being the only one not to make it."

I longed for the right words to take away her disappointment. "I know it hurts," I said. In the next days, I made a point to be there when Ann came home from school. We sat and talked at the kitchen table, and I laughed as she related the latest antics of the class clown.

319

Spending time together helped us make it through one more adolescent disaster.

In March, Ann came home full of news. "Guess what? Girls' softball is starting and I'm trying out for the team!"

I froze. Finally, I found my voice. "Oh, Ann," I said, "do you really think you should? I can't stand to see you disappointed again."

"It'll be okay, Mom. If I don't make the team, I can take it. If I can handle it, you can handle it," and we both laughed. This time, she made the team. With her teammates Sonja, Angie, and a group of other friends, she played a successful season as a catcher.

As I cheered everyone on from the bleachers, I realized what the experiences of the previous year had done for Ann. The rejection had been painful and confusing, but a wiser girl had emerged. She learned that goals aren't achieved without work, and the road to success may be peppered with disappointments. She also discovered that God had blessed her with special talents, some of which differed from the ones her friends enjoyed.

Most of all, I saw what those tough times had accomplished in our relationship. It was a bonding time for Ann and me. She needed a lot of support and encouragement to make it through the rough patches, and because I shared her struggle, we emerged a happier, stronger, and closer mother-daughter team.

—JEWELL JOHNSON

Family Forever

But Ruth replied, "Don't ask me to leave you and turn back. Wherever you go, I will go; wherever you live, I will live. Your people will be my people, and your God will be my God."
RUTH 1:16

Barbara and I didn't always get along. My mother-in-law had to discover that I would be good to her son. I needed to learn to appreciate her despite her loud ways. But we grew to love each other deeply. We shared our joys, as well as our sorrows. I held her when her younger son died tragically. Later, she held me when her other son, my husband, died after a traumatic illness.

During the eighteen years I was married to her son, Barbara and I made meals, attended births and funerals, went camping, watched movies, cleaned house, celebrated holidays, went fishing, shared secrets, and prayed to our Lord together. When my husband died, she never stopped being my mother. And I certainly didn't stop being her daughter. Three years later, when I thought of marrying again, I asked Barbara's blessing because she will always be my mother, my family, and my people. We are bound together by the same Heavenly Father!

When you believe in the same God, you share eternal love and a bond that cannot be broken.

—EVA JULIUSON

321

The Little Things You Do

Dear children, let's not merely say that we love each other;
let us show the truth by our actions.
1 JOHN 3:18

My daughter and her husband visit often. They usually arrive just before lunch, and often stay late into the evening. If I go to bed before they leave, I know there will be an e-mail from Emily waiting for me the next morning, letting me know they made it home safely and thanking me for a terrific time. It's a little thing, but it means a lot.

It's important to say, "I love you," but love is far more than just words. Movies and television characters prove their devotion with grand gestures, such as expensive gifts and flamboyant speeches, but real love is a lot less complicated. It simply means putting another person's needs before your own.

I demonstrate my love for my family daily in countless little ways. There's nothing very extravagant or impressive about laundry, cleaning, and cooking, but my family knows I do these things because I care. Just like Emily sending me a reassuring e-mail. That's love.

Put your words into action and demonstrate your love.

—SBT

Faults and Forgiveness

Make allowance for each other's faults, and
forgive anyone who offends you. Remember, the
Lord forgave you, so you must forgive others.
COLOSSIANS 3:13

The first time I took my daughter for a driving lesson, she practiced signaling and turning in the high school parking lot. After half an hour, she decided to end the lesson and got out of the car to switch places with me. I was still on the passenger's side when I felt the vehicle rolling backward. I unhooked my seat belt, stretched out my leg, and slammed on the brake.

"Why didn't you put it in park?" I yelled.

"You didn't tell me to!"

"It's common sense," I said. After I cooled off, I realized driving came automatically to me because I'd been doing it for over thirty years. My daughter was still learning the basics.

Later, I apologized. "I'm sorry," I said. "I shouldn't have assumed you knew something I hadn't taught you."

"That's okay, Mom," she said with a smile. "Can we go driving again tomorrow?"

Our children need to see us accept
responsibility for our mistakes.

—MARY LAUFER

The Payoff for Persistence

*Patient endurance is what you need now, so that
you will continue to do God's will. Then you will
receive all that he has promised.*
HEBREWS 10:36

My mother endured her share of struggles, but one of her greatest battles was fought with the scales. The medication she took to control her asthma caused weight gain, and this led her to try all sorts of diets and other weight loss products. She would lose a few pounds, become discouraged, and turn to a familiar and comforting friend—food.

Finally, she turned to the Lord. She prayed for Him to help her find a diet that would work, and she also asked to be released from her emotional need to eat. One of her friends suggested talking to a dietician at the local hospital. The dietician gave my mother a diet to follow, and the Lord gave her the strength to say no to comfort food. She lost fifty pounds, and the weight stayed off.

When the family gathered to celebrate her accomplishment, my father said, "I'm so proud of you."

My mother pointed toward the ceiling and replied, "I had lots of help."

Ask God for the strength to persevere.

—SBT

A Makeover for Mom

But if she has children or grandchildren, their first
responsibility is to show godliness at home and
repay their parents by taking care of them. This is
something that pleases God.
1 TIMOTHY 5:4

My mother-in-law lives in a delightful home, full of character, comfort, and love, but the years have taken their toll on the old place. Mildred has been a widow for several years, and despite her remarkable spirit and self-reliance, she has found it difficult to keep up with the maintenance and repairs. One of my husband's single brothers moved in just before his dad died. Kevin has been a tremendous help in keeping the wiring, plumbing, and construction in good shape, but when his four sisters got involved, they decided to do a little cosmetic surgery.

Despite being spread across the country, the girls arranged to meet for a few days at their mother's place. Once there, they went to work and redecorated the guest bedroom and upstairs bathroom. When we arrived for the unveiling, Mildred reminded me of a young girl on Christmas morning. Although she was delighted with her "new" rooms, I knew the real blessing was her daughters' thoughtful and loving gesture.

Think of a way to thank your mother
for everything she's done.

—SBT

Angels Watching Over Me

*Indeed, we all make many mistakes. For if we could control
our tongues, we would be perfect and could also control
ourselves in every other way.*
JAMES 3:2

One day, my daughter came home from school feeling humiliated and rejected. I pulled her to me and listened as the story came out between sobs. By the time she was done, I was so infuriated by one girl's comment that I jumped up and headed for the door. I didn't have a plan. God hadn't promised to send an army, or tell me to find three stones along the way. I decided I could do this on my own.

Just as I reached the door, my daughter ran to me with pleading eyes. "Mom, wait! You can't go over there. What kind of Christian example would that be?"

"Christian example? But . . ."

"Let's wait until we've calmed down and see what God says."

Her comment hit me like an unexpected blow and, suddenly, all I could think about was God allowing his only Son to die on a cross. As I held my daughter close, I realized God had sent an angel after all.

Turn your battles over to the Lord.

—JENNIE HILLIGUS

Attention to Detail

Furthermore, because we are united with Christ, we have received an inheritance from God, for he chose us in advance, and he makes everything work out according to his plan.
EPHESIANS 1:11

When I was eleven, my father accepted a new job halfway across the country. That summer, while I visited my Aunt Charlotte and Uncle Jack on their farm, my parents prepared for our move in the fall. In the letters my mother wrote to me while I was away, she filled me in on the family news, much of which detailed the huge task of getting ready for our new life.

In one letter, she told me how she had spent the morning packing up my bedroom. As I pictured her putting all of my treasured possessions in boxes, I felt a surge of panic. She put my fears to rest in the next sentence. "Don't worry, dear," she wrote, "I didn't throw anything out, and you'll be able to sort through everything when you get back."

Years later, it still moves me when I think about how well my mother knew me, and how she used that knowledge to anticipate my feelings and needs.

God takes care of every detail, no matter how small.

—SBT

Unfading Inner Beauty

*Clothe yourselves instead with the beauty that comes from
within, the unfading beauty of a gentle and quiet spirit,
which is so precious to God.*
1 PETER 3:4

Crowds swarmed into the huge church at Nyaga-hinika. It was June 26, 1988, our third Sunday in Africa. The sweltering heat was matched only by the warm smiles and gracious spirits of the Rwandese people who had enthusiastically welcomed our mission team of twenty-seven American teens and leaders.

As my sixteen-year-old daughter, Holly, and her translator, Sabamungu, approached the microphone, her face was radiant. "When I first came to Africa," she said, "I thought we had everything, and you had nothing. I assumed Americans had a corner on the market of Christianity, and we had come to teach *you*. But I had it backwards. Thank you for teaching me the true meaning of inner beauty."

Tears filled my eyes as she read 1 Peter 3:4 from her Bible and then continued her testimony. "Americans may have more earthly goods, but what you have in your hearts makes you very rich."

Inner beauty is true wealth in God's eyes.

—SANDI BANKS

The Window on Creation

Who but God goes up to heaven and comes back down?
Who holds the wind in his fists? Who wraps up the oceans in
his cloak? Who has created the whole wide world? What is
his name—and his son's name? Tell me if you know!
PROVERBS 30:4

As my mother's asthma worsened and restricted her activities, she discovered new, less strenuous interests. When she was in her fifties, she became an avid bird watcher without ever having to leave the house. Our living room had a huge picture window, making it possible for her to study a multitude of birds living in the wooded area on our property.

I would often come home from university and find her on the couch with her binoculars and the notebook in which she recorded her observations. I recall many wonderful afternoons when we talked about what she had seen that day and marveled together at God's amazing creation. Her enthusiasm for her feathered friends was contagious, and she often brought a smile to my face with her vivid descriptions.

Just as God cared for each and every bird that came to our yard, He cared for my mother by giving her a picture window and a passion for nature's wonders.

Even the smallest sparrow is a miracle of God's creation.

—SBT

The Feeling Is Mutual

I will comfort you there in Jerusalem
as a mother comforts her child.
ISAIAH 66:13

I sat and chatted with another mother while my daughter happily froliced on the playground. She raced from the climbing structure over to the seesaw, and I watched helplessly as her sandal caught on a branch. As if in slow motion, she tumbled face first to the ground. Shocked by the unexpected fall, her anguished howl didn't emerge until I scooped her up in my arms.

"Oh, sweetie. I'm so sorry you fell," I said and felt my face twist into a reflection of her agony. "I bet that really hurt, baby." As she looked up at me, gasping for calming breaths, I could tell that she knew I understood.

When we suffer, we can turn to the Lord with the confidence that he understands how we feel. The one who took on human suffering shares our pain, our fear, and our sadness. We can depend on the one who suffered for us.

The Lord feels what we feel.

—MARGOT STARBUCK

All You Need Is Another Hole in Your Head

The Lord is close to all who call on him,
yes, to all who call on him in truth.
PSALM 145:18

When my son Owen needed new clothes, my daughter Emily and her husband, Alan, offered to take Owen and me shopping. After we had finished, I assumed we would be heading home. That's when Emily announced she wanted to get her nose pierced. "For Pete's sake, why the heck would you want to do that?" I said, but Emily was determined.

That didn't stop me from asking God to inject some common sense into my daughter. Emily had a list of establishments where nose piercing was done, but we couldn't find the first place and began to look for the second. After an hour of searching, we gave up on the second place and began trying to find the third.

When we finally found it, Dylan and I waited outside while Emily and Alan went into the shop. A few minutes later, they emerged and Emily was visibly disappointed. "The guy who does the piercing isn't working tonight," she said. "Guess I'll have to come back." She never mentioned it again.

Pray about everything!

—SBT

Dressing Mother

*Treat older women as you would your
mother and treat younger women with all
purity as you would your own sisters.*
1 TIMOTHY 5:2

My two daughters have been dressing me since I was thirty-five. It started with shopping trips during which Rachel dropped not-so-subtle hints about what looked good on me. Recently, it has turned into a game where Alex misplaces items from the laundry that she thinks make me look old.

One morning, I couldn't find the sweater I always wear with my gray pants. "Girls, what do you think about this purple jacket?" I mused in a voice loud enough to draw their attention. Two teenagers rushed over and began to finger the items hanging in my closet. We are like three sisters; I am the nerdy one.

"This shirt would be great with your new jeans, Mom," Alex said. "And this fitted jacket is all the rage now." Rachel had already pulled the denim from the dresser and began to evaluate my shoes. She selected a trendy pair of slip-ons. I smiled as I perused my closet. Obviously, I would not be wearing my gray pants that day.

Mothers help us grow up. Daughters help us stay young.

—CASEY PITTS

Here I Am!

Then I heard the Lord asking, "Whom should I send as a messenger to this people? Who will go for us?" I said, "Here I am. Send me."
ISAIAH 6:8

When my daughter Emily was in elementary school, there weren't many things she loved more than playing soccer. She and her team played well, and it wasn't long before they were vying for the championship. At one point during the final game, I heard the coach ask for someone to fill in for an injured player. Emily's hand shot up, the coach nodded, and Emily jogged on to the field.

Unfortunately, her team lost that day, and the ride home was pretty dismal. "I just wanted to know what it felt like to be a champion," Emily said.

"Well, you might not be a soccer champion this year," I replied, "but you're definitely God's champion. I saw the way you responded when the coach needed someone. That's the mark of a true champion."

"Really?"

I nodded. "You bet, and I know if God called on you to do something, you'd be right there saying, 'Here I am. I'll do it!'" Emily grinned. "I wish we'd won the game, but it feels pretty good to be a champion."

God's champions are always on the winning side.

—SBT

Breaking the Mold

Ears to hear and eyes to see—both are gifts from the Lord.
PROVERBS 20:12

"May I stay home?" I couldn't believe six-year-old Jocelyn wasn't eager to join the rest of us in climbing a mountain. Her dad and I and her four siblings could hardly wait to see the view from the summit. She gave me her best smile. "I'd rather read a book."

"We'll call Grandma," I said. "You can stay with her."

It was the first of many times where my youngest daughter would choose books over long wilderness treks. It didn't bother her to be different, and she taught the rest of us that being a member of a family doesn't mean that everyone must enjoy the same activities. She may not have been my climbing partner but, to this day, she is my favorite movie or book buddy, and she never turns down a camping invitation—traveling by car. Of course, she always brings her book along!

We should allow our daughters to find their special niche instead of trying to mold them into our image.

—SANDY CATHCART

Engage Brain Before Speaking

*The wise are known for their understanding,
and pleasant words are persuasive.*
PROVERBS 16:21

After church one Sunday, my daughter Emily and I were in the kitchen deciding what to make for lunch. "It was great to see Donna," Emily said. "She told me she thought I'd lost weight."

I was distracted by our lunch preparations, but the truth is, I opened my mouth before I engaged my brain. "That was a nice thing for her to say. I do think your new haircut makes your face look thinner." As soon as the words left my mouth, I realized how terrible they sounded, and when I glanced at Emily's face, I saw tears in her eyes. "That's not what I meant to say," I said, but she had already left the kitchen.

A short time later, I went upstairs to her room and sat down on the bed. "I'm so sorry," I said. "Can you forgive me?"

She nodded slowly.

"Words are so powerful," I said. "I should be using them to build you up, not tear you down."

Seek forgiveness for the harsh words you've spoken.

—SBT

Portable Roots

Let each generation tell its children of your mighty acts;
let them proclaim your power.
PSALM 145:4

While wildfires ravaged our area, I listened to the radio by flickering candlelight and waited for evacuation announcements. "Pack one box each," my husband said.

"Things you love," I added. "The things that can't be replaced." Just like you two, I thought. I wondered about some of their choices, but we carefully tied each box closed. "Someday we'll tell stories about tonight," I promised. "Our Great Escape." I squirreled away items bequeathed to me by members of my family—objects with stories that signified God's healing and reconciliation. One day, I'd give these "portable roots" to the girls.

We were all grateful when the fires were brought under control, and I was also thankful for my recent wake-up call. Engulfed in shadows that smoky and terrifying night, I had been forced to refocus my priorities and take charge of our family memories. I still keep a list taped to the inside of a cupboard. It reads, "Things Worth Saving."

Whatever speaks of God's faithfulness is worth passing on.

—LAURIE KLEIN

Holding Hands

Yes, you have been with me from birth; from my mother's womb you have cared for me. No wonder I am always praising you!
PSALM 71:6

Emily and I had just finished lunch, and she asked if she could help me clean up. I knew she had been suffering from a headache all morning, so I told her to go and lie down for a while. She gave me a grateful smile and kissed my cheek. "You're such a good mom," she said.

I thought about what she had said while I washed the dishes. I knew I hadn't done it alone. God had taken me by the hand the day I discovered I was pregnant with my first child, and He had never let go.

He was there to comfort me when I lost two babies. And when I became pregnant again—with my daughter Emily—he calmed my fears. I felt his devoted presence when I had the ultrasound that let me know she was strong and healthy, and on the day of her birth, I pictured His smile and heard His loving congratulations. "Well done, Susan. I knew you could do it!"

God shares all of our joys and sorrows.

—SBT

The Hollers

So you see, faith by itself isn't enough. Unless it produces good deeds, it is dead and useless.
JAMES 2:17

In Middle Tennessee, the hollows or "hollers" lie between the small, steep hills. When Mother, rich in her love for the Lord, took me to help a poor family there, I saw faith in action.

At one wood-framed dwelling, Mother smiled at the frail woman standing in the doorway. "How are you today?" Mother said. "We've brought some things you might need."

A grin brightened the woman's face. "Tolerable," she replied. "Thanks." Four children peered out from behind her skinny frame. We watched as the woman took a small basin and, without ever changing the water, bathed each child in turn. When she was done, she dumped the basin's contents on the floor, scrubbed vigorously, and then swept the excess through the floor's open cracks.

As we left, I couldn't contain my astonishment. "Her walls were covered with newspapers," I said, "and it was cold in there!"

In the years that followed, it was a rare occasion when Mother had to remind me to count my blessings.

Our actions speak volumes.

—ELAINE YOUNG MCGUIRE

A Familiar Voice

My sheep listen to my voice;
I know them, and they follow me.
JOHN 10:27

I had just finished watering my pony when I heard the loud peeping come from one of the sheds. A chick had become separated from its mother, so I scooped him up and went on a search for his family.

I saw one hen with babies and put him down, but she chased him off. I remembered seeing a hen in the feed shed, and when I located her, I put the little guy down once again. She clucked, and he ran to her as fast as his little legs could carry him. He knew that voice, and he also knew exactly where he belonged.

I was reminded of the time Emily wandered away while we were shopping. When I realized she was missing, I began to call her name in a strong, clear voice and, within minutes, I saw her running toward me. Just like the chick, she knew my voice and wanted nothing more than to rejoin me.

The Lord's voice gives me clear direction
and a sense of belonging.

—SBT

Energizing Encouragement

*Let us think of ways to motivate one
another to acts of love and good works.*
HEBREWS 10:24

Ten-year-old Kelsey wasn't sure she was up to hiking to Ramsay Cascades, the highest waterfall in the Smokies. I said, "Of course you can! You're in great shape for a four-mile hike." Then I was the one who gave out. "I'm worn out," I said to the rest of the family. "I'll stay here until you come back." I ignored their teasing and sat down on a rock to wait.

After several minutes Kelsey came running back. "Come on, Mom," she said. "You can do it! The falls are so beautiful. I don't want you to miss them." I was so touched that she would return for me that I took a deep breath and allowed her to gently coax me the rest of the way up the path. The waterfalls were indeed incredible, but Kelsey's thoughtfulness in returning to encourage me was the best treat of all.

Our relationship is equally rewarding now that she's an adult, offering her mutual confidence and encouragement to me, whatever the circumstance.

*Mutual encouragement can bring unexpected
and delightful rewards.*

—LANITA BRADLEY BOYD

Comforting Chaos

For he has strengthened the bars of your gates
and blessed your children within your walls.
PSALM 147:8

I loved going to my Aunt Helen's small farm where I would quickly join whatever antics my six cousins had cooked up. With only one older brother, I relished the idea of being part of a large family, and Aunt Helen proved to be a wonderful surrogate mother. In contrast to the spotless home my mother kept, Aunt Helen's place was a haven of comforting chaos and disorder.

Years later, I had five children of my own. During a phone conversation with my aunt, I expressed my frustration in trying to keep my house in order. "It never seemed to bother you when we made a mess," I said, "and I never saw you frantically cleaning all the time."

"That's because I didn't want to waste a minute while my kids were growing up. I knew they would be gone someday, and I would have time—too much time—to keep my house in order." Her words prompted me to reexamine my priorities. The clock was ticking, and my children were waiting for me.

Your children don't require a spotless house to be happy.

—SBT

A Spirit of Adventure

Lord, through all generations, You have been our home!
PSALM 90:1

One autumn afternoon, my girls invited me outside to play. They brought me to their "house" under the tree and showed me their "food" of leaves, and their "money," which consisted of the pungent walnuts that had fallen from the tree above.

The girls had a playhouse, pretend food, and a cash register full of play money. However, they preferred the world beyond their tidy, plastic "home" where there was no pressure to assign values according to the world's standards. Unexpected elements such as the big gusts of wind and their beloved Collie added excitement not found inside four walls.

Our Christian life is best lived outside the safe confines of our home or church. We are called to seek a life of serving Christ where we may get dirty, and we may have to deal in a currency other than money. Risking the unknown can fill us with a wealth of joy that money can't buy.

God will give us what we need for all of our "adventures."

—ANITA LYNN RAMSEY

Safe in the Sky

The Lord is my light and my salvation—so why should I be afraid? The Lord is my fortress, protecting me from danger, so why should I tremble?

PSALM 27:1

One day in my women's Bible study, we were discussing God's protection, and my pastor's wife, Anne, told us about a time when she needed a reminder of God's faithfulness. After high school, her daughter Dawn enlisted in the army as a way to further her education.

Although Anne encouraged Dawn's determination to reach her goals, she couldn't help but wish there was a less dangerous path to law school.

When Dawn volunteered for the army airborne, Anne's fears for her daughter's safety became all consuming. The thought of her baby girl jumping out of airplanes was almost more than she could bear.

Dawn came home for a visit, and a tornado struck the store in which she was shopping. After an agonizing search, Anne and her husband, Ted, found their daughter unharmed. Later, Anne thanked God for keeping Dawn safe, and she realized that if He had watched over Dawn during a tornado, He would surely be there when she jumped out of a plane.

God protects those who love Him.

—SBT

A Life-Changing Melody

Let the whole earth sing to the Lord!
Each day proclaim the good news that he saves.
1 CHRONICLES 16:23

I was in the pediatrician's waiting room with my two preschoolers when two-year-old Claire and her brother decided to entertain everyone by belting out an enthusiastic rendition of "Jesus Loves Me" in perfect toddler pitch. The entire waiting room was held captive by the concert.

After trying half-heartedly to quiet them, I decided to sit back and listen. Soon, I became lost in the beauty of words I had heard all my life. My eyes grew misty as the simple song, coming from the lips of my precious children, suddenly became a clear and much needed reminder of God's love.

Claire's concert that day blessed a room full of frazzled mothers with a message more profound, perhaps, than the most eloquent sermon. Maybe next time I'll sing along!

The message of God's love is music to the ears.

—KELLY W. MIZE

Like a Kid in a Candy Store

*I tell you the truth, anyone who doesn't receive
the Kingdom of God like a child will never enter it.*
MARK 10:15

After watching a recent television special about the Atlanta Aquarium, I promised our son Connor, an aspiring marine biologist, that we would try to go to Georgia on spring break. When my daughter Emily found out about the trip, she begged to join us and before I knew it, she and her husband, Alan, were counting the days, too.

I've never been much of a traveler, and the thought of eight hours of driving each way didn't put me in a very good mood. In contrast, Emily was barely able to contain herself. She sang along to the radio, pointed out every sign and landmark, and kept telling me how much fun we were going to have.

She's acting like a kid in a candy store, I thought with a smile. I decided to forget about the long trip and take pleasure in the fact that I was getting two days off for the first time in ages. Thanks to Emily's childlike excitement, I ended up having a great trip and an unforgettable time in Atlanta.

Experience your life and your faith with childlike enthusiasm.

—SBT

Leaving the Nest

Come, my children, and listen to me,
and I will teach you to fear the Lord.
PSALM 34:11

My daughter Julie was packing for college. Boxes, clothing, shoes, CDs were strewn everywhere. Plagued by questions, I sat on her bed and surveyed the chaos. Was she ready? I wondered. Had I prepared her for college? Was she mature enough to handle all the stresses of college life? How would she survive without me? How would I survive without her?

The time had gone by so quickly. The pandemonium of these last few weeks had stolen so many precious hours. I was terrified that I was sending my lamb into a den of lions. "Can I take these bathroom rugs with me?" she asked as she came back into the room.

"Sure," I said and threw some shoes into a box.

She sat down beside me on the bed. "I sure hope that someday I will be a godly woman like you, Mom," she said. I hugged her, and I realized everything was going to be all right. She might not have all the answers, but she knew where to turn if she had questions.

God understands the pain of separation.

—CONNIE HILTON DUNN

Runaway

Oh, that I had wings like a dove;
then I would fly away and rest!
PSALM 55:6

"What's wrong?" my daughter asked me. She had called to tell me about her day, and I was uncommonly quiet.

"Oh, I'm just tired. I didn't sleep very well last night, and today has been crazier than usual. I realize it sounds childish but, sometimes, I feel like running away for a while."

"Well, you can run away for a while," she replied. "To the backyard, that is."

I laughed a little. "What are you talking about?"

"Why don't you go out back and just wander around," she said. "Get some brushes and groom the pony. Put some bread in your pocket and feed the pigeons and baby chicks. I know it doesn't sound very thrilling, but I bet it will make you feel better."

"Sounds good," I replied. I spent a couple of hours doing what Emily had suggested. I relaxed and enjoyed my animals, I marveled at God's creation, and, most importantly, I remembered how blessed I was.

We can stay at home and still get away from it all.

—SBT

Take Action

Get up, for it is your duty to tell us how to proceed in setting things straight. We are behind you, so be strong and take action.
EZRA 10:4

In 1970, I was a college junior. It was a time of campus demonstrations, antiwar protests, university closings, and National Guard troops on street corners. I watched as parents like mine came to take their daughters home.

Yet, in the midst of all this turmoil, I was determined to set my own course and return to campus for a summer job. But the job fell through, and I spiraled down into a funk. I moped around for days until my mother finally said, "Okay, get moving. It's time to look for something else." In other words, take action.

Her advice has served me well through the years. Take action. Face fears and work through problems. Have faith that everything will work out, and believe there will be better days. Of course, God said all these things first, but sometimes He uses our mothers to remind us.

Mothers who draw upon God's wisdom give strength to their daughters.

—KENDA TURNER

A Heavenly Wedding

For the Christian wife brings holiness to her marriage, and
the Christian husband brings holiness to his marriage.
1 CORINTHIANS 7:14

When my paternal grandmother, Maidie, was sixteen, she wanted to marry Robert, a forty-two-year-old
man who was boarding at her parents' house. Her mother
and father did their best to discourage the romance, but
my grandmother was unyielding. Rather than risk losing
their daughter, my great-grandparents gave the marriage
their blessing. When I asked my Aunt Helen why Madie
and Robert's relationship had been so successful, she said,
"Because they invited God to the wedding."

Many years later, I found myself with a strong-willed
daughter of my own. Emily was only eighteen when she
and Alan announced their intentions to get married. All
I could think of were reasons why they shouldn't get married, and then I remembered my grandparents.

Both Emily and Alan loved the Lord, and it was obvious
to everyone how much they cared for each other. So, like my
great-grandparents, I decided to transform my disapproval
into encouragement. Besides, I wanted to go to my daughter's wedding. I happened to know God would be there, too.

Invite God to the wedding and then
ask Him to stay for the marriage.

—SBT

349

Clutter Control

Therefore, since we are surrounded by such a huge crowd of witnesses to the life of faith, let us strip off every weight that slows us down, especially the sin that so easily trips us up. And let us run with endurance the race God has set before us.
HEBREWS 12:1

When my daughter, Cayla, and I visited my mother-in-law's new home, Cayla remarked, "Grandma, you've got too much stuff!"

My mother-in-law knew Cayla was right, and she spent the next month clearing out her clutter. God used my daughter's comment to stir something within me. I realized I had accumulated my own form of clutter. Managing three kids, work, and household obligations left little time for God. Limiting my devotional time to praying while driving and reading the Bible over breakfast was not the best recipe for spiritual growth.

After re-evaluating my priorities, I cut the clutter: unnecessary errands, kids' extra extracurricular activities, and my insistence on keeping a spotless house. Most important, I asked God for *His* priorities each day. On our next visit to Grandma's, Cayla exclaimed, "Grandma's house looks great without so much stuff!" Something tells me God thinks the same about my "spiritual house."

It's essential to control the clutter in our hearts and lives to make proper room for God.

—RENEE GRAY-WILBURN

A Spotless Birthday

For God is not unjust. He will not forget how hard you have worked for him and how you have shown your love to him by caring for other believers, as you still do.
HEBREWS 6:10

My birthday was approaching, and my daughter Emily had a confession. "I can't afford to get you anything for your birthday," she said, obviously distressed.

"It doesn't matter," I replied. "As long as you and Alan can come for my birthday dinner, I'll be happy."

"We'll be here," she said, but I could tell she was still upset. A few days later, Emily and Alan came over and, within a few minutes of their arrival, my husband insisted on taking me out for dinner. "We'll be here when you get back," Emily said. "Why don't you go and have a relaxing dinner with Dad?"

When we returned, Emily was in the kitchen, positioned like a guard in front of my incredibly dirty oven. "Ta da," she said and opened the oven door to reveal a sparkling, absolutely spotless interior. "Happy Birthday, Mom! I know how much you hate cleaning the oven."

"It's a wonderful present," I said, "but the best gift of all is the remarkable young woman who cleaned it for me."

A gift is sometimes forgotten, but a loving gesture is remembered forever.

—SBT

NOVEMBER

Tradition!

And now, dear brothers and sisters, we give you this command in the name of our Lord Jesus Christ: Stay away from all believers who live idle lives and don't follow the tradition they received from us.

2 THESSALONIANS 3:6

"*T*radition!" The song from the movie *Fiddler on the Roof* floated through my mind as I washed the turkey before stuffing it for Thanksgiving. I had been raised on Tradition with a capital T. All the family spent Thanksgiving on my grandparents' farm, and the menu never varied. As mandated by my grandfather, dinner was served at noon. There was no tolerance for late arrivals or, worse yet, not coming at all.

As the years went by, we moved too far away to visit the farm for Thanksgiving every year, but I still tried to keep up the traditions with my own three children. We built a house in the country with a spacious kitchen perfect for large family celebrations.

Eventually, my children grew up and long standing traditions began to crumble. I found myself facing Thanksgiving with one daughter in Phoenix and a son off on an out-of-state work project. Only my remaining daughter was scheduled to arrive, accompanied by her new husband.

I slapped the turkey into the pan. Thanksgiving dinner for four people was a waste of time, I thought. Where were the crowds of relatives I had counted on entertaining when we designed the house? I should have had several grandchildren by now, but our son was single, and our oldest daughter, Terry, had married an older man with three grown children. They didn't plan to have any more. In fact, they were expecting their first grandchild. My last hope for grandchildren was my youngest daughter, but she suffered from multiple sclerosis and wasn't sure she should even try to have a child.

The phone rang. It was my daughter, calling from Phoenix. She and her husband had gone there to visit his sons and taken a turkey for their celebration. One son was recently married and they were at his house. When I pictured the crowd of relatives gathered there, my mood worsened.

"Mom," Terry said. "When we got here, everyone expected me to make Thanksgiving dinner. I've never done it before. What am I supposed to do?" The tone of her voice reminded me of when she was a child and announced that she didn't ever want to be a grownup—it was too hard. Well, you're the grownup now, I thought. The rest of the family figure you should know how to do this.

"They don't even have a pan big enough for the turkey," she wailed. "They just moved in. Help!"

"Send Herb to the store for one of those big, disposable roasting pans," I said. "While he's doing that, I'll tell you how to get the turkey ready." My husband took over our preparations while I talked Terry through hers.

A little while later, the phone rang again. "Mom, could you tell me how Dad does the sweet potatoes? I know there are directions on the can, but I want mine to be just like his." Aha, I thought. Tradition! I put my husband on the phone.

Our other daughter and her husband arrived, and as we prepared to sit down for our dinner, she gave him a running commentary. "This is my Grandmother Campion's china and my other grandmother made the table-cloth. And these are our special mashed potatoes. They have secret ingredients. We have to have them every year." I smiled. Tradition was making a comeback.

Of course, the phone rang again. "Mom," Terry said. "How hot should the oven be for the pumpkin pie? Will this canned stuff be any good? I know you always use real pumpkins."

"Yes, Terry," I replied, "canned will be fine. I use it when I run out of the other. It tastes the same."

"Oh, that's good. I'm sorry I've interrupted you so much. Have a good dinner, Mom."

"You, too, sweetheart. And I'd like you to call once more. Let me know how everything turned out, okay?"

A few hours later, she phoned with the good news. "Everything was great. Herb and the boys loved it. I never imagined I could cook a whole Thanksgiving dinner!"

I couldn't resist teasing her a little. "I guess that officially makes you one of the grownups."

She laughed. "Yeah, and it was wonderful to have our traditional family dishes even though I wasn't at home."

I've since learned to let go of my expectations for the perfect Thanksgiving. With adult children who have new in-laws and friends, I can't always have it my way. The next year, anxious to show off her new skills, Terry invited us all to her house. The guest list included her in-laws and a man and his son without their wife and mother for the first time. She made everything except for a few side dishes the rest of us brought. Our younger daughter provided the secret mashed potatoes, after obtaining the recipe from me. Seeing my daughters taking their places among the adults made up for the fact that we weren't in my house.

I remembered the first Thanksgiving that my husband and I didn't spend with my parents. I worried how they would manage with just the two of them and hurried to their home that evening to console them. They were relaxing on the couch as my father watched football, and my mother knitted. The house was spotless. "You should have waited for me to help clean up," I said.

"There was nothing to clean up," my mother replied. "We had turkey TV dinners while your dad watched his game. It was wonderful. I didn't have to get up early. There was no cooking and no cleanup."

I was horrified. TV dinners for Thanksgiving! Suddenly, I understood that one of the reasons my mother preserved all of our traditions was so I could pass them down to my family. But traditions aren't cast in stone. When we marry, the Bible instructs us to leave our families and cleave to our new spouses. We may lose some of our family traditions, but that's how new ones are created.

This year, we were blessed with another generation to carry on our traditions. Our youngest daughter gave birth to a son. I wrapped him in a quilt my mother made for one of her nephews more than fifty years ago. A new baby in an antique quilt—how's that for passing on family traditions?

—Jean Campion

Returning the Favor

*And all the believers met together in one place
and shared everything they had.*
ACTS 2:44

Everyone was in an exceptional mood as we left the grocery store. I turned to my children and said, "Okay, who wants to ride the carnival horse first?"

In unison, my two elated children replied, "Me! Me!" I dug into my purse and realized with horror that I only had one quarter. How I hated to tell them they couldn't ride. Slowly, I began my disappointing explanation.

"That's okay, Momma," Kyra said. "Richy can ride this time, I don't mind."

Tears came to my eyes as I realized how she wanted to help by relinquishing her ride.

"All right, Richy," I said. "Climb up."

I heard an exclamation of glee. "Look guys, look," he said. "There's already a quarter in the slot. Now Kyra can ride too!" I'm quite sure my little girl left that day with a clear message of how God rewards us when we think of others first.

Give of yourself and God will return the favor.

—MELISSA FIELDS

Too Much Imagination

The name of the Lord is a strong fortress;
the godly run to him and are safe.
PROVERBS 18:10

For several years, I lived in a town nestled in the midst of a large wilderness area. Rarely, a cougar would find its way into town, but it usually wasn't long before the unwanted visitor was captured and relocated. A few days after one of these incidents, I put Emily in her stroller and headed down the dirt path behind my house to visit a friend.

Suddenly, I heard a rustle in the bushes beside me, and visions of the recently captured cougar filled my head. I tried to think of something else, but I kept listening for further noises and, before I knew it, I was practically running.

Abruptly, I came to a stop. "Enough is enough," I told my sleeping baby. I took several deep breaths and began to recite every prayer and Bible verse I could think of. My steps slowed and my heart stopped racing.

My friend greeted me at her door. "It's a beautiful day for a walk," she said.

I smiled and nodded. Especially if you remember God is walking with you, I thought.

You are never alone.

—SBT

Special Sandwiches

Blessed are those who are generous,
because they feed the poor.
PROVERBS 22:9

My thirteen-year-old daughter came home from her church youth group full of enthusiasm. "We're going to make peanut butter and jelly sandwiches for the homeless," she said.

"That's a great idea," I replied.

"We're going to take the food into the city, under the bridges where the homeless people live."

My stomach tightened. I didn't realize that the kids planned to deliver the sandwiches! I knew they'd be supervised, but there was crime in that area, and I feared for my daughter's safety. Part of me also wanted to protect her from seeing such a harsh side of the world.

But, after praying about it, I allowed her to go, and I was glad I did. The experience opened her eyes to the plight of the homeless and gave her the feeling that she made a difference in their lives.

We should encourage generosity in our daughters, even if it means extending their horizons beyond our comfort zones.

—MARY LAUFER

The Hunt for Happiness

*Take delight in the Lord,
and he will give you your heart's desires.*
PSALM 37:4

When I was a young girl, I was convinced that if I had a horse of my own, my life would be perfect. I adored my horse, but my life was far from ideal. As I grew older, my desires changed, and each time, I fell into the trap of expecting happiness from people and material possessions.

One day I told my mother of my growing disillusionment. "The Bible says that if I love the Lord, He will give me my heart's desire," I said.

"And what do you really want?" she replied.

I hesitated for a moment. "I guess I just want to be happy."

She smiled. "Well, I think you might have things backwards. Instead of looking for happiness in earthly pleasures, perhaps you should look to God. If you place Him above everything else, then you'll discover the true desires of your heart."

My mother was right. As my love for the Lord grew, and I put Him first in my life, I was blessed beyond anything I could have imagined.

Following God is the way to your heart's desire.

—SBT

Name Brand Needs

And why worry about your clothes? Look at the lilies and how they grow. They don't work or make their clothing.
MATTHEW 6:28

As we walked through the crowded parking lot, my daughter hung her head. "Cheer up," I said. "God knows you need school clothes."

"I don't want anyone to see me here. Only nerds shop here."

"If someone sees you, maybe it's because they're shopping here, too."

Her face relaxed in a smile. "I never thought of that." She carried her head a little higher.

The girls at school could be so cruel. I hated to see her teased, but we couldn't afford name-brand jeans.

On the way home, I reminded Heather that her new jeans looked nice. "You don't need name brands."

She nodded but, this time, there was no smile.

At church the following day, a friend gave me a bag of second-hand clothes. Perhaps there will be some stuff for Heather, I thought. We lugged the big bag to her room where we discovered lots of great clothes, including three pairs of name-brand jeans. "It's everything I need!" she said.

God knows exactly what you need.

—DONNA SUNDBLAD

Thanks for Everything

And give thanks for everything to God the Father in the name of our Lord Jesus Christ.
EPHESIANS 5:20

For my mother, saying "thank you" wasn't just a courtesy; it was a necessity. She taught my brother and I to write thank-you notes at an early age. "Someone took the time to pick out your gift and wrap it," she would say. "You can take the time to recognize their thoughtfulness."

The size of the gift was unimportant, and it didn't matter if I lacked the inspiration to thank Aunt Ruth for another pair of scratchy knitted slippers. Everyone received a note. Even now, gifts to members of our family receive an acknowledgment—all five of my children are veteran note writers.

It's not much different when it comes to thanking God. The Bible instructs me to thank Him for everything, from the tiniest blessing to the greatest miracle, from the most joyous gifts to the trials and tribulations that come my way. Because as my mother taught me, everything—even Aunt Ruth's scratchy slippers—deserves a thank-you.

Expressing gratitude to God is a spiritual essential.

—SBT

Remarkable Resolve

For you know that when your faith is tested,
your endurance has a chance to grow.
JAMES 1:3

My daughter Melissa could barely contain her excitement. "Guess what?" she said. "I'm going to Siberia to teach English and do mission work."

"Siberia?" I answered in a small voice. I immediately thought about the distance and frigid weather. My mind reeled with fresh worries. What about health care, I wondered? Was the country politically stable? Though I wouldn't attempt to stop her from testing her wings, I questioned the wisdom of her decision.

After she left, I finally found peace through prayer, but then the call came. "Mom, I had an accident," she said, obviously crying. "My knee is really torn up. I have to come home for surgery and rehab."

A twenty-four hour flight home with a full leg cast was only the beginning of Melissa's newest challenge. After surgery, she suffered through months of painful rehab. When she returned to Siberia, I was both amazed and inspired.

Patient endurance of testing and trials strengthens character.

—ELAINE YOUNG MCGUIRE

The Floodlight of Faith

If you are filled with light, with no dark corners,
then your whole life will be radiant, as though a
floodlight were filling you with light.
LUKE 11:36

The vast geographical distance between my father and me has limited our physical contact, but has done nothing to diminish the love we share. So when my brother phoned to tell me that our father was seriously ill, I could think of little else. Several times a day, I would find a place to be alone—never an easy task with five children—and pour my heart out to the Lord.

One afternoon, feeling particularly disheartened, I sat down at my computer to check my mail. The first message I read came from my daughter. It said, "Thanks for being in my life. I praise God every day for making you my mother."

Emily's love shone through her words and warmed my heart. She brought light to my darkened spirits, and I thanked God for reminding me of how blessed I am—no matter what happens.

Be filled with the light that comes from loving the Lord.

—SBT

Instructional Insomnia

I am leaving you with a gift—peace of mind and heart.
And the peace I give is a gift the world cannot give.
So don't be troubled or afraid.
JOHN 14:27

For three long years after the birth of my first baby, a good night's sleep was only a fond memory. Not only was she a fussy baby, daughter number two came along only a year later. They tag-teamed it, waking me up every few hours.

At first, I said, "This too shall pass," and invested in an economy size tube of under-eye concealer. When sleep deprivation became the status quo, I purchased my own espresso machine. I could whip up a skinny mocha triple-shot cappuccino in no time—even while jiggling a crying infant.

Those years didn't meet my picture book expectations of motherhood, but I did learn to depend on God to get me through the day. There were times when I cried out to Him as loudly as my little ones cried for me. This wouldn't have happened with contented, easy-going babies. It's a good thing my God is faithful, and the best part is, He never sleeps either.

Jesus didn't guarantee a stress-free life, but He promised to give us peace during our stressful times.

—MICHELLE GRIEP

Beneath the Surface

Look beneath the surface so you can judge correctly.
JOHN 7:24

I happen to think my daughter Emily is a beautiful young woman, but her response to my compliments rarely varies. "You have to say that," she argues, "because you're my mother."

Emily has never seen herself as attractive, and the other day I received a profound insight into part of the problem. We were watching television, and it seemed like every show we turned to was overpopulated with "perfect" people. Perfect bodies, perfect hair, and perfect smiles in abundance. I looked over at Emily and wondered how often she compared herself to these representatives of the world's idea of beauty.

Maybe it was time to remind her that I used to see myself in the same way. That is, until God changed the way I felt about everything including my appearance. I got up and turned off the television. "Hey," I said, "let's take the dogs for a walk. We haven't had a chance to talk since you got here."

God can help you change the way you see yourself.

—SBT

The Musical Connection

Are any of you suffering hardships? You should pray.
Are any of you happy? You should sing praises.
JAMES 5:13

For my fifty-fifth birthday, my daughter Melissa took me to an Anne Murray concert. As a foster child, she had witnessed my house cleaning ritual of playing an Anne Murray record while I worked. It wasn't long before she became a part of the routine, the two of us dancing to "Daydream Believer" and other great songs. Anne's wonderful music provided the soundtrack for much of our lives in those years.

On the night of the concert, as the lights dimmed, so did the difficult times we had known as mother and daughter. We watched Anne step onto the stage, singing an old familiar song and, suddenly, we were back in Nebraska, dancing around the living room together, dusting cloths in hand. During intermission, Melissa told me that the music reminded her of some of our best and craziest times together. Who could have ever known that a simple music ritual would connect our hearts so many years later?

God has given us the joy of music to connect our hearts in deep and lasting ways.

—KATHRYN WILSON

No Mistake

I knew you before I formed you in your mother's womb.
Before you were born I set you apart and appointed
you as my prophet to the nations.
JEREMIAH 1:5

I never tired of hearing my mother's account of how she and my father met. It sounded like a story straight out of one of my books of fairy tales. One day, she added a most intriguing detail. As it turned out, when she met my father, she was already engaged to a man named George. I relished this juicy tidbit for a few moments, although I was a little baffled. And then, it all made sense. "So, if you had married George," I said, "he would be my father."

My mother grinned and gave me a hug. "No, sweetheart," she replied. "God had it all worked out, even before you were born. In fact, He had everything planned before I was born, or anyone else for that matter. His plan is perfect, and He found the perfect father for you."

I decided to try and figure it out later. "Well," I said, "I'm really glad you didn't marry George because I'm happy with the father I've got." My mother just laughed.

Rejoice in knowing that God never makes mistakes.

—SBT

Operation Eighty Candles

Love each other with genuine affection,
and take delight in honoring each other.
ROMANS 12:10

For her eightieth birthday, my mother asked for a family celebration away from home. With everyone spread out across the country, my sister and I had to wonder: can we pull this off, and get everyone in one place? Thus, "Operation Eighty Candles" was born. We went to work on orchestrating the details and getting everyone on board with party plans.

With synchronized watches, charged cell phones, and a craving for coffee, eleven of us converged, one by one, on the "Emerald City." The weather in Seattle honored the celebration, too. Instead of rain, the sun washed over our weekend in the middle of January and lit up a brittle blue sky.

We knew our coming together under perfect conditions was no accident—God had orchestrated it. We raised our glasses to honor the woman who has never stopped serving us faithfully and loving us no matter what. Our cups overflowed with gratitude—mission accomplished!

When we honor our mother, we honor the life God gave us.

—DEBRA WHITING ALEXANDER

A Firm Foundation

Having carefully investigated everything from the beginning, I also have decided to write a careful account for you, most honorable Theophilus, so you can be certain of the truth of everything you were taught.

LUKE 1:3–4

As soon as I learned to read, I devoured every book in sight, but my favorite tales came from my mother. It didn't matter how many times I heard her anecdotes about life during the Great Depression or the romantic saga of how she met my father; everything she said fascinated me.

I now realize that my mother used her stories to teach me Biblical principles. In the same way that the Bible honored godly people by recounting their lives, my mother used her memories to pay homage to the significant people in her life.

As my children grew up, I discovered how much they enjoyed hearing stories about their grandmother, as well the ones from my own life. Emily, in particular, seemed to relish my trips into the past. Invariably, she would be the last one at the kitchen table, asking questions and wanting more. I'm not sure I've been able to fill my mother's shoes as family historian, but I will always be grateful for the opportunity.

Give your children roots by sharing your family history.

—SBT

Personalized Gifts

What sorrow awaits those who argue with their Creator.
Does a clay pot argue with its maker?
ISAIAH 45:9

I hated being me! My siblings were A students, but I was just average. When our report cards came home, I'd whimper to Mom, "I'm so sorry."

Mom would hug me and say, "You have many fine qualities. Someday, you'll realize how gifted you are." I felt there was an unwritten law requiring mothers to say that, so I didn't take her seriously. My entire world revolved around grades, but that changed.

God swept me into a life where I discovered my talents and put them to maximum use. My husband developed multiple sclerosis early in our marriage. I had always been gifted at nursing and willing to work hard. Thanks to God, I was able to take care of John for thirty years, until he went home to Jesus. I wish I could tell Mom how right she was, but I suspect she already knows!

God knows what we need and blesses us
with exactly the right gifts.

—LAURA L. BRADFORD

Revival

The Lord will work out his plans for my life—
for your faithful love, O Lord, endures forever.
Don't abandon me, for you made me.
PSALM 138:8

One afternoon, Emily and I discovered a hen sitting in a regal pose, her newly hatched chicks all tucked safely beneath her. As I closed the pen's door, I saw a chick lying in the mud. At first glance, I decided it had hatched and then died. "Poor thing," I said.

Emily picked up the tiny bird and cradled it in her hands. "I think it's still alive," she replied.

I put the chick in the incubator with some turkey eggs I hoped to hatch. A few hours later, we were in the kitchen preparing dinner and, suddenly, we heard muffled cheeping coming from the other room. Emily hurried to the incubator and lifted the lid. "He's alive," she said.

Sure enough, when I peered into the incubator, there stood the chick with his feathers fluffed out and his bright, black eyes staring up at me. That night, as I crept through the darkness to return him to his mother, I thought of the countless times my faith had revived me, and God's love had sustained me.

Allow God's love to give you new life.

—SBT

The Game of Life

The Lord leads with unfailing love and faithfulness all who keep his covenant and obey his demands.

PSALM 25:10

Recently, I bought a Monopoly game at the Goodwill store. I remembered the hours spent playing the game in my childhood, and I hoped my daughters would enjoy it as well. The game was in great shape, except the rules were missing. Unfazed, my girls invented their own rules.

I hadn't played Monopoly in twenty-five years and couldn't remember the rules. After a week of watching them play their way, I printed genuine Monopoly rules off the Internet. I was certain the girls would be glad to know the real way to play the game. To my surprise, they didn't like the real rules. They liked their version better and had to be convinced to play the right way. Too often in life, we make up our own rules. Rather than observing God's commandments, we prefer to do things according to how we think they should be done. However, I've learned that we can't break God's "rules" and expect His blessings.

To win at the game of life, we must play by God's rules.

—ANGIE VIK

Treasure the Time

Lord, remind me how brief my time on earth will be.
Remind me that my days are numbered—how
fleeting my life is.
PSALM 39:4

Like most children, I resisted returning to school after a vacation. My father taught at the university, so his breaks usually coincided with mine, and I recall my mother saying how much she hated to see us go back to school and work. Somehow, it softened my reluctance to know how much she would miss me.

Recently, at my women's Bible study, one of the mothers remarked how much she dreaded the beginning of spring break. While several women agreed with her, my friend Cheryl and I remained silent. "I guess there's something wrong with me," I whispered to Cheryl. "I love having the kids at home." She smiled and nodded. "Me, too!"

Admittedly, having the gang home for the holidays can be chaotic, exhausting, and stressful, but I know it won't be long before spring breaks and summer vacations are relegated to the past. So, for now, I'll cherish the draining and demanding days, and when the children go back to school, I'll make sure they know how much I'll miss them.

Treasure the special times before they become memories.

—SBT

375

Just a Minute

I love all who love me. Those who search will surely find me.
PROVERBS 8:17

My daughter, Lauren, called to me from the family room. "Mom, come and see what I've made with my Legos."

"Just a minute," I replied. "Wait until I load the dishwasher."

There was silence for a moment, and then I heard Lauren mutter. "Why don't you tell the dishwasher to wait a minute?" The exasperation in her voice made me wonder how many times a day I used that expression. How many times did I ask her to wait while I did some meaningless task?

How often do we say "just a minute" when we know we should stop and pray, or call a friend who's been absent from church? Minutes can easily turn into hours, days, and perhaps weeks. I need to stop and ask myself if what I'm doing is more important than seeking God's direction in my life.

Make a habit of putting God first.

—JEANETTE MACMILLAN

Fresh Mercies Every Morning

Great is His faithfulness;
His mercies begin afresh each morning.
LAMENTATIONS 3:23

"I've had a terrible day," my daughter Emily said, and I asked her to tell me about it. As is often the case, it hadn't been a major crisis, but a series of irritating and frustrating occurrences that spoiled her day. Things like the coffee maker overflowing, the arrival of the dreaded electric bill, and the cat being sick all over the couch.

I listened and offered my sympathies, and then I asked her a few questions. "Is Alan okay?"

"Yes, he's fine."

"Do you have a place to live and food in the cupboards?"

"I know what you're doing," she said. "And I've tried to count my blessings, but it's not working."

"I know how that feels," I replied. "Sometimes, I'm just grateful that the day is over, and I have a warm bed to crawl into. I thank God for my blessings and remember that He gives me a fresh start every morning."

"You know, Mom, today wasn't all bad."

"How so?" I replied.

"You called and cheered me up."

Even the worst day contains a multitude of blessings.

—SBT

Shall We Pray?

Pray in the Spirit at all times and on every occasion.
EPHESIANS 6:18

The clock chimed midnight. My girls clambered out of their sleeping bags at our friend's house, and we headed home. That evening's Bible study had been rich with the Lord's goodness and filled me with a sense of peace. Little did I know that I would be putting that night's lesson into practice in only a short while.

As I fumbled for my keys at the doorway of our pitch-black house, I made a horrifying discovery. I had no house key. It was now one in the morning. The neighborhood was dark and all too quiet. In desperation, I tried every key on the key ring. None of them worked, and I began to panic.

My seven-year-old daughter Laura's voice startled me. "We need to pray, Mommy!" she said and proceeded to recite a beautiful prayer, brimming with childlike faith.

I decided to try the office key again and, to my amazement, the door opened. "I can't believe it," I said.

"Why, Mommy?" Laura asked. "We prayed—remember?"

The faith of a child can work wonders.

—SANDI BANKS

Caring Correspondence

*Dear brothers and sisters, I close my letter with
these last words: Be joyful. Grow to maturity.
Encourage each other. Live in harmony and peace.
Then the God of love and peace will be with you.*
2 CORINTHIANS 13:11

I come from a family of letter writers. My mother communicated with her sisters via long, newsy epistles that she insisted on reading to me. And whenever I received a gift from one of my relatives, I was expected to send a thank-you note almost immediately. I continued the letter writing tradition after I left home, and whenever I received a letter from one of my aunts, I would phone my mother and share the family news.

When my brother sent my daughter, Emily, one of his original paintings as a wedding gift, my first words were, "Did you send him a thank-you note?"

"Yes, Mom," she replied in a somewhat exasperated tone, as if the effort had taken every ounce of energy she possessed. Consequently, I was surprised when, a few weeks later, she told me she had written a four-page letter to my brother. "Would you like to hear it?" she said.

"Of course," I replied. Three generations of letter writers, I thought. What a blessing!

*Reach out with a letter and let the special people in your life
know you're thinking about them.*

—SBT

Being There

Even if my father and mother abandon me,
the Lord will hold me close.
PSALM 27:10

I felt wistful as my husband and I stood in the darkness of our daughter's bedroom and watched her sleep. It was the week before her third birthday, and she was spending the night in her big girl bed for the very first time. The next morning found me in a nostalgic mood. "This morning you are two," I said to my little girl.

"Three!" she interjected proudly.

"Then you will be four, five, six," I said. "You will go to elementary school, and middle school, and high school, and college."

A look of concern appeared on her face. "Are you going to go to all those things with me, Mom?"

Oh, how I wish I could, I thought, and reassured her that she would be with me as long as she needed to be. Although I won't be present at every moment of my daughter's journey, I have every confidence that God will be there every single step of the way.

The Lord will never leave or forsake us.

—MARGOT STARBUCK

From Regret to Rejoicing

So now there is no condemnation
for those who belong to Christ Jesus.
ROMAN 8:1

A mother's death can be especially hard if the relationship between parent and child was fractured by negative feelings or unresolved differences. When my mother died, I felt blessed that I didn't have to deal with the additional pain of longing for a relationship that never existed. However, it wasn't long before I realized I had been left with the unwanted baggage of guilt, all the same.

I did my best to focus on positive things. However, like the taunting of a childhood bully, my mind kept taking me back to the times I hurt my mother's feelings, the thoughtless moments when I said something I later regretted, and the missed opportunities to show her how much she meant to me.

I knew God had forgiven me, but I was unable to forgive myself. It was only when I asked him to help free me from the darkness of regret that the brilliance of my beautiful memories came back. There are still a few tears when I think of my mother, but they are far outnumbered by the smiles.

God can help you replace guilt with gratitude.

—SBT

The Sweet Sound of Laughter

And so, my children, listen to me,
for all who follow my ways are joyful.
PROVERBS 8:32

In the years after I left home, I returned as often as possible to see my family. Some of my most treasured memories are of the evenings when we would sit around the table after dinner. We would talk about everything, and there was always laughter. My brother and father shared my dry, often sarcastic sense of humor and we frequently laughed until there were tears in our eyes. My mother, obviously amused by our antics, would smile and shrug as if unable to explain our foolishness.

I always dreamed of having a big family and hoped that once my children left home, they, too, would return often. My daughter and her husband have granted my wish with their frequent visits. And, as in years past, we gather around the table after dinner to talk and laugh.

One evening, after Emily and Alan had gone home, my husband smiled and told me how much he loved to hear me laugh. "I laugh because I'm happy," I said. "I never knew life could be so sweet."

Simple pleasures can bring great joy.

—SBT

Worth a Million

But let us who live in the light be clearheaded,
protected by the armor of faith and love, and wearing
as our helmet the confidence of our salvation.
1 THESSALONIANS 5:8

Parental chaperones are rarely popular. When Melissa heard we would be joining her youth group on a camping trip, she wasn't pleased. "Why do you guys always have to go?" she asked before proceeding to spend most of the trip with her friends.

Everything changed one starless night. I woke to the sound of the tent's zipper and heard a whisper. "Mom, are you awake? I need to go the bathroom. Will you come with me?"

"I'll get my shoes on," I replied.

"Mom," Melissa said on the way back, "I'm so glad you're here."

Suddenly, I didn't need any stars overhead—not with the light shining in my heart. As I rejoiced that my daughter trusted me in her time of need, I remembered how God is ready to help us. Even in the middle of the night. When I crawled back into bed, my husband stirred. "Everything okay?" he asked.

"Oh, yes," I replied. "I feel like someone just gave me a million dollars."

A mother's faith shines a light for her daughter.

—KENDA TURNER

A Plan for Panda

This foolish plan of God is wiser than the wisest of human plans, and God's weakness is stronger than the greatest of human strength.
1 CORINTHIANS 1:25

When my daughter's beloved Chihuahua died suddenly, I knew her heart was broken, but she resisted my best attempts to console her. On an impulse, I brought home a Pekingese puppy, which the family named Panda. I desperately wanted to bring a smile to Emily's face once again, but she barely acknowledged the dog's presence. After she moved out, it wasn't long before Panda and I became inseparable.

Over the next two years, my prayers were answered as Emily and I rebuilt our relationship and embarked on a wonderful new journey as friends. The other night, during one of her frequent visits, she offered to take the dog for a walk. "You know," she said, "I've never thanked you for buying Panda to cheer me up, and I'm sorry."

"That's okay, sweetheart," I replied. "God always works things out. He knew you needed to spread your wings, and He also knew I needed a sweet, little dog to keep me company when you were gone."

God will always work things out according to His wonderful plan.

—SBT

A Work in Progress

*And I am certain that God, who began the good work
within you, will continue his work until it is finally
finished on the day when Christ Jesus returns.*
PHILIPPIANS 1:6

My friend Steph watched twelve-year-old Lauren kick the soccer ball into the opposing team's goal as the game ended. She searched for the right words on the ride home as tears streaked her daughter's face. "Honey, you'll do better next time."

"I'm quitting," Lauren said.

Steph resisted the urge to help her take the easy way out. If Lauren quit now, she'd see herself as a failure for the rest of her life. "You're not the only one who has made that kind of mistake," Steph said. "Something similar happened to a young man in the first half of a college bowl game."

"I'll bet he never played again, either."

"Wrong. His coach put him back in after half time. People say he played the best game of his life in that second half." Steph put her arm around her daughter. "Please finish the season. If you still want to quit, you can do it then."

Lauren straightened her shoulders and took a deep breath. "Okay," she said. "It's a deal."

God doesn't stop working in our lives just because we fail.

—AVA PENNINGTON

Emily's Fruit

But the Holy Spirit produces this kind of fruit in our lives: love, joy, peace, patience, kindness, goodness, faithfulness, gentleness, and self-control.
There is no law against these things!
GALATIANS 5:22–23

Like most little brothers, Owen has always done his best to be a major aggravation to his four older siblings. At a very young age, he discovered exactly how to bother and annoy each one. His three brothers learned to deal with the persistent pest, but when Emily was still living at home, I had to referee daily battles. The relationship deteriorated to the point where Emily admitted that she couldn't wait to leave home and get away from Owen.

In the months since she left, I've been blessed to witness the miraculous results of God working in her life. Nowhere is this more apparent than in her relationship with Owen. Her love, patience, and gentleness have produced a powerful bond between them. Owen often phones her as soon as he comes home from school, and he has gone to stay with Emily and her husband, Alan, in Richmond on several occasions.

Emily is not the same young woman who left here just over a year ago. Just ask Owen!

God can repair even the most damaged relationships.

—SBT

Wisdom of the Heart

The greater my wisdom, the greater my grief.
To increase knowledge only increases sorrow.
ECCLESIASTES 1:18

My mother came from a family of four girls and one boy. Money was scarce, but my grandparents set up a fund so my uncle could attend university. When my mother talked about her brother's academic achievements, I could hear the longing in her voice, and I knew she wished there had been a way for her to attend university, too. A few years later, she married my father. He was a teacher who returned to university for graduate work. Although I attended college for only three years, my brother had a fairly extensive academic career.

My mother was gifted in so many ways but, on occasion, I think her "intellectual" family intimidated her. I now realize that true knowledge doesn't necessarily come from classrooms or books. As a grown woman with children of my own, I am less interested in gathering college credits than in obtaining the wisdom that comes from loving the Lord.

Turn to your Bible for inspired, infallible,
and inerrant knowledge.

—SBT

DECEMBER

God, The Father

Father to the fatherless, defender of widows—
this is God, whose dwelling is holy.
PSALM 68:5

*M*y heart ached as I held my hurting child. "Mommy, I miss him," Lydia whispered. Her brave front had finally crumbled. We clung to each other, seeking answers and comfort. Lydia's father had left our home two weeks earlier—only days before his fiftieth birthday. My husband and I had shared marriage and family, friends, and church leadership for almost twenty-nine years. How could I explain a situation to my eleven-year-old when it was a total mystery to me?

We sat together on her bed and continued our nightly routine. We talked about her day and, then, I asked her how she felt about her dad. My little prayer warrior had no words of her own, so we sang songs together, just as we had done at bedtime for years. We sang of God's love and faithfulness and how He would guide and care for us. After I wished her sweet dreams, I shut her door behind me and prayed that her plug-in nightlight would shine for her as hope in the darkness.

That was only the first of many incidents where we had to face the fact that the life we had known was over. Lydia and I were floundering in a sea of change. My older daughter had left for her first year of college just weeks before, and with my husband gone, I felt like the single mother of an only child.

Lydia and I were given plenty of opportunities to trust God and build our faith. She experienced rejection, abandonment, and confusion when she didn't hear from her dad for days at a time. We would pray together and ask God to be a Father to her in a tangible way. As I began to feel the pressure of my financial burdens, I asked Lydia to pray with me for peace in knowing that God would provide for us. We prayed about everything, and when something good happened, we praised God for working in our lives.

Meanwhile, I talked to my eighteen-year-old on the phone everyday. Amelia, an inexperienced freshman, seemed to be struggling with the thought of our broken family even more than the two of us left at home. As December approached and thoughts of the holidays loomed, she worried constantly about what Christmas would be like. Our traditions of going out to cut a tree, decorating the house, attending the Christmas Eve service, and opening gifts became sources of potential disaster instead of familiar enjoyment. It was obvious she longed for stability and certainty in the midst of chaos, but all I had to offer was God's faithfulness. I told her the same thing I had shared with Lydia. "Learn to let God be a Father to you."

When Amelia came home from school for Christmas break, she and I shared many conversations over coffee. Her boyfriend had also returned home for the holidays, so their relationship was a common topic. "With everything that has happened with Dad, I don't think I ever want to get married."

"Oh, Honey," I replied. "I still believe in marriage and family. I'm not angry, and I don't hate your dad. Don't let our problems steal the joy that you have with someone you love."

Tears filled Amelia's eyes. "Why doesn't God fix everything for us?" she asked.

I took a deep breath and attempted to explain. "I'm beginning to believe that God has a totally different idea of what He wants for us than what we think we want. He seems to be more interested in drawing us all closer to Him than He is in fixing our problems."

"That doesn't seem right."

I laughed. "It certainly doesn't feel right, and it sure doesn't make sense, but maybe it will someday."

Someone loaned us an artificial tree, and we christened it our "permanent Christmas tree." I decorated the house with our nativity sets one afternoon to surprise the girls when they came home from Christmas shopping. Surrounded by happy families with fathers, we made it through the Christmas Eve service, but Christmas Day was still ahead. What would things be like without a daddy and a husband?

I filled the stockings hanging on the fireplace and crawled into bed, not knowing what the morning would hold. I prayed for wisdom and repeated the Bible verse I had copied on a note card and mounted on the refrigerator. "We do not know what to do, but our eyes are upon You" (2 Chronicles 20: 12). I fell into a peaceful sleep with unspoken hope for a promise from God.

Christmas morning brought the usual excitement as the girls discovered the treasures in their stockings. Much to my amazement, the girls had also filled a stocking for me. I was overwhelmed by all the time and thought that had gone into their choices. They had included all of my favorite things: coffees, chocolates, jewelry, and lotions. The tears started early that day as I realized how much God had blessed me through my daughters.

After brunch, we moved on to the gifts underneath our adopted tree. There was no graceful way to avoid or ignore the obvious. Someone was missing from our family picture. As the girls looked to me for guidance, I couldn't help but think of all the women and children who had found themselves on their own today. With God's help, we will survive and thrive, I thought.

"Before we open presents I want to share something with you," I said to the girls. I recounted the many times when God had protected each of them, how He had blessed them in such unique ways, and how He was providing for us, even now. Soon, we were all crying and, this time, our tears came from gratitude.

—EVANGELINE BEALS GARDNER

Seasonal Overload

But as for me, I will sing about your power. Each morning I will sing with joy about your unfailing love. For you have been my refuge, a place of safety when I am in distress.
PSALM 59:16

My in-laws' living room was already filled with family and friends as we unloaded our gifts for the traditional Christmas Eve party. It had been a while since my young children had seen everyone, so they were feeling a bit overpowered by all the people.

As I began to talk to one of the relatives, my daughter nestled closer to me and took hold of my hand. I paused and turned to her. "Sweetie, do you want to play in the back room with the rest of the girls?"

"No," she said, shaking her head, "not yet." She stayed with me for a short time and, eventually, joined the rest of her cousins. At times, we feel overwhelmed, and we need to draw back to a place of safety and comfort. God knows this and He understands. He is always ready to take our hand and pull us close until we're ready to face the world again.

When life becomes too much, God's presence is all we need.

—MABELLE REAMER

The Gift of the Magi

*Three things will last forever—faith, hope, and love—
and the greatest of these is love.*
1 Cᴏʀɪɴᴛʜɪᴀɴs 13:13

One of my favorite stories is *The Gift of the Magi*, by O. Henry. It describes how an impoverished young married couple each sacrifices their greatest treasures to buy the other a Christmas gift. He sells his prized pocket watch to buy her tortoiseshell combs for her long, luxurious hair, and she sells her hair to buy him a fob for his watch.

Just before Christmas last year, Emily was in desperate need of some new clothes. She was thrilled when I told her I would give her some money so she could buy a few things. Then, I asked her what she planned to get for her husband, Alan. "I don't know. We're so broke, but this is our first Christmas together, and I want it to be special."

On Christmas day Emily confessed that she had taken the money I had given her and bought Alan a new video game. As it turned out, Alan had sold the game system to buy Emily some books she had always wanted. I suspect it was their best Christmas ever.

There is no gift greater than love.

—SBT

Amelia's Shining Light

Your word is a lamp to guide my feet and a light for my path.
PSALM 119:105

My daughter's e-mail threw my thoughts into momentary confusion. "Mom," she wrote, "I believe God is calling me to go into nursing." Amelia was in her first semester at a Christian college on a scholarship for graphic arts. Previously, she had planned on being a high school history teacher or psychologist. We had never considered a medical career.

I took a moment to pray. "God, show me that Amelia is headed in the right direction." When I opened my Bible, He led me to a familiar verse about His lamp guiding our feet. Later, when I was on my computer, He guided me to an Internet site on the symbols for nursing. I discovered that The International Council of Nurses uses the lamp or a candle to represent the light of knowledge as their signature symbol. I needed no further confirmation from God that Amelia would be able to shine her light to brighten the lives of others.

When God leads, we can follow with confidence.

—EVANGELINE BEALS GARDNER

Trick or Treat

Pride leads to disgrace, but with humility comes wisdom.
PROVERBS 11:2

When my daughter Emily was a senior, she and a group of friends decided to wear Halloween costumes to school. I was unaware that the new principal had announced, a few weeks earlier, that costumes would no longer be allowed. When Emily returned home that afternoon, it was clear her day had not gone well.

I wasn't sure how to respond when she admitted that she and her friends had been called to the principal's office after their arrival at school. "Meg convinced me it was a dumb rule," she said. "We figured other kids would dress up, and we wouldn't get into trouble."

"So what happened?" I asked.

"I apologized and told the principal that I was wrong for not respecting his rules. He said that my humility was refreshing and let me off with a warning. Are you going to punish me?"

"Not if you promise to think twice before letting someone talk you into something you know is wrong."

"I promise! Can I take off this stupid costume now?"

"You bet. I think Halloween is over for this year."

Sometimes, the most effective discipline comes from within.

—SBT

Migraine Misery

*But those who won't care for their relatives, especially those
in their own household, have denied the true faith.
Such people are worse than unbelievers.*
1 TIMOTHY 5:8

I suffer from migraines. Sometimes, they're quite mild, but a few weeks ago, I was in rough shape. When my headache began to worsen, I decided reluctantly that calling my husband at work was my only option.

When I picked up the phone, I dialed my daughter Emily's number by mistake. She was understandably surprised to hear from me at 5:30 in the morning, but as soon as I told her I was sick, she was concerned and sympathetic. "We can come right over," she said.

"But it's Alan's day off," I replied. "Besides, you're an hour away. I'm sure you don't feel like driving over here."

"We'll take you to the doctor's office as soon as it opens," she said. "You go and lie down, and we'll be there as soon as we can."

A few hours later, I was feeling great, and not just because my headache was gone. I knew God had led me to call Emily. I suspect He wanted me to know what a caring and thoughtful woman my daughter had become.

A person's true character comes through in a crisis.

—SBT

Quilting Our Faith

Now go and write down these words. Write them in a book.
They will stand until the end of time as a witness.
ISAIAH 30:8

As a small child, I was grateful for the sewing lessons offered by a neighboring grandmother, and when I had a daughter of my own, I was happy to teach her the skills I had learned. Some years later, we put our hands together to make a testimony quilt. My youngest son had been born with kidney failure, and throughout the years, we received many loving promises from God's word. I pieced together the scraps of colorful fabric, and in the center of each square my daughter cross-stitched a scripture verse.

Today, the quilt represents the love and abundant grace that covered us through that time. It is also a reminder of God's love for our daughter. When she was only five, we were told she might need to have her arm amputated due to a severe break. God knew of her wonderful gift and preserved that right hand to record His sustaining promises.

Use your gifts as a testimony of God's abundant grace.

—VERNA BOWMAN

Lip Service to the Lord

Unless the Lord builds a house, the work of the builders is wasted. Unless the Lord protects a city, guarding it with sentries will do no good.

PSALM 127:1

When my daughter was born, I vowed to do my very best as her mother. I chose her foods and toys carefully and supervised her activities. I strived to stimulate and nourish her intellectual and emotional development and worked to instill within her a love for all living things. But when it came to her spiritual development, I realize I paid only lip service to God's role in her life.

It was only when I welcomed the Lord into my life that I recognized how much I needed Him to help me become the mother I had always wanted to be. I realized that Emily was not only a gift from God—she belonged to Him. I was her earthly mother, but He was her Heavenly Father, and unless I welcomed Him as an active participant in my parenting, my best efforts would always fall short.

Your best parenting resource is the Lord.

—SBT

Someone Special

*In his grace, God has given us different gifts
for doing certain things well.*
1 PETER 4:10

My maternal grandmother was orphaned at ten and went to live with elderly relatives who were childless by choice. When I was ten, Nanny told me, "They put me in a big room on the third floor of the house. I was so alone and afraid." Her own children would never feel that sense of abandonment. Each would feel special, none more so than my mother.

She was born when Nanny was forty. There were already six children, and times were hard. Nevertheless, she always told Mother, "I was so excited when you were born. I wanted you even more than all the others!"

Nanny also had a knack for discovering each child's God-given talent and then encouraging and helping that gift to grow. How I wish she could attend our Fourth of July reunions where generations of her family come together to laugh and pray. I'm certain she would make sure everyone there felt like someone special.

God makes all His children feel like someone special.

—ELAINE YOUNG McGUIRE

Laying the Groundwork

*If I had the gift of prophecy, and if I understood all of God's
secret plans and possessed all knowledge, and if I had such
faith that I could move mountains, but didn't love others,
I would be nothing.*
1 CORINTHIANS 13:2

It was the powerful, enduring love my parents shared
which made their relationship something to be admired and
emulated. In the same way, my husband and I have discovered that our love—for each other and for the Lord—is the
strongest foundation possible for a triumphant marriage.

When my daughter, Emily, married Alan two years
ago, her obvious delight was a great blessing to me, but
like most mothers, I entertained my share of worries. I
knew the road they faced was full of detours, breakdowns,
and unfamiliar territory.

When they arrived for dinner the other night, I
greeted them and gave Emily a hug. "You look so pretty
today," I said. Alan nodded in agreement. "She looks
pretty every day."

Emily blushed and shot Alan a look of feigned annoy-
ance. A teasing grin appeared on his face, but when their
eyes met, I couldn't see anything but the obvious love they
had for each other. At that moment, I knew they were lay-
ing the groundwork for a joyful life together.

Our love for the Lord will see us through.

—SBT

My Parenting Partner

You watched me as I was being formed in utter seclusion,
as I was woven together in the dark of the womb.
PSALM 139:15

Even though I accepted the Lord as my personal savior at an early age, my daughter Emily was born during a period of my life when faith had taken second place to my worldly desires. I still prayed for my unborn child's well-being and praised Him when I delivered a strong and healthy baby, but I only had a vague idea of His profound role in my daughter's life—even before her conception.

After I dedicated my life to the Lord and began to spend time in His word, I made some amazing and life changing discoveries. Even before Emily was born, God had a purpose for her. He knew everything about her and, most importantly, He chose me for her mother.

These revelations brought the awareness that being Emily's mother was far more than changing diapers, worrying about a healthy diet, or deciding on the best education. Like everything else in my life, God had elevated motherhood from the ordinary to the divine.

Everything we do is for the glory of God.

—SBT

Christmas Pajamas

Thank God for His Son, His gift too wonderful for words.
2 CORINTHIANS 9:15

Christmas Eve at our house traditionally included a scrumptious dinner, the reading of the Christmas story from Luke, and a new pair of Christmas pajamas for our two daughters. As I watched them wiggle and giggle in their fuzzy gifts, I imagined how Mary felt on that cold and lonely night in Bethlehem with only scraps of cloth to swaddle her baby boy. I wondered if she felt the nervous excitement I clearly recalled from the night my first child was born.

Did Jesus receive a special gift when His birthday arrived each year? Family traditions offer security and meaning to a child's life especially when they are anchored in the reality of something as miraculous as Christmas—the gift of God's Son to the world. I hope my daughters will never forget the Christmas celebrations we shared, and I pray they may always love and worship God, the giver of all gifts.

Christmas gifts for others are a display
of our gratitude to God for Christ

—LINDA BLAINE POWELL

The Promise of a Reunion

God blesses those who mourn, for they will be comforted.
MATTHEW 5:4

In the years that followed my mother's death, my Aunt Helen helped ease the ache of loneliness and loss with her loving encouragement. Like my mother, she always seemed to know exactly what to say, and I could sense her great love for the Lord even over the telephone.

Our conversations covered a multitude of topics, ranging from the light-hearted to the bittersweet. I was often moved to tears when we talked about my mother or someone else who was no longer with us. One day, I was particularly saddened by the recent loss of two beloved family members. "Sometimes it feels like everyone is leaving me," I said.

Aunt Helen was silent for a few moments and, abruptly, I remembered that she, too, had suffered greatly in the past few years. "I'm sorry," I said. "I know how much you miss Uncle Fred and Dianne."

"I do miss them," she replied in a voice strong with conviction, "but I'll see them again. I have God's promise."

True comfort comes from the Lord.

—SBT

Understanding a Mother's Heart

*Furthermore, we have seen with our own eyes
and now testify that the Father sent his
Son to be the Savior of the world.*
1 JOHN 4:14

When my daughter Emily was a toddler, she suffered from frequent ear infections. This led to a decision by her pediatrician to put tubes in her ears. Although my mind told me it was the right thing to do, my heart held a different story. Despite the doctor's repeated assurances that it was a simple procedure designed to help Emily, I couldn't dismiss my growing fears.

What if something went wrong? Life without her was unimaginable, and I couldn't even begin to explain how much she meant to me. And then, one day a few weeks before her surgery, I came across a verse in the Bible I knew as well as my own name. However, this time it held a whole new meaning for me.

God had proven His love for me by sacrificing His only son. He knew exactly how I felt about Emily, and He understood my fears completely. In return, surely I could trust Him to do what was best for my precious girl.

Only God understands a mother's heart.

—SBT

Carry My Hand

Yet I still belong to you; you hold my right hand.
PSALM 73:23

When my daughter was tiny, she loved to be carried. From her vantage point over my shoulder she could view the world in comfort. Sometimes, however, it was necessary for her to walk. Then she would tug on my skirt and hold up a little hand and say, "Carry my hand; just carry my hand." With her fingers wrapped securely in my palm, we could go where we needed to go and still be connected.

Sometimes my Heavenly Father carries me, and sometimes He asks me to walk. Even as we plod through the trials in our life, we have His promise that, wherever we go, He is with us. And He does, indeed, carry our hand. If you are going through tough times in your life, watch for the signs that He is holding your hand. Maybe it is a comforting word from a friend, an unexpected blessing, a glorious sunset, or a verse in the Bible meant just for you.

Life may be unpredictable, but God's presence is unwavering.

—SUSAN LAWRENCE

Comfort Food

All praise to God, the Father of our Lord Jesus Christ.
God is our merciful Father and the source of all comfort.
2 CORINTHIANS 1:3

When I was a little girl, my mother would transform leftover rice into a culinary masterpiece known as rice pudding. Baked in the oven for a couple of hours, it filled the kitchen with the intoxicating smell of nutmeg and cinnamon. Long after she was gone, that wonderful aroma could transport me back to the kitchen of my childhood, and one taste of the creamy, sweet pudding brought to mind the love that went into making it.

In recent years, I've discovered that God is the ultimate source of comfort food. Spiritual sustenance is available the moment I open my Bible or whisper a prayer. I still make rice pudding on occasion, but there is no substitute for the calm and consolation I receive from my Heavenly Father.

Comfort food tastes great,
but God's Word will satisfy you forever.

—SBT

Focused on Fear

*Such love has no fear, because perfect love expels all fear.
If we are afraid, it is for fear of punishment, and this shows
that we have not fully experienced his perfect love.*
1 JOHN 4:18

The Bible is filled with proof that God does not want His children to be afraid. Sometimes, my husband teases me that if I can't find something to worry about, I will invent something. His comments are light-hearted, but there is truth in his words. I spend far too much time feeling fearful.

God makes frequent references to fear because he recognizes its destructive power. When I'm afraid, my focus on God is replaced by an obsession with things beyond my control. I lose sight of His promises, and my fellowship with Him suffers. Fear accomplishes little more than producing more fear.

If I want my daughter to grow up without fear, then I must ask God for help to release its tenacious hold on me. If I want her to become a person of faith and hope, I need to cling to the comforting words He has given me to drive my anxieties away forever.

There is no fear in God's perfect love.

—SBT

Taming My Temper

Kind words are like honey—sweet to the soul and healthy for the body.
PROVERBS 16:24

Three girls and one bathroom is a losing combination. As the mother of three teenagers, I was left with little choice but to put others ahead of myself. Accomplishing that with a cheerful attitude, however, took some time.

Walking into a jungle of curling iron cords and soggy towels snaked from shower to sink made me cranky. The rainforest atmosphere flattened my hair and soaked my clothes. By the time I left the humid wilderness, I was usually roaring like a lion.

I knew something had to be done when I overheard my fourteen-year-old rearranging a sleepover because she didn't want anyone to hear her crabby mother in the morning. Can you spell conviction? Short of adding a new bathroom, or trading in my girls for boys, I knew it was my attitude that had to change. So, each day before I stepped out of the tropical wasteland, I prayed. That small action put my focus back where it should have been all along—on God.

Turn to the Lord to tame your temper.

—MICHELLE GRIEP

A Dancing Dilemma

*Even if we feel guilty, God is greater than our feelings,
and he knows everything.*
1 JOHN 3:20

When I asked my mother for permission to take tap dancing lessons, she was thrilled. Unfortunately, the appeal of tap dancing for me lasted about ten minutes into my first lesson. When the instructor announced a recital in eight weeks, I couldn't stop thinking about how much my mother would love to watch me dance.

I thought I was doomed, but I came up with a plan. Every Wednesday, while everyone else was tap dancing, I would go to the library, and when the day of the recital arrived, I would feign some sort of illness.

Three weeks later, my scheme fell apart. "When were you going to tell me?" my mother asked.

"I didn't want to disappoint you," I said and burst into tears.

"I don't care if you want to dance," she replied, "but I am sad that you didn't tell me how you felt."

Just as my guilty secret did nothing to change my mother's feelings, God's love remains constant and unfailing—no matter what we tell Him.

Experience the freedom of confessing your sins to the Lord.

—SBT

Turning Stressful into Special

*Do not withhold good from those who deserve it
when it's in your power to help them.*
PROVERBS 3:27

With only three days until my wedding, my mother and I were hot and tired after another day of shopping. Looking forward to going home, we headed back to the parking lot. Suddenly, my mother stopped and touched my arm. "Wait," she said. "I've been thinking about that last dress you tried on. I really want you to wear it to your rehearsal dinner. Let's go back and get it."

"Oh, no!" I replied. "We've already spent too much on this wedding. I can wear something I already have."

She shook her head. "You've paid for a lot yourself. This is something I want to do."

And then, I understood. She wanted the dress to be her special going-away gift to me. I will never forget her thoughtfulness that day, especially at such a stressful time for both of us.

*Mothers can turn even the most stressful times into
something special and memorable.*

—LANITA BRADLEY BOYD

My Daughter, My Friend

The heartfelt counsel of a friend is as
sweet as perfume and incense.
PROVERBS 27:9

For the first few months after my daughter left home, she called about once a week to let me know she was all right. Our conversations were always friendly, but rarely lasted more than five minutes.

And then, one morning, the phone rang at 5:30. I answered and Emily said, "Oh, Mom, I'm so sick. I have a high fever and a sore throat, and I don't know what to do."

"You need to see a doctor. Can Alan take you to the emergency room?"

"Yes, but I don't want to spend the money."

"Don't worry about it. Just go. And call me later to let me know how you're doing, okay?"

"I will," she replied, and I could hear the relief in her voice.

When she phoned later, we talked for over an hour. She began to call daily and, in the weeks that followed, I found out how much my daughter loves to talk on the phone, but I also discovered a lot about my new friend.

It is a true blessing when your grown daughter becomes a
trusted friend.

—SBT

Everyone Is Invited

But the wisdom from above is first of all pure.
It is also peace loving, gentle at all times, and willing to yield
to others. It is full of mercy and good deeds. It shows no
favoritism and is always sincere.
JAMES 3:17

Whether you like them or not, birthday parties are an inevitable part of being a parent. Even if you never have a party, your children will, most likely, be invited to plenty of them.

I thoroughly enjoy hosting frilly, girly parties for my little princess, but I always struggle with the guest list. Whom should I invite? Will a parent be offended or a child feel left out? In an effort to discourage cliques as early as possible, I usually invite more girls than I originally intend.

I know it isn't realistic to think that everyone can be invited to every party but, as Christians, we should be careful not to form selective groups that discriminate. Are you consciously or subconsciously leaving anyone off the "guest list?" Christianity is one party where everyone is invited!

Everyone is on God's guest list.

—KELLY W. MIZE

The Christmas Tree Crisis

And the very hairs on your head are all numbered.
So don't be afraid; you are more valuable to God
than a whole flock of sparrows.
LUKE 12:7

When I was a little girl, I loved everything about Christmas with one important exception. When all the decorations had been removed, I would grieve for the once dignified and vibrant green tree, now limp and leaving a trail of browning needles as my father dragged it outside. One year, as my parents discussed getting the Christmas tree, I burst into tears and ran to my room.

Within seconds, my mother was sitting beside me on the bed. Between sobs, I tried to explain my outburst. I felt a familiar comfort growing inside of me as she listened patiently, her eyes filled with love and concern. Finally, she spoke. "Would it help if we got an artificial tree?" she asked.

I nodded eagerly. Instead of dismissing my emotions as childish or petty, she acknowledged their importance and did what she could to solve my dilemma. In the same way, God cares about every detail of my life, and when I share my worries with Him, I know I can count on His help.

God will never make you feel insignificant.

—SBT

Gingerbread Houses

*She carefully watches everything in her household
and suffers nothing from laziness.*
PROVERBS 31:27

It was Christmas Eve, and my granddaughters, six-year-old Hannah and three-year-old Katie, were busy constructing gingerbread houses in the kitchen with their mom. The walls of their creations stood tall as the thick icing hardened into edible cement, but the real fun began when the girls added the final touches. Red and green candy balls lined the roofs and the front doors, and brightly colored sprinkles were pasted on the outside walls. Laughter filled the kitchen whenever the tiny candy balls fell off the houses and bounced around on the counter and kitchen floor.

I was impressed with everyone's enthusiastic participation but, more importantly, my heart was warmed as I observed three young ladies working together in love. The icing may have held the gingerbread houses together that night, but love and devotion was the glue that would hold their home together in the years to come.

Love is the cement that holds our homes together.

—NANCY B. GIBBS

Unexpected Evidence

There are "friends" who destroy each other,
but a real friend sticks closer than a brother.
PROVERBS 18:24

It was not the sort of gift most women expect to receive from their daughter-in-law—a gift full of time, effort, and love. "Johanna, are you alright?" I asked through the locked bedroom door. It was Christmas Eve, and my eldest son's wife was missing the night's festivities. After entering our home a few hours previously, she had gone directly upstairs. "She's working on a last minute Christmas present," her husband said. "And she's adding the finishing touches."

When the time arrived to exchange gifts, Johanna emerged with the last present of the night. Suddenly, all eyes were upon me, and Johanna's beaming face. When I opened the gift, I found myself holding a beautiful, queen-size, hand-made quilt. "Until now," she said, "the only thing I ever quilted was a pot-holder in sixth grade."

My tears flowed as I realized the magnitude of such a gift. It was a remarkable gesture that left little doubt as to the proof of the friendship between my daughter-in-law and me.

Real friends eagerly offer their time, effort, and love.

—MARIBETH SPANGENBERG

Alone But Not Lonely

*No one will be able to stand against you as long
as you live. For I will be with you as I was with Moses.
I will not fail you or abandon you.*
JOSHUA 1:5

My husband's parents were in their eighties when his father, Richard, died suddenly. As the end of the year approached, I began to worry. I hoped celebrating Christmas without Richard wouldn't prove too difficult for my sweet mother-in-law.

We made plans to have dinner with Mildred at her house. Shortly after we opened our gifts on Christmas morning, I told everyone to get ready for the trip to Grandma's. I heard one of my children complain, "But it's still early!"

"Yes, but Grandma's alone this year, and I want to make sure she's all right," I replied.

Mildred greeted us all with a loving smile, but when she saw my face, her grin vanished. "What's wrong?" she asked.

"I was worried you might be lonely without Dad," I said. Her smile returned. "I might be alone now, but I'm never lonely. The Lord has always been with me, and He's not going anywhere."

You need never be lonely.

—SBT

Trust Takes Time

Don't you see how wonderfully kind, tolerant, and patient God is with you? Does this mean nothing to you? Can't you see that his kindness is intended to turn you from your sin?
ROMANS 2:4

When I was about ten, my aunt Charlotte placed a hen and her brood of chicks under my care. Full of self-importance, I imagined it wouldn't be long before they became affectionate and docile, much like the other animals I had befriended on the farm. Unfortunately, the hen continued to view me with suspicion and the chicks, sensing their mother's distrust, preferred to stay hidden under her protective wing.

One day, the hen bit me and, fighting back tears of pain and indignation, I informed my aunt that I was no longer interested in caring for the chickens. "Trust takes time," she explained and encouraged me to continue. By the end of the summer, the little family and I had become good friends.

For me, trusting God didn't happen overnight, but my caution and doubt have continued to fade under the enduring light of His endless patience and unconditional love.

God is waiting patiently for your trust.

—SBT

Glimmers of Faith

The Lord hears his people when they call to him for help.
He rescues them from all their troubles.
PSALM 34:17

"It's 3:00 A.M.," the radio announcer said. "Do you know where your child is?"

"No!" I cried and cradled my head in my hands. Two hours earlier, my daughter Michelle had packed all her belongings into a black plastic bag and climbed through the window. A piece of myself went with her.

Long days turned into weeks, and weeks turned into months. Often, my prayers were simply groans in the middle of sleepless nights. Would God honor such pleas?

That was over a decade ago. I wish I could claim that everything worked out and my daughter loves God with all her heart. I may be unable to say that, but I do know God heard my prayers. He restored my relationship with my daughter, and I see a glimmer of faith beginning to grow in her heart. For now, that's enough. The same God who heard the groaning of my heart will faithfully draw my daughter to Himself.

We can trust God to be faithful for our children,
just as He is for us.

—SANDY CATHCART

Wiping the Slate Clean

*He has removed our sins as far from us
as the east is from the west.*
PSALM 103:12

Apologizing to my mother wasn't easy, but it always had a happy ending. She never failed to forgive me. Every single time. Her forgiveness was a balm for the wretched feelings I invariably suffered for letting her down with my disobedience or misconduct. My mother's absolution was truly the gift that kept on giving. Once we had discussed the incident that had resulted in my apology, it was never mentioned again.

For years, I had been aware of God's forgiveness, but it wasn't until I began to study His word that I became aware of something important. Just like my mother, once I had asked for and been granted forgiveness, God treated my sins as though they had never existed. And also like my mother, His love for me hadn't changed one bit even though I had strayed from His teachings.

A clean slate is a thing of beauty.

—SBT

DECEMBER 29

Perfect Timing

*But the godly will flourish like palm trees
and grow strong like the cedars of Lebanon.*
PSALM 92:12

Like many people her age, my daughter Emily wondered about and, sometimes, agonized over what career she should pursue after graduation. "All of my friends know what they're going to do," she told me. "And I'm not sure at all. I'm not even very good at anything."

I thought about all the different jobs I had worked at during the years after I graduated, and then I tried to explain how long it had taken to discover some of my special abilities. "I didn't start my family until I was almost thirty," I told her, "and being a mom is the best job I've ever had. And I didn't start writing until I was forty-three. God has blessed you with certain talents," I continued. "Why don't you take your time and find out what they are?"

She nodded. "It would be nice to think about it a little longer."

I gave her a hug. "God will open the right door when you're ready. I promise."

What are your special gifts?

—SBT

Beacons of Wisdom

*For their command is a lamp and their instruction a light;
their corrective discipline is the way to life.*
PROVERBS 6:23

My mother was forty-two when I was born, and I can only imagine what it was like giving birth to twelve pounds of baby. She almost died giving me life, but God was gracious. We had forty-one years together, time Mother spent building my character. Every morning, she had breakfast with God, complete with buttered toast, coffee, and her Bible.

I accepted Christ one summer Sunday morning when I was eighteen. "Carol," my mother said, "never forget that you can't keep the birds from flying over your head, but you can keep them from building a nest in your hair."

She has been with Jesus twenty years now, but her wisdom remained with me. Whenever bad thoughts or temptations fly through my mind, I don't give them time to land. Rather I breathe a quiet prayer of repentance and of praise for the woman God trusted to nurture my healthy growth.

Some memories are like lamps in a window, leading us home.

—CAROL CLARK WARD

Equipped for Life

The teaching of your word gives light,
so even the simple can understand.
PSALM 119:130

When my daughter Emily moved into her first apartment, she had her bedroom furniture and personal possessions, but not much of anything else. I knew how much she loved to cook, so, one afternoon, I did a thorough investigation of my kitchen and came up with all sorts of dishes, pots and pans, and utensils I no longer used.

As she and her father loaded up the car with her new treasures, I took one last look for anything else she might need. I happened to notice my Bible sitting on the kitchen table. It was one of several Bibles I owned, and when Emily came back inside, I handed it to her. "I know you have a Bible, but I'd like you to have one of mine. Now, I feel as if I've given you the most important thing you'll ever need."

Emily grinned and flipped through the pages for a moment. "And I'll think of you every time I read it," she said.

I gave her a hug. "Yeah, I thought of that, too."

Your Bible equips you for life.

—SBT

CONTRIBUTORS

Debra Whiting Alexander, PhD, is a mental health practitioner and the author of *Loving Your Teenage Daughter* (*Whether She Likes It Or Not*). She lives in Eugene, Oregon with her husband of nearly twenty-five years.

Betty L. Arthurs has been writing for over twenty years. Her heart is captivated by the needs of those with broken lives who need to know of God's love. A speaker and teacher, she writes children's stories, personal experience articles, and devotionals.

Janet M. Bair is a freelance writer and a children's librarian. She enjoys going to the beach, reading, and belonging to a writer's group. Her two daughters, Joanna and Emily, are busy working, following their dreams.

Sandi Banks is an author, speaker, Summit Ministries worldview conference director, and Mom/Gramma to nine special young ladies. She is the author of *Anchors of Hope* has been published in *A Cup of Comfort® for Mothers*, and *A Cup of Comfort® Book of Prayer*.

Alma Barkman of Winnipeg, Manitoba, Canada is a freelance writer and author of seven books. For more info, visit her website at *www .almabarkman.com*.

Cindy Boose is the wife of a wonderful man and the mother of four beautiful young women, three of whom she homeschools. She writes from their home in South Carolina and has a special place in her heart for mothers and daughters.

Verna Bowman lives with her husband, Jeff, in Red Hill, Pennsylvania. She is the mother of four children and has five grandchildren. She has been deeply involved in the women's ministry in her church for many years.

Lanita Bradley Boyd draws on her life experiences to inspire others to a closer relationship with God. She is the founder of the Sisterhood of Christian Writers.

Laura L. Bradford resides in Walla Walla, Washington. She seeks to encourage others by writing of the countless ways God has touched her life.

Connie Sturm Cameron has been married to Chuck for twenty-nine years. They have two children, Chase and Chelsea, daughter-in-law Elizabeth, step-daughter Lori, and three grandchildren. Contact her at: *www .conniecameron.com* or connie_cameron@sbcglobal.net.

Contributors

LeAnn Campbell and her husband have six adult children, eleven grand-children, and two great-grandchildren. LeAnn coauthored *Moms Over 50 Devotions to Go* by Extreme Diva Media, Inc.

Jean Campion, mother and grandmother, bills herself as a free-range writer in southwest Colorado. She is also the author of two historical novels, *Minta Forever* and *Return to Rockytop*.

Sandy Cathcart is a freelance writer, photographer, and artist living in the mountains of Southern Oregon with her husband of thirty-six years. She often speaks and writes of her adventures with The Creator. You can view her art at *www.sandycathcart.com* and contact her through *sandycathcart .blogspot.com*.

Kendis Chenoweth is a minister's wife, mother of two, and a passionate communicator of her favorite topic—Jesus Christ. Her excitement, authenticity, and enthusiasm make her a popular teacher and speaker.

Gwen Rice Clark is a 2002 Amy Award Winner, a weekly inspirational columnist for the *Hillsboro, Ohio Times Gazette*, and has published more than 1,000 devotional articles.

Carol R. Cool is a speaker and an internationally published writer. Living in Bear, Delaware, she ministers as a church planter with her husband Les. Carol loves to encourage average people, like herself, to make a difference in their world and blogs about it on her website, *www.carolcool.com*.

Linda Crow is a mother of two daughters and one son. She is a writer who works in a youth ministry.

When **Dianne Daniels** is not busy enjoying her two young daughters, she writes Christian nonfiction to help and encourage other moms. You can find her work in several publications, including *A Cup of Comfort*® *Devotional for Mothers*.

Midge DeSart is a wife, mother, and grandmother. In addition to being the author of Maintaining Balance in a Stress-Filled World, she is a public speaker, church musician, and beading embellishment artist.

Jennifer Devlin is a speaker, ministry leader, and the author of *Verses We Know by Heart: Discovering the Details of Familiar Old Testament Passages* (2008) and *Life Principles for Christ-Like Living* (2006). For more information visit her website at *www.ministryforlife.com*.

Elsi Dodge is a single woman who travels in a 30-foot RV with her beagle and a cat who thinks he's a saber-toothed tiger. Retired after a quarter century of teaching special needs children, Dodge works with students and writes about God's guidance in her life. Her website is *www.RVTourist.com*.

Pamela Dowd is the author of a holiday novella, *All Jingled Out*. Four of her stories have been published in *A Cup of Comfort® Devotional for Women*. She and her husband, Rodney, have three daughters, three sons-in-law, and one grandson. Contact Pamela at *pam@pameladowd.com*.

Iris G. Dowling, from Cochranville, Pennsylvania, writes church program materials, puppet skits, stories, teaching articles, and her work is published in many collections by Standard Publishing, Lillenas, Bible Pathways for Kids, ABWE Missions, and National Drama Service.

Connie Hilton Dunn believes in pursuing life passionately. She is a wife, mother, systems specialist, writer, and aspiring life coach. You can check out her website at *www.spirit-led-coaching.com* or contact her at *www.shoutlife.com/connie_dunn*.

Liz Hoyt Eberle and her husband live in the Texas hill country. Between enjoying their busy retirement and large blended family, Liz writes about everyday people who bless others. She can be reached at *eberle2@hotmail.com*.

Sally Ferguson is learning about being a child of God through being a mom. Sally has had over fifty-eight articles published, in addition to her coloring book, *What Will I Be When I Grow Up?* For information on her speaking calendar, go to *www.sallyferguson.net*.

Melissa Fields has lived in Massachusetts with her fabulous husband for fourteen years. She homeschools their two adorable children. Her writing can be found in *His, All My Bad Habits I Learned From Grandpa*, and the upcoming *Life Savors*.

Suzanne Woods Fisher's first novel, *Copper Star*, a World War II love story, is inspired by true events. Its sequel, *Copper Fire*, picks up as the war in Europe winds down. Fisher is a wife and mother, and a puppy raiser for Guide Dogs for the Blind. She writes for many magazines.

Darlene Franklin, award-winning author and speaker, resides in the Colorado foothills with her mother and her cat Talia. She has two grown children and two grandchildren. Visit her website blog at *www.darlenehfranklin.com*.

Phyllis Qualls Freeman is retired from secretarial work in the medical field. She has more than 225 devotionals published by three publishing houses. She loves teaching Sunday school and being a grandmother to five.

CONTRIBUTORS

Evangeline Beals Gardner has been a freelance writer for twenty-five years. She has written short stories, inspirational articles, newspaper interviews, and Sunday school curriculum. Her two daughters, Amelia, age eighteen, and Lydia, age eleven, make her home an exciting place to be.

Nancy B. Gibbs is a pastor's wife, mother, and grandmother. She is also a weekly religion columnist and a motivational speaker. You may visit Nancy's website at *www.nancybgibbs.com* or e-mail her at *Nancybgibbs@aol.com*.

Renee Gray-Wilburn is a mother of three who writes and edits in the foothills of Pikes Peak. She has over fifty articles and stories published in the adult, children's, and inspirational markets, including *A Cup of Comfort®️ Devotional for Mothers* and *A Cup of Comfort®️ Book of Prayer*.

Michelle Griep has been writing since she first discovered Crayolas and blank wall space. Following in her Master's footsteps, she strives to impart Biblical truths in story format.

Pam Halter is a former homeschooling mom, a children's author and, most recently, a grandmother. She lives in New Jersey with her husband, Daryl, two daughters, and three cats. Pam also has a granddaughter. Visit her website at *www.pamhalter.info*.

Jennie Hilligus lives in the Kansas City area and has been married for twenty-seven years. She was a freelance artist for Hallmark for nearly fourteen years. She enjoys spending time boating with her best friend/husband. They have two adult children and a new son-in-law.

Cynthia Agricola Hinkle is the children's author of *The Thankful Leper* and contributed anthologies including *A Cup of Comfort®️ Devotional for Mothers*. She is the senior editor for the regional Christian monthly, *Jubilee Magazine*. She and her daughter live and pray together in southwest Ohio.

Imogene Johnson is a retired secretary with Virginia's Department of Correctional Education. She lives in rural Virginia with her husband, O.W. She loves retirement, southern gospel music, and singing praises to the Lord in her church choir.

Jewell Johnson lives in Arizona with her husband, LeRoy. Besides writing she enjoys walking, reading, and quilting.

Eva Juliuson is a mother and grandmother who shares God's love through writing, teaching, and working with kids. She sends out regular short free e-mail prayers to help jump-start others into a deeper prayer life with God. To receive them, e-mail her at *evajuliuson@hotmail.com*.

Charlotte Kardokus is a freelance writer from Salem, Oregon. She is a wife of thirty-three years, a mother of two, and a grandmother of three. Her devotionals have appeared in various publications including *A Cup of Comfort® Devotional for Mothers*.

LaRose Karr is a freelance writer and speaker. She lives in Colorado with her husband and is the mother of four grown children. Her work has appeared in numerous compilation books, devotional guides, newsletters, and on websites. E-mail: *larosekarr@bresnan.net*.

Karla Kassebaum is a freelance writer with a heart for parents and family. Her website, *www.karlakassebaum.com*, provides encouragement for parents. She lives in Grand Junction, Colorado, with her husband and daughter.

Jami Kirkbride has a master's degree in counseling. She's a freelance writer and certified personality trainer. She's inspired by her husband, Jeff, and four children. She's a contributing author to When God Steps In and Laundry Tales. For more information, visit *www.JamiKirkbride.com*.

Laurie Klein's award-winning works appear widely in Christian and secular journals, anthologies, hymnals and recordings. Co-founder/consulting editor of *Rock & Sling: A Journal of Literature, Art and Faith*, and recent winner of the Merton Prize for Poetry of the Sacred.

Mary Laufer's work has been published in The Christian Communicator, Hunger Enough—*Living Spiritually in a Consumer Society*, Chicken Soup for the Girl's Soul, and Her Story—*What I Learned in My Bathtub*. She lives in Forest Grove, Oregon, with her husband and daughter.

Susan Lawrence is a freelance writer who has recently retired from elementary teaching to write and speak full-time. She is the author of *A Family Garden of Christian Virtues* and *A Young Child's Garden of Christian Virtues*. She lives with her husband, Gary, near Des Moines, Iowa. She has three grown children and four grandchildren.

Kathryn Lay is the author of over 1,400 articles, essays, devotionals, and stories for adults and children. Her children's novel, *Crown Me!*, was published in 2004 and republished in paperback as *How to Rule the School* by Scholastic Books. Check out her website at *www.kathrynlay.com* for information on her books, online writing classes, and speaking information, or e-mail her at *rlay15@aol.com*.

429

CONTRIBUTORS

L. A. Lindburg is a stay-at-home mother of two boys. She and her family reside in Nebraska near the Omaha metro area. She participates in and/or teaches Bible studies for youth and adult. She also enjoys a good walk on a summer evening.

Lynn Ludwick is a mother of three and grandmother of seven. She lives in a funky little house, and surrounds herself with her books, her quilts, her family, and her friends.

Joyce Starr Macias is a retired newspaper reporter whose freelance articles have appeared in *Family Life Today, The War Cry, Purpose, Live, Mature Living,* and *His Forever.* Joyce conducts nursing home services and co-chairs the seniors' group at her church in Spring City, Pennsylvania.

Jeanette MacMillan is an English major who's taught her middle school students to research and write creatively. She and her husband reside in Indiana near their three married children and eight grandchildren. She's currently working in a school media center.

Sandra McGarrity lives and writes in Chesapeake, Virginia.

Alice M. McGhee is a writer living in Littleton, Colorado. She teaches Bible studies in her church, and is active in mission activities. Reading, needlework, and playing with her grandchildren are some of her favorite pastimes.

Elaine Young McGuire, from Lilburn, Georgia, is a retired teacher who enjoys participating in short-term mission efforts. A journal she wrote to guide others in this process is scheduled for summer publication and promotion.

Karen McKee has a degree in English from Regis University and works as a librarian. She resides in Palisade, Colorado, with her husband of forty-one years. She has two grown sons and seven grandchildren.

Nancy Mitchell lives and writes in Colorado with her husband and five of their nine children. She values mentoring women including her three daughters, reading George MacDonald, and playing board games.

Patricia Mitchell writes from Kansas City, Missouri.

Kelly W. Mize is a wife, mother, and freelance writer living in Madison, Alabama. A former teacher with a master's degree, Kelly's work has appeared in a number of publications for both children and adults.

Laurie Modrzejewski's work has appeared in *Christian Communicator, Pockets, Clubhouse, Shine Brightly,* and *Spirit-Led Writer.* A wife and mother of three, Laurie and her family live in Mechanicsville, Maryland.

Sandy Moffett works as a funeral singer and has written the lyrics for many of the songs she sings. She writes inspirational prose and poetry and speaks to women's groups. She and her husband Greg live in Bakersfield, California. They have four children and one grandchild.

Dena N. Netherton is a musician, teacher, and author. Her passion is creating and sharing stories and characters that inspire, comfort, and teach Biblical principles. Living in the Colorado Rockies, she's been married to Bruce for twenty-nine years and has three grown children.

Ava Pennington is a freelance writer, speaker, and Bible teacher, with an MBA from St. John's University. She has published magazine articles and contributed stories to eight *Chicken Soup for the Soul* books and two *Cup of Comfort®* books. For more information, visit *www.avawrites.com*.

Laurie A. Perkins lives with husband, Philip, in Needham, Massachusetts. She is a former children's librarian. Laurie's story "Stretching My Prayer Muscle" is published in *A Cup of Comfort® for Christians*. She has published a novel, *Blood Diamonds: A Cryptic Crime Suspense*.

Casey Pitts is the wife of an Air Force chaplain and the mother of five children. Much of her time is spent managing her busy home, participating in organizations such as the Protestant Women of the Chapel, and writing various projects.

Connie K. Pombo is an author, speaker, and founder of Women's Mentoring Ministries in Mt. Joy, Pennsylvania. When not speaking or writing, Connie enjoys photography—one of her greatest passions.

Lori Poppinga is a pastor's wife from Northwest Iowa. She and her husband, Jeff, have eight children. She recently completed her first freelance project with Group Publishing, Inc. and has had articles accepted by *Proverbs 31 Woman*, *Hearts at Home*, and the MOP's website.

Linda Blaine Powell is a retired elementary teacher. She's been married for forty-four years and has two married daughters and four grandchildren. She enjoys writing in a variety of genres and has had an article published in the February 2005 issue of *Mature Living* magazine.

Susan Estribou Ramsden lives in California with her husband, Howard. They are the proud parents of Kimberly and grandparents of Olivia and Luke, who bring them endless delight. Susan enjoys encouraging others through her poetry, devotionals, and speaking engagements.

Anita Lynn Ramsey lives in Smithville, Missouri, with her two sons, three daughters, a collie, and two cats.

Contributors

Mabelle Reamer has been married for twenty-seven years. She has three adult children and one grandson. She has a master's degree in Christian counseling and serves on the women's ministry team at church.

Carolyn Byers Ruch learns many valuable lessons from her daughter and the many "daughters" the Lord has brought into her life. She is the cofounder of Tamar's Redemption, a ministry to survivors of childhood sexual abuse. Contact her at *tamarsredemption@comcast.net.*

Deborah Scheuffele, a native of Seattle, Washington, grew up writing stories on rainy days. Balancing home and work she writes for several publications in various genres. Deborah currently lives in Carlsbad, California, with her husband and four children.

Lori Z. Scott, an award-winning author and former elementary teacher, has contributed to more than a dozen books. Visit *www.MeghanRoseSeries.com* and discover her laugh out-loud children's book series written with her own daughter specifically in mind.

Donna J. Shepherd's devotionals and stories appear in *Daily Grace for Women, Anytime Prayers for Everyday Moms,* and *The Best Grandma in the World.* Visit Donna on the web at *www.donnajshepherd.com.*

Karen Sherrill is the mother of four (includes three daughters and twins). She has been married to her husband Robert, a Family Life Pastor, for thirty-one years. She is a speaker and webmaster of her site *www.ineverydaylife.com.*

Maribeth Spangenberg and her husband, Steve, are the proud parents of nine children. She writes for homeschooling magazines and websites and counts it a blessing to be able to encourage other mothers to stay the course.

Sherron Slavens has fifteen published devotionals including one in a previous *Cup of Comfort®* publication. She and her husband, Jim, have three children and three grandchildren. Sherron facilitates spiritual retreats for Colorado Women of Vision.

Yvonne Curry Smallwood writes from Upper Marlboro, Maryland. Trained as a biologist, she has worked more than twenty years in science administration. Her stories appear in several publications.

Margot Starbuck, a writer and speaker, lives in Durham, North Carolina. She is a daughter by birth and by adoption as well as a mother by birth and by adoption. Margot is a minister in the Presbyterian Church. Learn more at *www.MargotStarbuck.com*.

Michele Starkey suffered a ruptured brain aneurysm and survived by the grace of God. She and her beloved husband, Keith, live in the beautiful Hudson Valley of New York where they enjoy life to the fullest.

Donna Sundblad resides in Georgia with her husband, Rick. Among her published works are *Pumping Your Muse*, *Windwalker*, various inspirational short stories, and a second YA fantasy novel soon to be released. Visit her website at *www.theinkslinger.net*.

Vicki Tiede is a homeschooling wife and mother. She is the founder of Grace Lessons Ministries (*www.vickitiede.com*), a speaking and writing ministry designed to encourage and equip women to face the inevitable challenges of marriage, motherhood, and walking with Christ.

Donna Collins Tinsley, is a stay-at-home mom of four daughters who aspires to write while homeschooling one daughter, and chasing after her four-year-old grandson. She has just finished writing a book called *Somebody's Daughter*.

Kenda Turner lives with her husband in Cincinnati, Ohio, where she enjoys writing, reading, photography, and walks in all seasons. She has been published in various periodicals and devotional magazines.

Angie Vik lives in Northwest Iowa in an old farmhouse with her husband, six daughters, and one son. She is a pastor's wife, busy mom, part-time librarian, and compulsive reader. She enjoys visiting with friends, writing, camping, and snuggling with her little girls when they get in bed with her in the morning.

Carol Clark Ward has been employed in the thoroughbred horse industry for over twenty years. She studied creative writing at the University of Kentucky and completed the apprentice program at Christian Writer's Guild. Most recently, she has been writing devotionals for her church's (8,000–10,000 attendees per week) website.

Karen H. Whiting (*www.karenhwhiting.com*) has a heart for encouraging families to stay connected and bring the presence of Christ into the home. She has five grown children and five grandchildren. She and her husband live on Maryland's eastern shore.

CONTRIBUTORS

Donna L. Wichelman is the author of several published articles and short stories. In November 2007, she completed the journeyman level of the Christian Writers Guild. She has a master's degree in mass communication from San Jose State University.

Kathryn Wilson is the author of *Stone Cold in a Warm Bed* and a contributor to the *One Year Life Verse Devotional* and *Living the Serenity Prayer*. With her husband, she leads the recovery ministry of her church and is a support group facilitator.

Paula Wiseman lives in Robinson, Illinois, with her husband Jon, and children Lauren the drama queen, Alan the Lego Brickmaster, and Rachel the terrific toddler. She has written for children and teens and has contributed to several devotionals. She is currently working on a series of novels.

Karen Witemeyer is a deacon's wife and mother of three who is passionate about helping women navigate the path to spiritual maturity and grateful for the direction she receives in return.

Jamie Speak Wooten is a unique combination of writer, speaker, and Bible teacher. She creatively relates biblical truths to daily living in her monthly e-Devotional for women entitled *Hey Girlfriend . . . It's Almost Friday!* To join her e-mailing list, contact her at *speakforchrist@kc.rr.com.*

Debbie Zile is a working mother and a pastor's wife with three children. Her work as a writer includes a weekly column published in a city newspaper, employment as a community reporter, poems written for civic organizations, and children's plays. She also speaks at Mother-Daughter banquets.

Subject Index

Scripture Index

441

COME SEE WHAT'S BREWING AT
CUP OF COMFORT.COM

Be inspired. Be uplifted. Be involved.

www.cupofcomfort.com

With our enhanced, community-focused website, readers can:

- Enjoy featured stories

- Share their thoughts, experiences, ideas, and more in our communit' forums

- Submit stories for possible inclusior in future volumes and receive professional feedback

- Subscribe to our *Cup of Comfort*® newsletter

- And more!